Dividing Classes

Dividing Classes

HOW THE MIDDLE CLASS NEGOTIATES
AND RATIONALIZES SCHOOL ADVANTAGE

ELLEN BRANTLINGER

RoutledgeFalmer
New York • London

Published in 2003 by
RoutledgeFalmer
29 West 35th Street
New York, NY 10001
www.routledge-ny.com

Published in Great Britain by
RoutledgeFalmer
11 New Fetter Lane
London EC4P 4EE
www.routledgefalmer.com

RoutledgeFalmer is an imprint of the Taylor & Francis Group.
Printed in the United States of America on acid-free paper.

10 9 8 7 6 5 4

Library of Congress Cataloging-in-Publication Data

Brantlinger, Ellen A.
    Dividing classes: how the middle class negotiates and rationalizes school advantage / Ellen Brantlinger.
      p. cm.
    Includes bibliographical references and index.
    ISBN 0-415-93297-1—ISBN 0-415-93298-X (pbk.)
     1. Educational sociology—United States. 2. Students—United States—Social conditions.
  3. Social stratification—United States. 4. Middle class—United States. I. Title.

LC205 .B73 2003
306.43—dc21   2002036705

Permissions

An earlier version of Chapter 3 appeared as "Self-Interest and Liberal Educational Discourse: How Ideology Works for Middle Class Mothers," by Ellen Brantlinger, Massoumeh Majd-Jabbari, and Samuel L. Guskin, in *American Educational Research Journal*, (33) 3: 571–598, 1996. Copyright 1996 by the American Educational Research Association. Adapted with the permission of the publisher.

An earlier version of Chapter 4 appeared as "The Conflicting Pedagogical and Curricular Perspectives of Middle-Class Mothers," in *Journal of Curriculum Studies*, (30) 4: 431–460, 1998. Reprinted by permission of Taylor & Francis, Inc. www.tandf.co.uk.

Contents

Acknowledgments

In doing a critical ethnography, one is not always kind to the individuals who take part in a study. But I strongly believe that participants should be the first to be recognized for their contributions. In spite of my often unrelenting criticism of participants—as well as others in the community who they represent—indeed, because of the criticism, I am particularly grateful to the 20 mothers, 30 school personnel, and 4 school board members whose narratives are featured in this book. Many of them knew me and my agenda regarding social class relations in Hillsdale* long before they agreed to take part in my research and were still brave enough to risk being part of my story even though they knew they were unlikely to be portrayed in a positive light. Many participants are fond friends and acquaintances. I hope they understand that my intentions are not to accuse them of personal wrongdoing but rather to illustrate the nature of social class relations and the pernicious outcomes of certain ways of thinking and acting related to social class. At any rate, I have conscientiously attempted to maintain confidentiality and disguise individual characteristics in ways that interviewees will not be recognized. Many thanks to these people who all believe in the importance of research and were generous in giving their time and efforts to this project. In addition to the actual interview data, this book contains some observations of school administrators and board members. Because I am especially critical of them, I must add the caveat that public officials must be held accountable for their actions. Furthermore, they are used to reading portrayals of their behaviors in the local press and should under-

---

*A pseudonym, as are all names of people and places in this book.

stand that this book is another venue in which an author has reacted to their public actions.

There were a number of people who contributed to this book by conducting interviews or putting me in contact with participants and informants. Michelle Henderson interviewed school board members and wrote chapter 8. Thanks to the Proffitt Foundation at Indiana University for awarding funding to graduate students to interview some participants and transcribe interviews. I am grateful to Massoumeh Majd-Jabbari and Mark Simon for sensitive interviewing and careful transcribing. My colleague and friend, Anna Ochoa, is an emeritus faculty member in Curriculum Studies who interviewed some school personnel. Samuel Guskin, another emeritus professor, took part in the conceptualization of the study and in writing the proposal for Proffitt funding. I appreciate the knowledge I have gained through my conversations with Zeynep Alat, Jim Ansaldo, Jean Anyon, Debra Baker, Gina Blackburn, Wanda Blanchett, Leslie Bloom, Purnima Bose, Cathy Bowes, JoAnne Bunnage, Cary Buzzelli, Sandra Cade, Carrie Chapman, Hae-Jin Chung, Kim Cosier, Scot Danforth, Ashley deWaal-Lucas, Lori Ernsperger, Mary Gaither, Deb Garrahy, Lonni Gill, Karen Grady, Joan Hart, Sally Harvey-Koelpin, Hester Hemmerling, Steve Hinnefeld, Dodie Hodges, Marlissa Hughs, Susan Johnstad, Ji-Yeon Lee, Mi Young Lee, Nancy Lesko, Angela Lexmond, Bradley Levinson, Hsi Nancy Lien, Suzanne Pack Marrero, Mary Lou Morton, Rungnapa Nutravong, Cecilia Obeng, Pilanut Phusawisot, Elli Poelzer, Joe Ramsey, Anne Smith, Edy Stoughton, Carla Teed, Wendy Walter-Bailey, Sandra Washburn, Paul Worfel, and Jia-Chyi Yan. Thanks also to Joe Miranda, Acquisitions Editor, and Nicole Ellis, Production Editor, at RoutledgeFalmer for their timely support. It is always humbling, especially for a senior professor, to see how many errors can be found in what was thought to be a meticulously edited manuscript.

Special thanks to my family (Patrick, Andrew, Susan, & Jeremy), who live gracefully with their opinionated, radical, and activist partner/mother, as well as to their loved ones (Leroy, Jayla, Byron, & Jackie). I am particularly appreciative of their own critical thinking and of their efforts for social justice and equity.

Preface

A s with many current article and book titles, *classes divided* is a double entendre that alludes to more than one kind of class and more than one type of division. *Classes* refers to society's hierarchical socioeconomic structure as well as various levels of tracked classrooms and children class(ifi)ed as they are assigned to those levels. *Divided* captures how classes live in isolated residential areas (Wilson, 1987; Young, 2000) as well as how children are educated in classes and schools with spatially bounded (class-wise and racially) enrollment patterns (Oakes, 1985; Orfield, 2000; Orfield, Eaton, & Harvard Project, 1996). High-income people cluster in gated communities and prestigious schools and receive high-status epithets (e.g., bright, gifted, talented); lower-income people, whether working or "under" class, are relegated to less desirable neighborhoods (e.g., ghettos, housing projects, rural slums, trailer courts, older inner-ring suburbs with small homes) and underfunded, poorly situated schools with lesser facilities and fewer resources. Their children are dubbed at risk, culturally deprived, and often disabled. Social class divides how students participate—or do not participate—in activities, and it influences peer acceptance and rejection. This book focuses primarily on social class; however, the high correspondence between class and race/ethnicity is widely acknowledged. As Orfield et al. (1996) note: "A student in an intensely segregated African American and Latino school was fourteen times more likely to be in a high-poverty school (more than 50 percent poor) than a student in a school that was more than 90 percent white" (pp. 55–61).

When I first decided to put together my studies of affluent constituencies in Hillsdale[1] for this book, I had in mind the title, *Class Deficit Upside Down*. In the field of education the term *deficit* is tied almost exclusively to intellectual or achievement criteria and is thus associated with those who do not do well in school. By virtue of their poverty,[2] children become culturally, socially, and intellectually deficient and at risk for nonspecific but certainly negative outcomes;[3] they are expected not to do well in their school or postschool lives. Academic achievement is often the sole criterion used to gauge both school and student effectiveness (Schneider, Teske, & Marschall, 2000), yet other quality indicators should be considered. For example, people who are generous, kind, well adjusted, and have a good sense of humor make good friends. People with an interest in others and their community are good companions. To build a strong democracy (Barber, 1984; Young, 2000), citizens should have constructive ideas, be articulate and assertive in expressing opinions, and be motivated to engage in debates about topics related to local or global conditions that are modifiable by personal or collective action. They should be tolerant of others' views and willing to compromise. People who help others when times are hard or things go wrong and who generally take others' interests into account are valued neighbors. Thus, risk must be based on criteria relevant to the well-being of communities. People should be judged on whether they act within a reciprocal morality that spans across class, ethnicity, race, nationality, gender, age, ability, and sexual orientation. In my alternate title, *deficit* refers to people who do not display morality or a democratic spirit in their everyday lives. Certainly such deficits are of more consequence than a few IQ points or right or wrong items on achievement tests.

As I considered the statistics about widening income gaps and threatening environmental, economic,[4] and social conditions, the idea that moral deficits were particularly problematic grew in importance. Unlike the portrayals of deficit that pertain to the poor, this version of deficit applies to people of higher classes—in the case of this book, to educated middle-class parents who do not think beyond their own children when they interact with schools, or to teachers and administrators who cater to prominent people's interests to retain employment, advance in careers, or avoid inconvenience. Moral deficiencies encompass those not directly within sight of my ethnographic lens—and invisible to many mainstream Americans except indirectly through ads or media messages sponsored by them—the managers of transglobal corporations whose personal financial gains and political power are increasingly based on others' loss and oppression (Medovoi, 2002; Seldon, 1990). According to my criteria, such dominant and domineering people have a social and moral deficit that interferes with our country's achieving the best forms of democratic community (see Glendon, 1991; Gutmann, 1996; Rorty, 1998; Schudson, 1998; Sober & Wilson, 1998; Tilly, 1999; Unger, 1987a, b; Worsham & Olson, 1999).

Typically, middle-class parents are viewed as the model for educational values, goals, and participation in children's education. The statement, "Middle-class parents expect their offspring to do well in school and believe schooling is the means to postschool career and social success," seems a banal synopsis of class standpoint and straightforward assertion of fact. When the ideological grounding of the statement is examined, however, its simplicity and neutrality become clouded. Because it is well documented that schools facilitate middle-class agendas—that members of this class are winners in the U.S. educational and occupational systems—notions of doing well (i.e., better than others) and getting ahead (i.e., creating social hierarchies) are problematic. The downside of some classes perpetually winning is that it depends on others losing; to state the obvious, social ranking stratifies and divides.

This book provides an overview of how members of the professional class—and I situate myself in this class and accept responsibility for complicity in class politics—use (our) agency in crafty ways to secure the best of what schools have to offer for our own children. In interviewing educated middle-class people, my goal was to understand the thinking that accompanies the pursuit of school privilege for children of one's own class. I designed the studies to learn whether the proponents of stratified structures were aware of the detrimental impact that unequal school conditions have on children of other classes. As I detail how the educated middle-class negotiates[5] school advantage and rationalizes[6] their actions, it is important to note that these same individuals are esteemed as the most intelligent, liberal, and well-meaning people in society. In this book, I cast a slice of Hillsdale citizens as villains. My aim was not to portray particular individuals or a whole class as evil but rather to show how certain flawed moralities and self-centered acts sway society away from an ethics of reciprocity and the best expressions of democratic community life.

To document the thinking of professionals who dominate school policy and practice, this book mainly draws from interviews conducted in the town where I have lived and worked for 34 years and have done a number of research projects related to social class. All my studies centered around local informants' educational values and goals, perceptions of local schools, and views of relations between people of different social classes.

In chapter 1, I review literature about stratified schooling, including the nature of social class and school structure formation as well as causes for class-related differences in educational attainment and achievement. I provide a short history of how *deficit* thinking about losers and *merit* thinking about winners shape American schools. Drawing from E. O. Wright (1985,

1989), I argue that the middle class is a contradictory class in terms of its status relative to lower socioeconomic groups as well as its thoughts about social life and schooling. Hypotheses about the extent to which the middle class monopolizes advantages and how ideologies veil both intentions and advantages are introduced in this chapter. I review theories about how neo-liberal perspectives of the middle-class managers of social institutions combine with those of global capitalists to undermine the possibility of equity and democratic community building in schools.

In chapter 2, I provide an overview of my own background as it relates to this research, the nature of the town of Hillsdale, the findings of my earlier studies of low-income residents, and the methods used in the studies reported in this book. In chapter 3, I address how affluent mothers, selected because of their involvement in school affairs, describe children and parents of their class and those of other classes. My analysis of their narratives makes use of British sociologist John B. Thompson's (1984, 1990) ideas about ideology as well as theories about women's roles in status production for the family. I describe the dissonance created by the clash between liberal values regarding equitable public schools and preference for segregated and advantaged educational circumstances for offspring of affluent mothers. In chapter 4, I focus on the conflicts between mothers' sentiments about progressive education and the desire for a tightly framed, traditional curriculum in which their offspring can establish measurable superiority.

In chapter 5, I examine the narratives of 22 teachers and 4 principals and make the case that personnel at mixed- or low-income schools differ in background, present status, and educational outlook from those employed at schools attended by children of high-income families. This chapter includes information about school personnel's awareness of the impact of social class on Hillsdale schools. I take a particular look at teachers who are first in their generation to go to college in chapter 6. Their narratives reveal their opposition to stratified school practices but indicate that their low status relative to affluent parents and teachers at high-income schools leads to a passivity on their part that leaves school hierarchies soundly in place.

I start chapter 7 with a selective history of central administration and school board impact on Hillsdale schools and end with summaries of the perspectives of former superintendents and assistant superintendents. Chapter 8 includes the research of Michelle Henderson, who interviewed school board members and a west-side[7] middle-class parent who had been in a position to follow school board affairs for several years. In chapter 9, I emphasize the importance of correctly identifying the sources of school disparities and provide a rationale for supporting equitable, democratic practices in schools and society.

1

Class Position, Social Life, and School Outcomes

---

everal facts are known about American social classes, schools, and students. First, adult wages vary widely, with the income gap increasing over recent years (Anyon, 2000; Sleeter, 2000).[1] Second, per capita pupil expenditure correlates with social class; hence schools differ in the quality of their facilities, materials, and human resources (Burton, 1999; Kozol, 1991; Orfield, 2000; Wenglinsky, 1998). Third, there is a high correspondence between student class status and school achievement and attainment (Jencks & Phillips, 1998; Lee, 2002).[2] Although these strong links between class status, school structures, and student outcomes are well known, social class is still ignored or treated as if it were relatively unimportant to schooling. Regardless of evidence to the contrary, because schools are thought to reward capacities rather than social standing, they are believed to be meritocracies in which students have equal chances to succeed. Meritocracies, however, are not based on an egalitarian principle of success for all; rather they differentially reward high intelligence, athletic competence, work ethic, and other types of student merit.

Americans waiver between assuming that students are essentially the same or very different. Based on the first assumption, all are expected to achieve above a statistical norm and are penalized if they cannot do so. For example, although school attendance is mandated to age 16, some states have legislated that students be denied a diploma if they do not pass graduation exit exams. A rationale for this draconian measure is that it sends a reality message to corrupted adolescents, neglectful parents, and inept or uncaring teachers (Fairtest, 1999–2000a). Such "for your own good" logic also undergirds competitive grading and castigating discipline—and is the same reason given for violence in child rearing (Miller, 1986). So, in spite of inflicting penalties that create hardships for certain students, proponents of these measures see themselves as caring about them. The contrasting sense that students are essentially different results in their being subjected to ranked grouping and competitive evaluation—practices leading to the failure of many students and/or limited access to enriched curricular and pedagogical resources.

Hierarchies are structured into meritocracies, yet in theory schools are to operate in fair and impartial ways so that children have equal chances to move up in social class rank and improve their life conditions. In reality, educational circumstances are not equal; wealthy white children inevitably are advantaged (Burton, 1999; Gamoran & Berends, 1987; Kohn, 1998; Kozol, 1991; Mills, 1963; Orfield, 1992, 2000; Ryan, 1969, 1981; Sexton, 1961). In *Schooling in Capitalist America,* Bowles and Gintis (1976) introduced educators to the now widely accepted theory that instead of facilitating social mobility, schools reproduce the stratified class structure of society by socializing children for predetermined class-related adult roles and circumstances. Sociological research confirms the validity of this theory by documenting the connections between families' class positions and the nature and quality of children's education (e.g., Anyon, 1980, 1981; Bernstein, 1971, 1973; Kohn, 1969, 1994; Kohn & Schooler, 1983; Kohn & Slomczynski, 1990; Lareau, 1989). For example, in *Learning to Labor,* Willis (1977) writes about how the resistance of British working-class youths to schooling and their consequent lack of school success results in their ending up with the same low-status jobs as their fathers. Many of these studies document the "way things are" rather than "why they are that way"; that is, little attention is paid to understanding human intentions or actions in school hierarchy creation. Morrow and Torres (1994) criticize classic renditions of correspondence theory (e.g., Althusser's structuralism) for dwelling on systemic phenomena that reduce people to interpellated, passive subjects. Structural-level analyses imply that stratification happens without deliberate human agency as perhaps the unintentional fallout of arbitrary social habits and benign conditions of practice. Scholars did ask Gramsci's (1971/1929–1935) perennially imperative "who benefits" from stratification question but did not explore how people deliberately negotiate and justify their advantage.

In *The Hidden Injuries of Class,* Sennett and Cobb (1972) include the anthropological and psychological concept of pseudospeciation, which refers to the inner solidarity and cohesion of a tribe (e.g., middle-class people) becoming so strong that they see their customs as universal. Such insiders are proficient at aligning institutions with their customs and, of course, at meeting their own standards. When they excel, they attribute success to superior traits and behaviors, hence believing they are more deserving than others and that rankings are legitimate, necessary, and even neutral. This account of hierarchy creation echoes Gramsci's theory of how hegemony confounds the thinking of bourgeois and working classes, so, in spite of contrary evidence, both believe that schools are fair and enable social mobility; they are meritocracies.

In contrast to the common assumption that stratified institutional structures, practices, and outcomes *just* happen, drawing from the work of prominent Marxist theorists (e.g., Apple, 1993, 1996; Bourdieu, 1977, 1984, 1996, 1998; Eagleton, 1990, 1991; Gramsci, 1929–1935/1971; Thompson, 1984, 1990; Young, 1990, 2000; Zizek, 1994; 1998), I examine implications of the view that social stratification is not a benign, chance occurrence but the result of people's intention and informed agency. Indeed, this book is grounded on the belief that dominant classes actively pursue advantage and that social class formation depends on the discursive and actual development of subordinates. Given the prevalence of school hierarchies and their resistance to change (Fullan, 1993; Tyack & Tobin, 1994; Weinstein, Madison, & Kuklinski, 1995; Weiss, 1995), it is reasonable to hypothesize that existing structures and practices are durable precisely because they correspond to influential people's desires, hence from their power to create and retain them (Bersoff, 1999; Connell, 1993; Schnog, 1997; Shor & Pari, 1999).[3] Although I do not deny that elites at the summit of hierarchies have the most to gain from stratification, educated middle-class individuals also benefit because they are relatively high up the social ladder. To set the stage for my analyses of the narratives of local educated middle-class people, in this chapter I give an overview of (1) the nature of dominant and subordinate group formation; (2) the characteristics of the educated middle class's position and perspective; and (3) the ways that ideology functions to support class distinctions. Additionally, because local social class relations do not exist in a vacuum, I provide theories about the impact of global capitalism and corporate control of the media and money on schooling and on social class relations.

DOMINANT AND SUBORDINATE GROUP FORMATION

Exploring the etiology and functioning of power in shaping activities within and between groups, Apfelbaum (1999), a Jewish refugee to France during World War II, theorizes that dominant groups develop standards based on their own characteristics and customs and expect others to emulate their styles and assimilate to their customs whether it is feasible for them or productive for society. They also create myths[4] about human features related to race, ethnicity, class, and gender that mark, label, brand, and stigmatize others as outsiders. Dominant group members imply that outlooks within their collective are homogeneous and that outsiders have little in common with them (Shanahan & Jones, 1999). Their power is maximized when the *us* and *them* binary is seen as fundamental and irreversible (Bourdieu, 1984). Apfelbaum points out that centering one group simultaneously marginalizes the Other.[5] Due to their low position in status hierarchies or history of unfavorable relations with dominant groups, peripheral groups have little access to goods and services (Nielsen, 1997). Privileging central groups in education is widespread, as is limiting the access to the best education of those on the periphery (Anderson & Saavedra, 1995; Bannerji, 1995; Bryson & de Castell, 1997; Coleman, 1988; Deyhle & Swisher, 1997; Sleeter, Gutierrez, New, & Takata, 1992).

The creation of dominant/subordinate group binaries (or hierarchies) is not purposeless but represents an important set of interdependent relations: superiority needs inferiority, normality/abnormality, success/failure, ability/disability, winners/losers. The role, status, and even raison d'être of dominant groups hinges on the existence of subordinates (Stallybrass & White, 1986). Basing ideas about empire building on Lacan's (1982) signification, Bellamy (1998) claims the colonizer's identity depends on a lack that can only be filled by a colonized Other (p. 342). Domination always results in subordinate oppression (Eagleton, 1990). Young (1990) delineates the components of oppression as (1) exploitation—structural relation in which some exercise their capacities under the control of others; (2) marginalization—expulsion or exile from labor or social life; (3) powerlessness; (4) cultural imperialism in which the dominant group's experience and culture are established as the norm, so the oppressed groups' perspective is rendered inferior and/or invisible; (5) violence—intimidation, humiliation, harassment, incarceration, physical attack (pp. 197–198). Based on his meta-analysis of anthropological studies, Brown (1991) concludes in *Human Universals* that people create power and status hierarchies to varying degrees, with distinctions based on sexuality, gender, class, or family (ethnic, racial) ties.[6]

Implicit to class reproduction is a pattern of distinction making or bias that prevents an equal distribution of benefits to groups. Tinney (1983) distinguishes three levels of bias: *individual* (prejudice, stereotyping), *institutional* (structural inequities), and *collective* (normative). Personal prejudice is most likely to be recognized and thus is easiest to address. In contrast, the institutional customs within and outside schools that locate some students in disadvantageous positions are rarely visible (as bias) to dominant group members (Corson, 1992). Normative bias is the most difficult to recognize because it permeates symbols and language (e.g., the term *black* has a host of negative denotations and connotations—sin, evil, crime, dirt, depression, death; Dyson, 1993; Morrison, 1993). White people do not see skin color as a privileging force (Bell, 1994; Cose, 1993; Henry, 1995; hooks, 1989; Ladson-Billings & Tate, 1995; Lawrence-

Lightfoot, 1994; Walker, 1997; Weis, 1990), men do not see masculinity as advantaging them (Connell, 1998; Gerschick, 1998; Haraway, 1988; Harding, 1998; Jensen, 1997; Lorde, 1984),[7] affluent people do not name the benefits of financial assets (Conley, 1999; Oliver & Shapiro, 1995; Ryan, 1971, 1981; Sennett & Cobb, 1972), and scholars do not see how their cultural and social capital allow them to dominate professional organizations (Brantlinger, 1997).[8] Teachers, who are largely middle class and white (Newman, 1998), uphold Eurocentric canons and customs that distance, dislocate, underrepresent, and misrepresent Others (Asante, 1991; Banks, 1997; Bannerji, 1995; Kozol, 2001; Marshall, 1994; Spivak, 1988, 1994) and are unaware of their complicity in systems that stratify and oppress (Britzman, 1997; O'Brien, 1998; Weiss, 1995; Wright, 1994). Given the damage inherent in biased norms and institutions, a goal of this book is to show how hierarchies are normalized by discourses and how the human intentions that bring them about are managed to be played down and denied.

CONTRIVING LEGITIMACY FOR DOMINATION: THE ROLE OF IDEOLOGY

Because of the importance of psychological dynamics in class positioning and school structure formation, I focus less on what affluent people do to create hierarchies and more on what they say (i.e., think) about what influences education. Many constructs that are used for thinking (e.g., perceptions, opinions, attitudes, beliefs, social constructs, tacit and explicit knowledge, internalized scripts, mental representations of reality, ideologies; Pajares, 1992) could have provided a reasonable framework for analyzing study participants' narratives. Alexander, Schallert, and Hare's (1991) *tacit knowledge*—deeply embedded, subconscious[9] sociocultural thought—could have worked as could Nespor's (1987) *beliefs* with their strong "affective components that reside in episodic memory" (knowledge is stored semantically; pp. 311–321). I settled on ideology as a central analytic construct because of its historic links to critical theory and Marxist analysis but mostly because of its aptness in explaining the processes of domination and subordination that were apparent in the narratives of the educated middle-class people interviewed for this book.

Ideology is "meaning in the service of power" (Thompson, 1984, p. 7) or the "production of principles, ideas, and categories that support unequal class relations" (Apple, 1992, p. 127). According to Gramsci's (1929–1935/1971) theory of hegemony, ideology is integral to the struggle of dominant groups to keep subordinates in designated places and counter resistance from them. Force can be used to establish and maintain power—as it has been historically—but it is nicer and more efficient to convince those in low positions of the legitimacy of hierarchy and disparity. In democracies, dominant groups must have some degree of permission from subordinates to exert control over them; that consensus is achieved by circulating ideologies that obfuscate the rankings and power imbalances that work against equity for peripheral groups. By permeating language and thought (Bakhtin, 1981; Zizek, 1989, 1998), ideology allows privilege to redound to the powerful without people's conscious knowledge of whose interests are served (Eichstedt, 1998; Lukes, 1974). Ideology "allows the dominant class to appear not as a class but as representative of the whole society" (Larrain, 1992, p. 52). It also insulates beliefs from criticism and establishes a basis for group solidarity (Burbules, 1992).

Ideologies are systems of representations (images) or complexes of narratives composed of familiar and respected (religious, scientific) texts (Althusser, 1974/1976; Barrett, 1994; Zizek, 1994). As "anonymous discourse on the social" (Thompson, 1984, p. 27), ideologies mediate people's understanding in profoundly unconscious ways (Althusser, 1971; Bakhtin, 1983). Coterminous with institutional structures (Bourdieu, 1996),[10] ideologies work like a "network of templates or blueprints" through which experience is articulated and orientations to actions are (re)constituted (Geertz, 1973, p. 11). Institutions become bureaucracies with an excessive commitment to norms. As norms become rigid, rational situational responses are prevented (Sergiovanni, 1991). Thus, institutions resist change and defend uniform behaviors; they regulate oppression as they generate ideologies that naturalize their existence (Popkewitz, 1991). As with individual neurosis, institutional pathologies have damaging consequences (Habermas, 1978).

Rationality's place in ideology is debated. Boudon (1994) maintains that although the irrational has a residual place in their creation, ideologies start "*not in spite of but because of* human rationality" (italics in original; p. 24). As "common sense beliefs about political and social matters," ideologies are based directly or indirectly on scientific authority (p. 73). At the same time, ideologies resonate with people's needs, anxieties, passions, and fantasies (Cookson, 1992). For example, a common ideology, the "egalitarian myth," comforts American middle classes while offering hope to the poor (Boudon, 1994, p. 180). The master signifiers (identity-bearing words) embedded in ideologies are important to the psyche (Lacan, 1982).

Bucking a trend by some scholars to neutralize ideology, British sociologist John B. Thompson (1990) formulates a critical conceptualization of ways that "symbolic forms[11] intersect with relations of power" so that "meaning is mobilized to establish and sustain relations of domination" (p. 56). Thompson asserts that "social location and entitlements associated with positions endow individuals with varying degrees of power to make decisions, pursue ends, or realize interests." He further clarifies that domination occurs when "established relations of power are systematically asymmetrical" and "particular agents have durable power which remains inaccessible to others" (p. 59). I use Thompson's (1990) ideological operations and symbolic construction strategies (see Table 3.1) to identify manifestations of ideology in participants' narratives; my critique illustrates how an interlocking stock of ideas backs normative cultural practice to support the elevated status of dominant groups, thus allowing stratified social relations to seem right, natural, and inevitable (Rochon, 1998). Polanyi (1957) notes that the ideas and customs that support stratified social relations become so internal and visceral that they are taken for granted regardless of social actors' class position. As Bourdieu (1996) writes, "social hierarchy dissimulates itself to those it dignifies no less than to those it excludes" (p. x).

Ideologies that mystify class relations take various forms including storytelling. This chapter presents familiar versions of ideological storytelling that are circulated by dominant class scholars, educators, and parents to account for class distinctions in educational and occupational outcomes. In the early to mid-1900s, lay and scholarly stories focused on genes, race, and ethnicity; that is, tales of biological determinism were widespread. Theories about genetic inferiority were accepted as proven by scientific evidence (see Gould, 1981, 1995) and the eugenic remedies that were acted upon by public officials had dire consequences for "contaminating groups."[12] The most dramatic example is the deathly ethnic purging (extermination) of Jewish and Roma peoples by Germans in the Holocaust of the 1930s and 1940s. Subsequently, genetic explanations for human distinctions lost their appeal. Nevertheless, when explanations of genetic differences in intelligence emerge (e.g., Jensen, 1969; Herrnstein & Murray, 1994), they get considerable public exposure in the popular press—some indignation and condemnation, but much is rather ambiguous.[13]

During the 1960s and 1970s, when genetic theories were mostly out of style, the idea of cultural deprivation was featured in social science and lay theories about social class differences in student achievement. For example, the classic ideological "American dream of social mobility," combined with tales of "school as a meritocracy," cause a range of students to believe that the playing field is level and those who excel do so by virtue of natural talents while those who fail are lacking. Another popular portrayal (ideology) is that poor people do not care if they fail in school and choose to live in poverty. The happy ending of these stories for high achievers is that they are entitled to rewards and need not worry about the negative school and life circumstances of Others. Because the affluent are distanced geographically and psychologically from poor people's lives, their impressions have little connection to reality.

Cultural deprivation arguments were debunked a generation ago (Keddie, 1973). Still, an enduring social construct is that poor children's unsuccessful school careers are due to insufficient intellectual stimulation at home and parents' not caring about education.[14] In spite of the criticism of victim blaming (Ryan, 1971) and of locating problems in those subjected to racism rather than in racists (DuBois, 1965), discerning inferiority in Others continues to dominate public discourse and social science research (Brantlinger, 1997; Valencia, 1997; Wright, 1993). Deficit sentiments (ideologies) also reverberate through the rationale of policy makers. Ray and Mickelson (1990) cite U.S. Secretary of Labor Cavazos's espousal of a defective worker philosophy in his claim that trade and budget problems cannot be resolved without overcoming educational problems. National projects such as *A Nation at Risk,* 1983, (U.S. Department of Education, 1983) and *America 2000,* (U.S. Department of Education, 1991), based on assumptions of deficient workers and declining global competitiveness, passed with bipartisan support (Arons, 1997). By constantly criticizing schools and students and proposing actions that have little relevance to solving actual problems, political and corporate leaders divert attention from disadvantaging school conditions (Natriello, 1996, p. 8) and ignore the self-serving actions of powerful people. Using these tactics, corporate and government officials abdicate responsibility for the dire economic circumstances of many families.

In contrast to theory based on presumptions of poor people's inferiority, a seemingly kinder way is understanding the poor as culturally different. British sociologist Basil Bernstein (1971, 1973) locates the cause of working-class students' lower school performance in the disjuncture between their restricted code and the elaborated communication style of middle-class school personnel—that is, to code mismatch. In spite of the emphasis on cultural relativity rather than inferiority, the terms *restricted* and *elaborated* are semantically loaded and imply a hierarchy in which one style is better. Others who subscribe to difference theory[15] also expect the dominant class to understand differences while the onus is on subordinates to change (e.g., learn elaborated or standard code).

Whether they explicitly proclaim a conviction about parental lacks, family literacy projects also function under versions of deficit and difference hypotheses (see Auerbach, 1989). It can be argued that the burgeoning technorational enterprise[16] aimed at improving the educational outcomes of low-achieving children is undergirded by deficit hypotheses because inadequacies are found in children or families and remedies are designed to change them. Similarly, the standards and accountability movement is based on the complementary premises that some teachers and/or students are inadequate and either/both must improve. Although not as destructive as Nazi death camps or as great a violation of human rights as forced sterilization or institutionalization, public revelations of low test scores and enforced sanctions for failing schools and students inflict substantial symbolic violence on subordinates in the current system. The onus is on them to "catch up" with high achievers to improve their personal chances for a decent life and/or resuscitate the nation's economy. What is lacking in these scholarly and public discourses is mention of a need to equalize school expenditures or raise low-income families' salaries to reduce the disparities in educational and life circumstances.

In answering the question of who benefits (Gramsci) from recent educational trends, I argue that the educated middle class gains from expanded professional roles and accumulated evidence of their own superiority and the corporate class benefits from the sale of remedies (Metcalf, 2002) and from having a scapegoat to blame for the nations' supposed economic woes.[17] Ideological tales divert attention from their superior conditions and selfish actions. Subordinates are not asked how they feel about segregated or lesser status nor are they seriously included in decisions that affect them. It is implied that remedies benefit them or the whole society. Yet benefits are partial—*only* for the dominant. Harvey (2001) quotes Marx as stating that whenever there is a hoarding of resources (including social status) by some, the accumulation of misery for Others is a necessary condition (p. 28).

THE ROLE OF THE EDUCATED MIDDLE CLASS IN SOCIAL LIFE

Most Americans describe themselves as middle class (Brantlinger, 1993; Felski, 2002); hence, in some ways, class is an amorphous and ambiguous construct. However, there are many ways this comfortable self-definition of class status is fractured. Anyon (1980) distinguishes an affluent professional (equivalent to my "educated middle") class from lower-salaried white-collar workers. Locating what he calls the "new middle class" in a contradictory position between the polarized capitalist and the working classes, E. O. Wright (1989) points out that, lacking capital, they do work for wages and thus in a classic Marxist sense are capitalistically exploited. Because of financial assets, they tie their interests to upper classes and believe they benefit from capitalism. Educational credentials[18] raise them to the status of a cultural bourgeoisie with the specialized expertise to shape institutions, establish official knowledge, set standards, define social space, and generate cultural distinctions (Bourdieu, 1977, 1984, 1996). Composed of such highly skilled wage earners as managers, social workers, teachers, and psychiatrists (Gouldner, 1979), the new middle class is empowered to "contain the struggles of subjugated classes" (Wright, 1989, p. 24).

Real authority ultimately lies with capitalists; nevertheless, credentialed workers or "faceless professionals who are competent members of a social class going about the business" of using "technical expertise to work within a discipline" (Foucault, 1980, p. 7) comprise a "reign of experts" (Troyna & Vincent, 1996) who police social life with a "technocratic certainty that they understand other people's happiness better than they do"

(Bourdieu, 1998, p. 27). They control[19] the masses through the major disciplinary instruments of hierarchic surveillance, normalizing sanctions, and examination (Foucault, 1977). A tacit consensus exists among educators, scholars, and elites that only expert knowledge is legitimate (Tyack & Hansot, 1982). Others' cultural traits and preferences are not represented in the governance of public institutions, and, because they are devalued, attempts are made to eradicate them (Banks, 1997; Foster, 1997; Sleeter, 1995).[20] Funding initiatives supposedly aimed at helping the poor have increased professional jobs for the college educated. While the ranks of the poor expand, their conditions worsen, and their isolation becomes more profound, jobs in the social service sector have proliferated as have the credentials needed to obtain them. Some (Brown, 1995; Danforth, 1996; Gordon & Keiser, 1998) question the value of these proliferating specialized fields and people's dependence on credentials garnered through higher education[21]— phenomena that result in an ever-expanding professional middle class with ever-tightening standards to secure their monopoly of higher ranks (Gouldner, 1979; Wright, 1985).

In modern times, social divisions are solidified and officially sanctioned by legislated regulations and professional protocols. The Individuals with Disabilities Education Act (1990) authorizes disability categories and due-process guidelines for practice. States mandate high-stakes tests and accountability measures to control teachers and students. Roles of providers and consumers of services are monitored to ensure compliance with established procedures. Power imbalances between local actors are depersonalized—professionals only do their jobs—so power relations are disguised as they are perpetuated. For these reasons, Ringer (2000) challenges the "received view" that the relation between educational expansion and democratization of nations is constructive (p. 158).

Professionals put forward members of their class as models to emulate. Educated parents are touted as the ideal in terms of valuing education and encouraging achievement (Epstein, 1990; Epstein & Scott-Jones, 1992; Mayer, 1997; Will, 2002). They constitute an unstudied but positively imagined control group against whom Others are unfavorably compared. Few in the educated middle class consider how their class might have a detrimental impact on society or Others in their community, yet studies of middle-class parents and educators show that they endorse class-partial practices (Eichstedt, 1998; Kozol, 1991; Packer, 1992). Sieber (1982) details how affluent parents who moved into renovated brownstones in an urban area demanded advanced classes for their children, thereby creating the two-tier system in which substantially more resources went to affluent children. Lipman (1998) quotes an administrator who said that upper-middle-class white parents say they are supporters of public schools but want their children isolated and tracked in them (p. 1). In Ontario, Canada, Olson (1983) documents how funds meant to improve relations between English- and French-speaking people went to French-language immersion programs attended only by advanced middle-class children.

Horvat, Lareau, and Weininger (2002) note the propensity of affluent parents to be knowledgeable about school affairs and integrated into school functions and information networks. They control their children's course and program choices and intervene in decisions regarding them. The information resources, attitude of advocacy, and critical surveillance of practice that affluent parents bring to their school interactions are powerful and effective (Lareau, 1989). Furthermore, middle-class people believe that advocating for school advantage for their children is integral to being a good parent (Brantlinger, Majd-Jabbari, & Guskin, 1996). David (1993) documents how this trend toward "parentocracy" means children's educational conditions depend on mothers' actions. Other scholars describe how educated parents unite in collective actions to secure advantages for children of their class (Graue, Kroeger, & Prager, 2001; Kohn, 1998; Lareau & Shumar, 1996; Lipman, 1997; Useem, 1992; Valdes, 1996). Whitty (2000) claims that the British middle class has effectively colonized public education for themselves. Parents of the educated middle class are strong advocates for their children and, unlike their poor or working-class counterparts, are positioned to exert considerable influence over schooling (Apple, 1992; Ball, 1994; Bersoff, 1999; Farazmand, 1999; Grimes, 1997; Oakes, Gamoran, & Page, 1992; Tooley, 1999). As they pursue preferences for their children (i.e., hoard opportunities; Tilly, 1999), they determine the nature and quality of education for all children (Lovelace, 2002; Oakes & Guiton, 1995; Thomas & Moran, 1992; Wells, 2002; Wells & Serna, 1996).

RELEGATING OTHERS TO LESSER STATUS

Eagleton (1990) notes that it is the oppressors' privilege to decide what the oppressed should be. In schools this translates into separating children from poor and working-class backgrounds from the mainstream and referring to them with disparaging epithets (Apter, 1996; Caplan, 1995; Capshew, 1999; Kutchins & Kirk, 1997; McDermott & Varenne, 1996; McLeod & Hertog, 1999; Varenne & McDermott, 1998). Classifications impact how others see children as well as how they see themselves (Kailin, 2000). Segregated placements inevitably result in decreased school and postschool success (Ansalone, 2001; Dunn, 1968; Wells & Crain, 1992). Reynolds and Wolfe (1998) report that children who receive special education services have lower reading and math achievement scores than comparable students left in mainstream classes and that students separated for longer times have the lowest scores. Low-achieving students placed in high tracks make academic gains within a short period of time (Mehan, Hubbard, & Villanueva, 1994; Oakes & Guiton, 1995). Even when students select their track placements—what some school patrons mistakedly call detracking—students' track choice is influenced by their sense of identity as well as invisible institutional barriers, so lower-income students and students of color still end up in lower tracks (Yonezawa, Wells, & Serna, 2002).

According to Bourdieu, schools have taken over the task of sanctifying social divisions through generating inequalities and stigmatizing even average performance (cited in Roth, 1992). Classification is a "practice of power deeply inscribed on the oppressed" (Ladwig & Gore, 1994, p. 234). Inequality and stigma inflict symbolic violence (humiliation, alienation, and rejection) on those labeled and educated in the lower echelons of stratified schools. Yet technical labels are touted as scientifically correct and objectively determined; hence, they are impervious to criticism (Howe, 1997). It is this pretense of objectivity and neutrality that makes ranking and classifying systems especially pernicious (Delamont, 1989; Fine & Roberts, 1999; hooks, 1994). Because ranking systems are officially endorsed by professional and governmental guidelines and due-process procedures,[22] they happen with the collusion of subordinates, although subordinates are never sufficiently informed nor can their participation be seen as voluntary (Ball, 1994; Bourdieu, 1996; Brantlinger, 1986b).

Although professionals often maintain that schools geared to distinctive characteristics of students are humane in preventing students' frustration and failure,[23] there is evidence that people whose children end up in second-rate alternatives are opposed to such arrangements. Kantor and Lowe (1995) claim "no black constituency demanded compensatory education; nor did any organized black group participate in the formulation of federal legislation that endorsed compensatory practices" (p. 9). My studies reveal that working-class and poor youth and their parents are bitter about low-track and special education placement (Brantlinger, 1986b, 1993).[24] Wrigley (1982) writes of how Chicago working classes historically fought vocational programs through labor organizations. They wanted their children in comprehensive schools because they were aware that separate systems were inherently unequal and limiting.

EXPLANATIONS FOR SOCIAL CLASS AND SCHOOL OUTCOMES CORRESPONDENCE

Agreement exists among educational researchers that students' achievement and attainment corresponds to their social class status (Coleman, 1988; Coleman et al., 1966; Jencks, 1972). Disputes arise about how to account for differences. Regardless of myths and stereotypes about working-class and low-income people, my interviews with parents and youth indicate that lesser educational outcomes are not due to language or intelligence deficits nor are they the result of families not valuing education (Brantlinger, 1985a, 1986a, 1993). Similarly, others have found that lower-income people share the reverence of the middle class for education and the good life as well as the conviction that social mobility depends on school success (Dibos, 2002; Kozol, 2001; MacLeod, 1987). Admittedly, because they are rational in judging their life circumstances, working-class and poor children and their parents have lower expectations for educational and occupational attainment (Brantlinger, 1986a). They cannot afford private supplementary advantages during their K–12 education or the expenses of higher education (Orfield, 1992; Ryan, Sheldon, Kasser, & Deci, 1996). Because they rarely benefit from it, the competitive school structure does not play the same motivating role for them as for middle-class students (Brandau & Collins, 1994). Class advantage may be invisible to those who benefit, but subordinates are acutely aware of barriers to opportunity (Delpit, 1995). And, past struggles either alienate students from school or leave them resigned to the likelihood of future unfavorable circumstances (Brantlinger, 1985a, 1993); that is systemic bias has a cumulative effect on morale (Mickelson, 1993). Some oppressed students protest bias and resist domination by engaging in opposition to school authority (Ogbu, 1995; Willis, 1977). Creating counteridentities to oppose stereotypes and discrimination may sometimes be advantageous; (Fraser, 1989; Mehan, 1992, 1995), however, refusal to conform often results in retaliation by those in charge, which worsens students' chances relative to mainstream school agendas (MacLeod, 1987; Willis, 1977).

The most salient reason for school achievement disparities is that poor, working-class, immigrant, inner-city, and minority children are hampered by the character and quality of their schools (Burton, 1999; Fields & Feinberg, 2001; Gamoran & Berends, 1987; Jencks, 1972; Kozol, 1967, 1991, 2001; Ludwig & Bassi, 1999; Orfield, 2000; Seiler & Tobin, 2000; Sexton, 1961; Wilson & Corbett, 2001) and inadequate family income (Bales, 1999; Polakow, 1992; Rubin, 1976; Ryan, 1969; Weis, 1990; Wildman, 1996; Wilson, 1987, 1996). Local control of school finance means that along with better life conditions, students from wealthier families receive a better education. Yet inequities are rarely addressed by politicians, the media, or scholars. Although not legitimate in a wealthy country that could revise the tax base and resource distribution, given the local property tax–based funding of public schools, quality differences between districts might be expected. But disparities are also common within districts. Lipman (2002) notes extreme differences within the Chicago Public School System and claims they result from three levels of policy implementation: (1) *Rules* seem fair to all (2) but are *enacted* distinctively according to each school's student (class) composition; and (3) at the *symbolic* level, students, parents, and school personnel react to rules from their class positions. Powerful parents insist on the best resources for their children's education (Wildman, 1996). Less influential parents have similar hopes for their children's schools, but their wishes go unrealized (Brantlinger, 1985c; Harry, 1992; Lareau, 1989). Although school personnel might be responsive if poor people were more assertive, because subordinates are resigned to life's disparities, they tend to expect school inequities and do not feel entitled to make demands (Brantlinger, 1985a, b).

Lower-income people do not choose inadequate schools (Lauder et al., 1999; Lee, 1993, 1995; Lee, Croninger, & Smith 1996; Thrupp, 1998), but policy failure at various levels means they have little control over school quality (Anyon, 1997; Apple, 2001; Orfield, 2000). They also do not have the power of the pocketbook to buy houses in neighborhoods known for good schools (Schneider et al., 2000). Even when they attend heterogeneous schools, tracking results in students of different classes not having the same opportunities for learning (Ansalone, 2001; Oakes, 1985; Oakes, Gamoran, & Page, 1992; Oakes & Guiton, 1995; Ryan, 1981; Sexton, 1961; Varenne & McDermott, 1998; Wells, 2002). Because of the intersection of social class status and race/ethnicity, children of color are overrepresented in low-status classes and underrepresented in high-status ones (Artiles & Trent, 1994; Barton & Oliver, 1997; Brantlinger, 1986b, 1993; Connor & Boskin, 2001; Harry, 1992, 1994; Oswald, Coutinho, Best, & Singh, 1999; Patton, 1998; Tomlinson, 1982, 1999). Teachers select Eurocentric middle-class–oriented curriculum, which, when combined with the messages taught through the stratified school structure, causes poor children and children of color to believe that they are not as smart and deserving as their middle-class white counterparts (Brantlinger, 1993; Carlson, 1999, 2002; Dibos, 2002; Graue, Kroeger, & Prager, 2001). Some are so alienated that they give up on the biased system before they reach high school (Brantlinger, 1993; MacLeod, 1987; Willis, 1977).

If working-class and low-income people value an enriched curriculum and social class–inclusive classes and schools, and if they do better in mixed and enhanced circumstances, citizens—especially educational scholars—must ask why segregating practices exist and why curriculum and pedagogy vary according to social class status. Because I was convinced that discrimination and social class, ethnic, and racial apartheid were not unintended, I designed studies of educated parents and school personnel to shed light on these issues. However, before I turn to the findings of my ethnographic work, it is important to connect ideas about the educated middle class to the broader context of national and international politics in which people and schools in communities such as Hillsdale are situated.

GLOBALIZED CAPITALISM, NEOLIBERAL IDEOLOGY, AND SCHOOLING

In thinking about modern society, the idea of drift captures how globalized capitalism[25] evolves without conscious planning or rational deliberation on the part of a broad base of citizens (Glendon, 1991; Hamilton, 1998; Wolfe, 1998). People naively believe that expanding markets and production automatically result in improved material and social conditions (Childs, 2000; Gupta, 2000; Hall, 1983; Harvey, 2001). As Bourdieu (1998) puts it, people "collectively, in the mode of consensus, have an atavistic faith in the historical inevitability of productive forces" and "utter a fatalistic discourse which transforms economic tendencies into destiny" (p. 18). Carlson and Apple (1998) build on Gramsci's theory that in advanced capitalist societies (in a Fordism era of mass production), consumerism drives industrialization, human thinking, and the organization of public institutions (pp. 6–7).[26] Challenging the idea that the spread of capitalism is progress, Weil (1999) claims:

> Postmodern capitalism, with all its emphasis on material acquisition at the expense of human sovereignty and dignity, has created a society whereby heroes and heroines have been replaced by celebrities, artists replaced by producers, and citizens replaced by consumers. It is a society marked by insipid individualism, rabid consumption, material acquisition, and a collective loss of reason and historicity. (p. 91)

Similarly, Kincheloe (1999b) writes that "even conservative analysts have come to understand the negative psychological impact of market-driven capitalism with its commodification of desire and its decimation of community" (p. 5). Yet, even if negative effects are in view, if the United States resembles France, the public chooses "political candidates according to narrow-minded, regressive, security-minded, protectionist, conservative xenophobia" (Bourdieu, 1998, p. 18).

Jones (2000) reports on how the organization of economic activity transcends national borders and jurisdictions with globalized capitalism; thus, transnational corporations (TNCs) avoid the taxation and regulatory discipline that conventionally has been the concern and responsibility of national governments. Acknowledging this trend, Stromquist and Monkman (2000) claim that not only are TNCs the primary agents of globalization but they are its major beneficiaries. Hirst and Thompson (1996) believe that corporate leaders and the free-trade liberals[27] who support them feel that politicians have no other task than to protect unfettered worldwide trading. Calling the federal deficit a "license to steal, because it lets the upper class manipulate accounting procedures and transfer funds to themselves without changing taxes," transferring "the burden to future generations," Kalra (1995) elaborates on the consequences of neoliberalism:

> The function of (the myth of the free market) ideology is to divert the attention of the sheep from reality. This is done by repeating shibboleths like free markets, free trade, performance, double taxation, capital formation, and jobs like a mantra over and over again. The idea is that the sheep will believe what they are told and blame one another for the travails. (p. 147)

Worsham and Olson (1999) concur that "the neo-conservative right has mastered the logic of hegemony in recent years" (p. 130).

Ahmad (1992) argues that the modern time period has witnessed an unprecedented growth of capitalist technological power—a "global triumph of colonialism" in "an imperialized world" (p. 17) that has a great impact on local cultures and civil relations within and between national borders.[28] Yet, curiously, while capitalism expands globally, its influence goes unnoticed. Americans do not call themselves capitalists (Kailin, 2000). The United States is the largest imperial power in history, yet this is rarely mentioned.[29] When global capitalism is brought up within the neoliberal enlightenment discourse, it is not framed as imperialism but rather as freedom and progress (Sleeter, 2000).

Bourdieu (1998) claims that neoliberalism succeeds in presenting itself as self-evident because nothing is put forward to oppose it. Others warn that the problem with counteracting corporate control of public thought rests mainly with the media (Scatamburlo, 1998). Whereas in the first part of the 20th century newspapers and radio stations were locally owned by citizens of a variety of political persuasions, currently the small number of large communication networks are owned by fewer than two dozen enormous profit-making corporations (McChesney, 1997). Messages supporting corporations and bureaucratic institutions have worldwide circulation (McChesney, 1999; McLeod & Hertog, 1999; Viswanath & Demers, 1999). Regardless of general knowledge that workers are exploited, the rationality of the market and the importance of entrepreneurs taking advantage of economic opportunity are touted (Glendon, 1991; Harvey, 1996, 2000, 2001; Huntington, 1996). The media ignores or negatively portrays anyone who protests the system (Glasser & Bowers, 1999).

Another tactic to distract the public from concerns they should have about poor conditions for workers and corporations' colonization of land and people (Martin & Schumann, 1997; Sleeter, 2000) is to focus news on crimes and Hollywood, and keep the public entertained with soap operas and sitcoms. Instead of reporting the poor conditions in American schools, which reveal the need for public expenditures or tax increases (Carnoy, 2000;

Natriello, 1996; Neill, 2000), the media focuses on inferior students, teachers, and workers (Mortimore & Mortimore, 1999). Britzman (1992) calls the highly publicized idea of declining teacher quality (and similar media messages) an "arranged, slippery history that hides its interestedness and politics of selection" (p. 73). Educational coverage consistently recommends business-oriented measures to correct the problems they identify (Metcalf, 2002). The ideological messages connected with globalization refute scholars' claims that school funding and quality do matter in terms of student outcomes (Krueger, 2000). Corporate intervention in school governance encourages technical and test-oriented schools that reproduce and aggravate the current social class and wage structure (Neill, 2000). Economic globalization discourses are not unique to the United States but frame educational policies the world over (Ball, 1993, 1998; Hargreaves, 1994; Hatcher, 1998a, b; Medovoi, 2002; Mintrom, 2000; Morley & Rassool, 1999; Reay, 1998; Taylor, Rizvi, Lingard, & Henry, 1997).

One message that has dominated the media is the supposed decline of schools. This hype may have been generated to fill the vacuum left when the communist threat was no longer a sensation.[30] Certainly a cold war logic infuses the anxiety about inadequate workers and risk of losing in global markets or in high-tech battlegrounds. Pronouncements of pending doom are not unique to the United States; hyperbolic concern about lacks in functional literacy tied to fears of national vulnerability is evident in England (Ball, Kenny, & Gardiner, 1990) and Australia (Taylor, Rizvi, Lingard, & Henry, 1997). Nevertheless, informed critics provide statistics to refute the validity of claims that literacy is declining (Baron, 2000; Bracey, 1997; Rothstein, 1999) or that economic troubles are due to ill-prepared workers (Berliner, 2000; Kenway, 1998; Noddings, 1995).

Berliner and Biddle (1995) call the agitation about academic decline and the United States losing ground compared to other nations a "manufactured crisis." Smyth and Schacklock (1998) reject the position that schools can or should be engines for economic restoration. Apprehension about the scarcity of competent graduates in technical fields (U.S. Department of Education, 1983, 1991) is contradicted by the evidence of high unemployment rates among graduates with advanced degrees in mathematics, science, and technology (Boutwell, 1997; Noddings, 1994; O'Brien, 1998). Furthermore, the actual high educational attainment rates in the United States have not prevented jobs with sustainable salaries from disappearing (Wilson, 1996). Even if achievement were declining, it is unlikely that tougher standards for student performance would effectively improve schools or the economy (Kohn, 1998; Kozol, 2001; Meier, 2000; Ohanian, 1999; Starratt, 1994).

Members of the educated middle class probably do not consider themselves imperialists, capitalists, or even advantaged; nevertheless, they are enthusiastic consumers of material culture and cherish the commodified credentials that enable them to manage public affairs. Sleeter (2000) argues that elites increasingly call the shots about education and legislate social controls that bind students to the existing social order. Kalra (1995) concurs: "the upper class has an institutional monopoly" and "the electoral system ensures that no matter who wins, upper class control of the government remains unaffected" (p. xi). Wells (2000) documents a free market rationale for those who support school choice (e.g., charter schools, public vouchers for private schools), which she sees as a backlash against redistributive reforms aimed at decreasing disparities in education and society.

Lykes, Banuazizi, Liem, and Morris (1996) warn that a sharp conservative turn in U.S. politics in the mid-1990s promises to undo progressive social politics that were fought for and won in the 1960s and 1970s because "an ideological crusade by the neo-conservatives has sought to persuade the middle and working classes that their own stagnant economic position is not due to unfair advantages accorded to privileged groups but to the slothfulness of 'welfare mothers,' the overburdening of our schools and social service agencies by immigrants, and the undue advantages enjoyed by those who have been helped by affirmative action programs" (p. 8). Piven and Cloward (1996) call welfare bashing an easy political strategy that is integral to "the new class war." As corporate officials condemn the undeserving poor for putting a drain on the economy (Gans, 1996) and use scare tactics about recessions that would come from businesses folding, they relocate their companies to third-world countries without wage and environmental regulations, or, for that matter, compulsory education. Meanwhile, TNCs make huge profits and colonize citizens of rich and poor nations (Sleeter, 2000). Ahmad (1992) claims that "economic realities surround and saturate us" (p. 70), so "corporate repressions and an expanding compliant, affluent bourgeoisie [professional and managerial class] are interrelated" (p. 36).

While the workings of capitalism have remained invisible and social inequalities have been reluctantly acknowledged (O'Brien, 1998), the income gap between classes has widened. Referring to the material losses of the working class as a "pauperization of wages," Anyon (2000) observes that globalization has meant a concentration of extreme wealth in relatively few international families and increasing poverty and hopelessness among large sectors of society.[31] In England, Garmarnikow and Green (2000) report poverty at 33% with increasing class polarization. As social classes are polarized financially and divided spatially, whether due to false consciousness of class interest or misperception of the enemy, the struggle over limited resources is more often within classes than between them. Desperate economic conditions pit weaker citizens against each other[32] while elites compete for high-paying or high-status positions (Lasch, 1993). Some project that while the middle class may benefit temporarily from the hierarchies they create,[33] a political equality in which each person influences the political process through elections and other means is central to democracy. So, when inequalities escalate, democracy is under threat internally (Lasch, 1995; Miller, 1996; Osbourne, 1996; Rorty, 1998). The decline of social responsibility among elites (Lukas, 1998) and feelings of powerlessness in subordinates (Lukacs, 2000) generally result in alienation and political passivity among American citizens (Eliasoph, 1998).[34]

The impact of global politics on schools is not the focus of this book; however, it must be acknowledged that the attitudes and behaviors of the various middle-class people in my studies do evolve in a polarized social world in which there are disproportionate benefits and injuries from capitalism and class standing (Piven & Cloward, 1979, 1996) and that the social, political, and economic climate shapes human thinking and actions. As Anijar (1999) points out, "individual enterprises [her example is slavery] exist in an 'all encompassing economic system' " (p. 56). Ahmad (1992) claims that economic realities surround and saturate us (p. 70), so corporate repressions and the rise of a compliant and affluent bourgeoisie (college-educated professional and managerial class) are interrelated (p. 36).

The spectacle made of education in the political arena and the media has caused state and national legislation (e.g., U.S. Department of Education, 1983, 1991) demanding student and teacher performance on a narrow range of measures (Anderson, 2002). Education is turned into a ritual performance rather than being an authentically meaningful experience (McLaren, 1986). Corporate messages inculcate an orientation that only technical knowledge that contributes to the market is of value (Brock, 1999; Gelberg, 1997; Harvey, 2000; King, 1995; Lukacs, 2000; Stromquist & Monkman, 2000; Weil, 1999). This technical expedience mentality impacts what students learn or do not learn (Fairtest 1999–2000a, b; Hatton, 1997; McNeil, 1995, 2000a, b). Hinchey (1999) claims that "instrumental rationality turns learning into a mechanistic, depersonalized activity" (p. 128). Leistyna (1999) adds that teachers are reduced "to passive, objective, and efficient distributors of technical information" (p. 7). Similarly, by emphasizing distinctions between types of learners and specialized instructional techniques, teacher education is a conservative determinant of teacher practice (Brantlinger, 1996; Britzman, 1991, 1997). Once on the job, external pressures for students to score well on standardized tests inevitably intensify teachers' job demands, causing teaching to seem like meaningless busyness (Hall & Harding, 2002). Some teachers are so anxious about the negative repercussions of their students getting below-average scores that they resort to cheating (Associated Press, 2000, June 8).

Most educators admit that the accountability and standards movement embedded in this technocratic educational milieu results in certain students' failure. But Carlson and Apple (1998) warn of the negative effects of this kind of schooling on the identity formation of successful students. All pay a price for excessive competition, strict focus on credentialing, and knowledge packaged into measurable pieces. In *Competitive Ethos and Democratic Education,* Nicholls (1989) claims success is defined as superiority over others. He regrets that losing diminishes students' feelings of accomplishment and winning exacerbates egotism. Those who excel have a sense of superiority and entitlement (Brantlinger, 1993) or an "individualistic and narcissistic orientation" (Anyon, 1980, p. 74). Americans are dominated by "the egoistic conception of equality as equality of opportunity to compete for society's prizes" rather than a "noncompetitive conviction that all people are equally and uniquely valuable, and have the same claim on the respect of their fellows and the benefits of the society" (Watt, 1994, p. 227). Saavedra's (2000) claims that opulent people's demand for commodification of knowledge damages all students.

Regarding the themes of this book, corporate notions of inferior workers correspond to the ideas of the educated middle class about the inferiority of other people's children. Perhaps because they gain from the market economy (Dale, 2000; Rizvi & Lingard, 2000), affluent professionals find global capitalists' perspectives credible. Privileges and wealth are concentrated in these classes, so both subscribe to the neoliberal optimism that progress is tied to market development—what Harvey (2000) calls the teleological inevitability of global capitalism (p. 13). The neoliberal ideology that translates democracy into individual rights and freedoms provides the justification for unrestrained competition on the economic front as well as in classrooms (Gutmann, 1996; Koggel, 1998; Lamont, 1992). Monopolizing the best neighborhoods, schools, and courses is legitimated by a market mentality. Consumption and expansion are the order of the day. Queries about whether this mentality amounts to progress are discouraged. Referring to the extensive use of cars and tremendous growth in house size and suburbs reported in Census 2000, Kunstler (2000) tallies the huge economic, social, environmental, and spiritual costs that America pays for its consumer-crazed lifestyle.

WHAT IS STUDIED AND SAID; WHAT IS IGNORED OR SILENCED

Although the public continuously hears about low-achieving students, there is a remarkable silence in scholarly journals and the media about the nature and worth of current achievement goals, the prevalence of practices that advantage some children, and the impact that privileging systems have on the persistence of social rankings. Instead, educational scholars, political theorists, politicians, and media pundits reiterate a multitude of theories about flaws in the disadvantaged to explain the correspondence between social class and school outcomes. Because everything is political and ideological (Zizek, 1994)—and actions are purposeful—it is reasonable to assume that what gets studied and announced or hidden and silenced is a product of influential groups' intentions and is based on their desire to sustain their own personal (class) interests (Thompson, 1984, 1990). In analyzing the trends in discourse and practice, it is important to keep in mind that dominant groups are constantly energized to come up with new theories to support their hegemony (Gramsci, 1929–1935/1971). Although subordinate groups are not content with the consequences of the current social class dynamics, dominant groups not only are satisfied but they take the social class divisions in society for granted and are motivated to further entrench and expand them. Most scholars do not conjecture about the class structure, recent intensification of social class distinctions, or proliferation of tools designed to solidify and reify distinctions. They do spend time trying to explain the class-correlated differential educational outcomes in ways that are not attributed to their own desires or actions.

This chapter has provided a summary of theories relevant to the nature of social hierarchies, the position of the educated and credentialed middle class relative to global capitalism, and the function of ideologies in creating and sustaining hierarchies. Though cursory, it is hoped that this overview has clarified my ideas about social life, thus providing the grounding for the studies of educated middle-class individuals included in this book.

2

Examining Social Class Reproduction at Micro and Emic Levels: A Critical, Interpretive Study

My long-term interest in how social class influences intergroup relations and life outcomes turned into a formal research agenda when I observed friends and neighbors' reactions to a series of school closings in Hillsdale in the early 1980s. Because low-income families rarely attended the school board meetings and did not air their views in letters to the editor of the local newspaper—as their affluent counterparts did—I decided to go to low-income people to find out how they felt about the state of educational affairs. The events surrounding the school closing and the ramifications from them are described in somewhat more detail in a brief recent history of administrative and board actions in chapter 7. To clarify what aroused my interest in social class issues and particularly what motivated me to study social class relations in Hillsdale, I begin this chapter with an autobiographical sketch before I detail the methods used in the studies of parents and school personnel.

NOTICING CLASS

I grew up in a small town in Minnesota in the 1940s and 1950s. My mother was a second-grade teacher and my father, who started out as a high school teacher, became a case worker for Social Security when he returned from World War II. In 1946, the year I started first grade, my parents bought an old summer cottage on White Bear Lake, and after a few winters of huddling around a space heater in the living room, my parents saved enough money to winterize the house. A short story by Fitzgerald, "Black Bear Lake," gives a fictional account of life at the summer mansions on an island and a peninsula across the lake from my family's modest home in the small town of Mahtomedi. Located about 20 miles from St. Paul, which at that time took about 30 minutes by an interurban streetcar[1] and 45 to 60 minutes by winding road, the area on the south shore of the lake consisted of resort homes of varying sizes along the lakeshore and farms and working-class families' residences away from the lake in the surrounding area.

Perhaps my first encounter with class distinctions was watching the summer folk with their expensive clothes, boats, and homes. Occasionally I was temporarily friends with summer children, but those of us who lived in Mahtomedi year-round were set apart and mostly quite intimidated by the lifestyles of our wealthier neighbors.[2] As a teenager I worked as a maid, house cleaner, and babysitter for some of these people. In the winter, when the affluent people left us, our town became similar to other small towns in rural Minnesota. I went to school in the same building with mostly the same 40 classmates for 12 years. The majority of my schoolmates did not go to college. Although we were tracked across grade levels in math and science in high school, students were otherwise grouped together. Participation in school activities and friendship patterns crossed class lines. In winter, class distinctions were not an obvious part of daily life.[3]

Because my parents were politically left wing, they encouraged me to go to Antioch College in Ohio. It had no honors sections, competitive athletics, or Greek system. A sense of community responsibility was the pervading ethos of college life; competition and materialism were frowned upon. After several years of teaching secondary social studies and special education in Ohio and in the Boston area while my husband was in graduate school, in 1968 we moved back to the Midwest. My husband became an English professor and I a doctoral student at the large state university in Hillsdale. We bought a house in an older part of town close to the university, had one child, and adopted two more. Our neighborhood elementary school had a social class mixture because an adjacent lower-income residential area was in its catchment zone and some rural children were bused to the school.

Our children may have been in a somewhat mixed school; however, our family socialized almost exclusively with university people. Through the years, I noticed that these neighbors and friends were selective about their children's playmates and extremely forward in demanding privileged school circumstances for their children. Most had grown up in suburban areas on the East or West Coast or in large midwestern cities, and a number had attended private elementary and secondary schools. They talked about the local people with suspicion and disdain, conveying that these people were considerably different from themselves. Some worried that the local dialect of Hillsdale teachers and children would rub off on their children. Perhaps because I had attended a school with social class[4] diversity, I was puzzled by these attitudes and became increasingly bothered about them.

In 1978, after completing my doctorate, I began to teach special education courses and coordinate field experiences, and continued to do so for two decades. I placed approximately 100 preservice teachers per year in preschool to adult general and special education settings mostly in Hillsdale but also within a 60-mile radius of the university, which included inner-city, small town, and rural schools. Most of the field placements were in public schools, but some were in other programs.[5] My typical schedule was to supervise field experience students from Monday to Thursday mornings and student teachers on some afternoons and Fridays. I observed students, discussed their work with them and their supervising teachers, and met with principals to make arrangements or deal with problems. By 1993, I had spent at least 5,000 hours observing in schools, adding 2,000 more during the 5 years until I resigned from directing undergraduate programs in 1998 to coordinate the curriculum studies doctoral program. Although I have done mainly interview studies, my thorough acquaintance with Hillsdale and its schools provides a contextual exposure that merits calling my studies ethnographies.

When my youngest child was in third grade, the neighborhood elementary school closed. One plan suggested by the board of school trustees was to zone the neighborhood children to one of two nearby low-income schools. At that point, the previously latent feelings about social class surfaced as full-fledged terror in my university-affiliated neighbors. These supposedly liberal parents vociferously opposed any suggestion of desegregating schools along class lines. Yet, a few years earlier, many of these same people had condemned the resistence of whites to racial desegregation. Of course, they had watched racial desegregation from a safe distance because fewer than 5% of Hillsdale's population were African American. In contrast to other parents, I tried to convince my neighbors and the school trustees that if our children were zoned to the closest low-income school, it would then be a mixed school. This stand irritated neighbors.[6] Based on an attempt to satisfy high-income patrons on both sides of this debate, the trustees decided to allow families a choice of attending either Richards, a high-income elementary school at a greater distance from most homes, or Southside, a low-income school within walking distance for most families. Of the 134 elementary-age children in the neighborhood, only 4, including my youngest child, a 9-year-old, went to Southside. Admittedly, Southside was dilapidated, lacking resources, and the grounds were not attractive, but my husband and I reasoned that if we believed in neighborhood schools and class integration, then Southside should be our choice.[7]

At the time of the school closings, because of my daily contact with friends and neighbors, I was aware of how high-income people felt about schooling, and because I visited all Hillsdale schools on a daily basis, I was familiar with the inequitable conditions. On the other hand, I had no idea about the perceptions and opinions of low-income people in Hillsdale, although neighbors who opposed social class desegregation assured me that "*they wanted to keep to their own.*"

In 1984, my intrinsic curiosity about low-income people's thoughts and opinions led to my first study of social class in Hillsdale.[8] Theories about social class correspondence (Bowles & Gintis, 1976) resonated with my understanding of phenomena I observed during my own earlier years of public school teaching and later supervisory experiences in Hillsdale. I was convinced that class bias permeated school and community life, but I did not know how local low-income people felt about local schools. In this study, I contacted parents by going door to door in low-income neighborhoods[9] on evenings and weekends, told prospective informants that I was a teacher educator interested in how parents felt about schools, and often interviewed them immediately. I eventually interviewed 26 mothers and 9 fathers (Brantlinger, 1985a, b, c, 1986a, b). At least 75% of contacted parents agreed to be interviewed. Among other things, I learned that low-income parents were aware that better programs and conditions existed at schools in high-income neighborhoods, surmised that district lines were deliberately drawn to separate classes, and felt that most teachers did not particularly like their children and would prefer to teach at higher-income schools. Parents were bitter in recalling the pain of their own schooling. Most felt there was a stigma attached to the low-income schools and that class desegregation would mean their children would have access to a better education; however, they also spoke of the rejection and low status that were likely to occur if their children were to go to mixed elementary schools because they had witnessed this happening to their children in the class-heterogeneous secondary schools in town.

A few years after the study of low-income parents, I interviewed 40 adolescents (aged 13–18), again using a residential census approach in housing projects and other neighborhoods in the catchment zones of schools with high free-lunch counts. The interviews took place in their homes, yards, or nearby public areas (parks, playgrounds, parking lots). As with low-income parents, these youths spoke of painful experiences in school that they attributed to their social class status. They envied affluent class advantage while also indicating a strong but somewhat ambivalent identification with their own class. Consistent with ideas of hegemony, many adolescents internalized negative views of themselves and believed that more affluent students were brighter and generally more worthy of advanced school placement and better school outcomes. Subscribing to the ideology of schools as meritocracies, they judged schools to be mainly fair, although they were extremely angry about their interactions with some uncaring teachers, their failure, and their low placement in tracks or special education. Their bitterness had a profound impact on my thinking. While documenting the extensiveness of their insight into class dominance, I also noted the debilitating nature of the negative images they held about their class and how they echoed the meritocratic ideologies of dominant classes.

After studying these working-class and poor people, I noted and wrote about their intelligence, insight, and common humanity but perhaps was still influenced by the pervasive view that the answer to problems having to do with inequities lay within them. Eventually, however, after years of informally listening to my advantaged neighbors, friends, and colleagues (and perhaps to my longings for myself and my own children), I saw the need to turn my scholarly gaze inward and upward at professional classes and observe what Wexler (1992) refers to as the "textured nature of the psycho-dynamics of institutional life" (p. 8) and the impact of class status on students' interpersonal relations in schools and on their self-dynamics (i.e., the construction of identity through cultural signs and social class symbols).

In addition to my studies of low-income parents and adolescents, while doing field experience supervision, I conducted an informal survey of various school practices by observing in buildings and talking to teachers and principals. I checked with principals and/or guidance counselors who were responsible for making ability group or achievement track arrangements at each school about how they made placement decisions. I learned that regardless of student achievement, some deliberately took students' class status into account and justified this class-based sorting on the grounds that "they knew" that certain students either were or were not going to college or that certain parents would or would not protest low placements and/or demand high ones for their offspring. In 1984, I wrote a report, *What a Model Community Sweeps Under the Rug: Class Discrimination in the Schools,* which I gave to school trustees, central administrators, some principals, and the local press. Although there was no public recognition of this report, it did trigger a number of changes (e.g., remodeling and/or rebuilding of low-income schools, an equitable fee distribution policy, discontinued use of a biased teacher transfer policy, some modification of grouping practices) that somewhat reduced class disparities in schools. It also appeared to have inspired some reporters to do more stories about equity in local schools and to include more coverage of the events at low-income schools in the newspaper.

LEARNING TO TURN THE SCHOLARLY GAZE INWARD AND UPWARD

As the reader will ascertain, in this book I do not follow the tradition of studying historically marginalized groups to explain social class reproduction but look upward and inward at segments of the middle class who have high levels of educational attainment as well as high levels of influence on schools. Borsa (1990), Bourdieu (1984), Ellsworth (1989), and Wright (1993) recommend that researchers study their own groups. Following this advice, I chose participants similar to myself in ethnicity, educational experience, professional careers, gender (in the case of the study of middle-class mothers), and social class.

After hearing low-income parents and teenagers discuss their perceptions of the attitudes and actions of upper classes, I decided to turn my scholarly gaze upward, first focusing my attention on 34 affluent adolescents. The results of that study were reported along with those of low-income youths in a book entitled *The Politics of Social Class in Secondary Schools: Views of Affluent and Impoverished Youth* (1993). Next, because of the power of middle-class adults to shape education through their professional positions and actions as influential parents, I decided that an understanding of their thoughts about schooling was especially important.

Although my previous studies had not been funded, colleagues and I received enough funding from the School of Education Proffitt Grant to hire two graduate students for two of the studies included in this book (high-income parents, school personnel) to do some interviews and transcribe the audiotapes of interviews. For a variety of reasons, including illness and retirement as well as the graduation of the doctoral students, I have done the analyses and interpretations of data and written the report of results from these studies myself.

Early social class reproduction theories were based on analyzing the generalized meta, macro, structural, or systemic levels of social life; thus they were often reduced to pessimistic accounts of class determinism in which people of each social class were reduced to descriptions that seemed to give them essential and eternal class-bounded characteristics. Correspondence theorists did not look closely at the agency or thinking processes of dominant people. And, relatively few acknowledged the insight and resistant agency of poor and working classes. Some ethnographers do examine the micro level of reproductive schooling by observing interactions among actors in social settings and they study the emic level of people's understandings by overhearing conversations or directly listening in interviews (e.g., MacLeod, 1987; Willis, 1977). Fine (1991) examines school structural factors as well as adolescents' views in her attempt to understand the complexities of school dropout phenomena. Scholars have begun to gaze upward at affluent or high-achieving students and elite schools (Mathews, 1998; Peshkin, 2001; Powell, 1996; Proweller, 1998). Eder (1995) observes how affluent middle-school students occupy the prestigious spaces of school that are closed to poorer students. Offering insights into antisocial acts by middle-class students, Merton (1994) looks at the behaviors of parents to conclude that home and community pressures are at the root of bullying and put-downs in middle-school social relations. Some studies of class reproduction include people's "improvised acts" and "idiosyncratic meanings" (Holland, Lachicotte, Skinner, & Cain, 1998, p. 279).

In contrast to "neutral" ethnographies in which researchers confine their reports to description and hesitate to incorporate explanations and interpretations that differ from those of participants, I analyze the underlying, tacit meanings of narratives and am often highly critical of certain participants' thinking and actions. In studying dominant-class individuals, the qualitative researcher's purpose clearly is not to give voice to "the traditionally silenced." Dominant voices, by definition, already are loud and influential. Furthermore, educated middle-class individuals are neither oppressed nor marginalized. They do not need researchers to advocate for them—they are extremely competent at self-advocacy. It may be unfair to criticize the actions of generous participants or, especially, to deconstruct the narratives of the unsuspecting. Yet, the truth value of research with dominant people is more important than kindness and more likely to have an impact on equitable schooling than respect for participants. In this book, the results of interviews with affluent mothers, school personnel, and school board members are analyzed and reported. Because these people are similar to myself, my critical analyses may be construed as self-scrutiny. Indeed, I discern my own thoughts reverberating through the narratives of mothers and teachers. Therefore, to some extent, my criticism of participants is self-criticism.

Like others (e.g., feminists, postmodernists, Marxists, poststructuralists), I am open about how my position and perspectives ground and guide my work and shape the lens through which I see and interpret social life. Although some recommend that researchers bracket their own lives and ideas so as not to influence findings, I maintain that none of us begin any study—qualitative or quantitative—without ideas about what we will find. Most of us have fairly developed theories about social life and, whether we are aware of it, we do try to substantiate our views through our empirical work. Hence, I do not deny that I bring by understandings of macro-level concepts to my studies and fuse them with the observations of micro-phenomena that I glean through the data collected in interviews. It is important to be straightforward in admitting that because I believe correspondence theory provides a valid explanation for class relationships, I very deliberately devised ways in planning my studies to explore how agents' class-embedded personal meanings and class-oriented activities coalesce to form social class identities and produce influential discourses that reproduce class hierarchies within schools and throughout society. Thus, I do not always take participants' narratives at face value but rather scrutinize them for deeper, tacit meanings that might explain relations of domination and subordination. Because of my interest in the psychodynamics related to people's social class positions, I do an ideological critique of participants' thinking and the tacit sociocultural knowledge embedded in their discourses.

RESEARCH APPROACH

Making the claim that social class is salient in determining the nature of interpersonal interactions in schools, Wexler (1992) cites the need for empirical studies of the psychodynamics of teachers, administrators, students, and parents. Giddens (1987) contends that for institutions to make sense, the thinking that undergirds them must be understood. My interest in subjectivity, tacit knowledge (Bakhtin, 1981), and deep thought structures (Kincheloe, 1993), as well as in "unpackaging culture" (Cole, 1996), led me to use interpretive inquiry to explore professionals' thinking about their children and schooling and to gauge their preferences for certain school structures. Drawing from the fields of anthropology, sociology, and linguistics (Atkinson, 1985; Bakhtin, 1981), interpretive research is based on the premises that meaning is created through affective and contextualized processes and language has constitutive power (Gaskins, Miller, & Corsaro, 1992). Mehan (1992) claims that interpretive studies can get close to the processes by which social stratification is generated, so this approach offers a means to understand the complexities and conflicted views of a dominant class. Interpretive studies are not always in the critical genre; however, my ideas are consistent with the tenets of critical theory that unequal power relationships among people are ubiquitous and that a primary goal of scholarly work is to explore the nature of power differentials and act to reduce them. My aim was to add the cultural and psychodynamic elements of participants' active sense-making to macro theories of social class reproduction (Mehan, 1992).

A perusal of academic journals and books is likely to reveal a proliferation of qualitative techniques and/or terms to describe them, as well as a blurring of boundaries between research methodologies and scholarly disciplines. The language used for research undertakings reflects scholars' particular fields but also their idiosyncratic circumstances, social contexts, educational backgrounds, and political or philosophical orientations. I call my studies interpretive, but because the interviews are embedded in a knowledge of context that comes from my long-term observation in Hillsdale and in its schools, they amount to an ethnography designed to "describe and interpret cultural behavior" (Wolcott, 1987, p. 43). Thus, because my class analyses come form a critical theory perspective, this book might be considered to be a "critical ethnography" (Anderson & Irvine, 1993).

I do narrative analyses (Elbaz-Luwisch, 1997) and discourse analyses (Fairclough, 1992) of participants' stories about themselves, their children, and schooling, using deconstruction as a tool to scrutinize texts and discourses. I incorporate such concepts from literary criticism as verisimilitude, metaphor, prototypes to describe the rhetorical images, and good stories (believable but not necessarily true accounts) that add to the credibility and persuasiveness of the ideological texts I examine (see Keller, 1994, pp. 28–30). According to Ewert's (1991) self-reflective criteria, the study might be hermeneutic. It also fits van Manen's (1990) idea of a phenomenological method that gets information about people's practical knowledge. Consistent with the advice of Morrow and Torres (1994), my research is a "historically specific theoretical formulation that integrates the agency-structure dialectic in analyzing processes of social and cultural reproduction" (p. 48).[10] My long-term observations of social and institutional life in Hillsdale have informed me about the macro level of class relations. Through interviews with a range of individuals, I believe that I have come to understand much about the emic level of social life and the psychodynamics of discourse and identity construction of various groups in town.

SETTING AND PARTICIPANTS

The studies reported in this book were conducted in "Hillsdale," a Midwestern city with a population of about 65,000. The town is dominated by a large (35,000 students) state university. Class bifurcation is evident in residential life (high-income people live primarily on the east side and low-income people on the west side of town), so children of different classes mainly attend separate elementary schools. The two high schools and junior high schools[11] are located on the north and south sides of the city, thus cut across the east/west class-related residential patterns and have similar class heterogeneous enrollments. Nevertheless, tracking results in substantial social class segregation of pupils within secondary schools.

Study of Educated Mothers   Parents of Anyon's (1980) "affluent professional" (rather than "executive elite" or "white-collar") class were selected for the study[12] (see Table 2.1). An initial round of eight families who had been active in school affairs (e.g., library volunteers, Parent Teacher Organization members or leaders, coordinators of such extracurricular activities as theater groups or foreign-language instruction) were identified. Interviews were conducted in participants' homes by a Middle Eastern graduate student.[13] Participants were contacted by telephone and arrangements were made for home interviews. On completion of each interview, participants were asked to suggest others they knew who had been active in school affairs

Table 2.1

Educational and Occupational Attainment of Mothers and Spouses

	N	%
Highest Degree Earned by Mothers		
Doctorate	4	20
Master's, plus	3	15
Master's	7	35
Bachelor's, plus	1	5
Bachelor's	4	20
Attended college, 2 years	1	5
Occupations of Mothers		
Professionals	18	90
writers/editors/researchers	5	25
public school teachers	4	20
professors	4	20
administrators (welfare department, shelter for abused women, home day care, group home for adults with mental disabilities)	4	20
librarian	1	5
Clerical worker	1	5
Homemaker	1	5
Personal Schooling of Mothers		
Mainly attended private schools	11	55
Mainly attended suburban schools	7	35
Attended class-comprehensive schools	2	10
Occupations of Spouses		
Professors	15	75
Businessmen	2	10
Minister	1	5
Press editor	1	5
High school teacher	1	5

who might take part in the study.[14] In each household contacted, mothers agreed to be interviewed. All were white.[15] Participants had between one and five children (mean of 2.75), the youngest of whom was 7 and the oldest 28. The children of 18 had attended secondary schools; the offspring of 2 had already graduated from high school.[16] Three mothers had grown up in the state but none in the town where the study took place. Eleven attended private schools for at least part of their school careers.

My intent was to include either or both parents; however, mothers usually answered the telephone and agreed to participate.[17] The few fathers who answered promptly turned the phone over to their wives.[18] Interviewing only women was unintentional; however, when I began to see the pattern as more than coincidental, I decided that including only mothers was an adventitious occurrence that added to the strength of the study. My primary interest was social class, and I had not thought much about its intersection with gender. A subsequent literature review revealed that theories of gender in social class reproduction, though underdeveloped, were significant (Atkinson, 1985; Walkerdine, 2000). Women's roles are heavily overlaid with domestic and status production work for the family (Collins, 1992). More generally, Connell (1987, 1998) writes of a systematic connection between economic exploitation of capitalism, paternalism, subordination of women, and the relegation of domestic work to women. Concern with children, schooling, and family status apparently are the domain of women; it is mothers who negotiate with schools regarding children (Biklen, 1995; David, 1993; Lareau, 1989; Useem, 1992).

Study of School Personnel   Thirty-one Hillsdale school personnel, including 4 central administrators, 4 principals, 22 teachers, and 1 school secretary,[19] were interviewed (see Table 2.2). Principals and teachers were selected to include the spread of elementary to secondary grade levels as well as to represent schools in high-, mixed-, and low-income residential areas. Because I wanted the participants to be well informed about Hillsdale and its schools, I selected mainly people who had several years of experience. Information about teaching experience, income level of the school's student body, and parental status of participants is included in Table 2.2. Interviews were conducted by two faculty members (one of whom is the author) and a graduate student. Interviews took place in participants' homes or workplaces. Each was audiotaped and transcribed.

DATA COLLECTION AND ANALYSIS PROCEDURES

As with my earlier studies of social class (i.e., low-income parents and high- and low-income adolescents), this research with affluent mothers and school personnel was centered around informants' perceptions of education, their

Table 2.2

School Personnel Interviewed

		Years of Experience
Teachers—Elementary		
*Kindergarten	High-income school	17 (some at low-income schools)
*3rd grade	Low-income school	23
*3rd grade	Low-income school	20
*3rd grade	Mixed-income school	23
*3rd grade	High-income school	14
*4th grade	Low-income school	22
4th grade	Low-income school	31
*4th grade	Mixed-income school	23
*5th grade	High-income school	17
*5th grade	Mixed-income school	30
*5th grade (G&T)	High-income school	11 (some at middle, low-income)
*5th grade	Low-income school	16 (some at middle school level)
6th grade	High-income school	23
*Physical Ed.	Low-income school	24 (half at middle school level)
*Librarian	Low-income school	13 (some high & mixed schools)
Art	Low-income school	3
Teachers—Secondary		
Science (general sections)	Middle school	28
*English (2 honors, 1 basic)	High school	27 (10 as elem. sp. ed.)
Social studies (general sections)	Middle school	8
Social studies (honors sections)	High school	4
*English (general sections)	Middle school	17
*Social studies (advanced)	High school	21
Administrators		
*Retired superintendent		41 (6 as teacher and 20 as principal)
*Former interim superintendent (1 yr.)		25 (11 as principal, 9 as teacher, 3 as personnel director)
*Asst. superintendent—elementary		19 (4 as elem. ed. teacher)
*Asst. superintendent—secondary		24 (20 outside this district)
*Principal—middle school		17 (11 as teacher)
*Principal—low-income elementary		16 (8 as teacher)
*Principal—high-income elementary		13 (8 as teacher)
*Principal—high school		8 (6 as teacher)

*Person is a parent.

values and goals regarding education, their understanding of education in the local area, and their views of the relations between social classes in the town of Hillsdale and its schools. The interviews consisted of three stages of questioning. Stage 1 explored their general feelings about education (e.g., concerns about current education, strengths and weaknesses of local education and education elsewhere, the education of this generation of children compared with their own education, purposes of schooling, preferences for certain types of pedagogy and curriculum). Stage 2 focused on local education and social class issues (e.g., the equivalency of all schools in the district, schools they would or would not want their children to attend, what they believed low-income parents and children thought about local schools, their contact with people of other social classes). Stage 3 used two forced-choice items: (1) whether they would support redistricting to allow for social class desegregation of schools, and (2) whether they approved of banning ability grouping and tracking. Stage 1 was designed to partly gauge whether participants would bring up social class on their own as well as explore their own ideas about schooling. Stage 2 directed them to talk about class issues. Stage 3 required participants to commit to specific positions about social class relations. All interviews were tape-recorded and transcribed.

Narrative analyses involved developing themes and identifying issues that emerged during the interviews (Merriam, 1998). Because of my interest in tacit knowledge (Bakhtin, 1981) and ideology, language usage and meanings embedded in narratives were closely examined. The approach resembles what Kincheloe (1993) calls "post-formal concern with deep structures" (p. 148); with uncovering the tacit sociopolitical forces "to get behind the curtain of ostensible normality" (p. 149). Attempts were made to evaluate the affective tone of discourses as well as the significance of the sequence in which topics were addressed. In chapter 1, I reviewed the literature on ideologies and introduced Thompson's (1984, 1990) modes of operational analyses that guided my search for evidence of ideology in affluent mothers' narratives. Because this approach is mainly used in chapter 3, I provide more information about it in that chapter.

3

Affluent Mothers Narrate Their Own and Other People's Children

---

To understand social class disparities in educational and occupational outcomes, social scientists inevitably have looked at or hypothesized about poor people and minorities—those previously called "cultural deprived" and presently called "at risk." Deficit-oriented scholars come up with theories about what poor people do wrong that keeps them in subordinate positions and what we—white middle-class professionals—can do to help them better themselves. Although the intentions behind such research seemingly are benevolent, recommendations that scholars be funded to seek solutions and/or professionals to provide services may ultimately be more self- than other-serving. The remedy is never to increase the money that the poor receive. Even champions of the left use such concepts as false consciousness in a partial way to explain how working classes are duped into subscribing to ideologies that strengthen the position of dominant classes—a theory that implies they are not as intellectually astute as their affluent and educationally advanced counterparts. Thus, the poor not only lose out in power relations and material distribution but also in negative aspersions about their intellectual attributes. To combat such injustices, in this book I show that false consciousness is common to dominant classes. To win educationally, and ultimately materially and morally, such classes use obfuscating ideology and rhetoric to convince Others, but perhaps mostly themselves, of their superior intelligence and work ethic, while still crediting themselves with the moral high ground of being benevolent toward Others and thus liberal. They negotiate win/win[1] situations for themselves, which result in the ubiquitous lose/lose conditions for Others.

In this chapter, as well as in chapter 4, I examine middle-class mothers' narratives about children and schooling, and conjecture about the self-serving purposes of their stories. To understand domination and subordination patterns and ferret out deceptions in mothers' stories, I use Thompson's (1990) ideological operations and strategies to illustrate how their depictions of their own and Other people's children provide the rationale and justification for the case they make for their children's need for distinctive and separated school circumstances. I show how mothers readily relegate Other people's children to segregated settings and lesser conditions while claiming that such arrangements are in the Other's best interest. Yet, they would never tolerate low tracks, special education placements, and schools with predominantly low-income enrollments for their own children. Finally, I document how mothers still perceive themselves (and expect to be seen by others) as liberal regarding social class relationships. As noted in chapter 2, in my ideological critique of mothers' narratives, I make use of Thompson's (1990) modes of ideological operations and symbolic construction strategies (see Table 3.1). Specific uses of particular operations and strategies are in italics.

SOCIAL CLASS DISTINCTIONS AND SELF-LOCATION IN THE CLASS SYSTEM

When asked about their class background, none of the mothers called themselves "upper class," three said they were "upper middle class," and one joked she was a "yuppie." In spite of referring to multiple layers of classes and noting distinctions within the middle class, consistent with Thompson's ideological operation of *symbolization of unity,* mothers located themselves within middle-class boundaries. *Naturalization, eternalization,* and *universalization* strategies of symbolic construction allowed them to portray their middle-class traits as an inevitable and permanent essence of themselves and others of their class. However, the fear of their children's falling away from that symbolic center and class position surfaced as a real concern and as influential in mothers' preferences for certain school structures and practices.

Though amorphous and ambiguous, the middle-class category is a positive collective with which to identify.[2] Being in the middle—neither a "have" nor a "have not"—means not taking on the negative characteristics associated with class extremes. The rich, for example, are commonly portrayed as snobbish and greedy; the poor as ignorant, mentally slow, lazy, unclean, and violent (Brantlinger, 1993). In my class analysis of *Good Will Hunting* (Brantlinger, 1999b), I noted how members of upper classes (Harvard students) were represented as competitive and hostile while lower-class hoodlums fought Will and his buddies and Will had flashbacks of his abusive father. Will and Skylar were exceptions to their respective classes, a comforting portrayal that meant the American dream is alive for the deserving poor and that middle-class people like Skylar—and the viewers—are not prejudiced about class. In the study reported in this book, mothers did not directly distinguish themselves from pushy stereotypes of the rich, yet their

Table 3.1

Thompson's (1990) Modes of Ideological Operation and Strategies of Symbolic Construction

---

Legitimation—when relations of domination are represented as just and worthy of support

Rationalization—a chain of reasoning that defends a set of social relations or institutions and seeks to persuade an audience of its worthiness of support

Universalization—represents institutional arrangements that serve the interests of some as serving the interests of all

Narrativization—embeds justifying actions in stories

Dissimulation—when relations of domination are concealed, denied, obscured, or represented in ways that deflect attention

Displacement—when positive or negative connotations are transferred to other objects or individuals

Euphemization—when institutions, actions, or social relations are (re)described in terms that elicit a positive evaluation.

Unification—allows individuals to be embraced in a collective identity, irrespective of any differences and divisions

Standardization—when a certain framework is promoted as the shared and acceptable basis of symbolic exchange

Symbolization of unity—construction of a collective identity diffused through a plurality of groups

Fragmentation—dispersal of individuals and groups capable of mounting a challenge to a dominant group

Differentiation—focus on divisions, distinctions, and characteristics that disunite individuals and groups

Expurgation of the other—construction of an enemy, either from within or without, which is portrayed as evil, harmful, or threatening and must be resisted

Reification—represents a transitory, historical state of affairs as if it were natural, permanent, and outside of time

Naturalization or Essentialization—a social creation is portrayed as the inevitable outcome of innate characteristics

Eternalization—deprives phenomena of social-historical character by emphasizing their permanent, unchanging nature

Nominalization—focuses attention on certain central and salient themes at the expense of other marginal or decentered ones

Passivization—ignoring and deleting certain actors and agency.

---

avoidance of the upper-class category for themselves perhaps indicates they eschewed those unflattering images and thus located themselves in the nebulous and neutral middle.

Being in the middle implies a three-tiered class system. Yet, because the rich were not mentioned in mothers' narratives and because they constantly contrasted their own middle-class traits with those of the poor, it is reasonable to conclude that mothers constructed a social class dichotomy that separated middle from lower classes. Binary distinctions play a key role in all social categorization regarding gender, intelligence, sexual orientation, worthiness, race, ethnicity, or class. Derrida (1982) maintains that dichotomous oppositions in language fix boundaries between what is acceptable and unacceptable; then distinctions are reinforced by emulating the acceptable and avoiding the unacceptable. In spite of rhetorically placing themselves in a social middle, mothers anchored themselves on the upper end of a two-tiered class system. In turn, as quotations in this chapter show, they constructed class superiority by playing their characteristics against the less desirable traits of poor people.

Although only a few mothers had substantial contact with poor people, the lower class was symbolically visible in narratives as a problematic group who possessed few redeeming qualities and shared virtually no commonalities with mothers. Mothers also spoke of the middle class as homogeneous, rarely mentioning within-class distinctions. By referring to themselves and their children as "ordinary," they implied that Others were not. Such *unification* operations using the ideological strategies *standardization* and *symbolization of unity* allowed mothers to enclose the group with whom they identified while creating a less-than-ordinary Other. In an earlier study (Brantlinger, 1985b), low-income parents similarly used "normal," "regular," and "ordinary" for children of their class, contrasting them with "hotshot kids," "those with money," "snobs," "to-do's," "status people," and "your respectable ones."

The creation of binaries is not neutral or benign. In analyzing group formation dynamics, Apfelbaum (1999) points out that using centered and decentered categories has deleterious consequences for those on the periphery. In my study, mothers eagerly established themselves as middle class and declared who was not in their collective. Thus, the *fragmentation* ideological operation with its *differentiation* and *expurgation of the enemy* strategies is apparent in this distinction-making process. As in all societies with hierarchical social divisions, the high continuously reinvent themselves as superior to retain power (Bourdieu, 1984). In *The Sublime Object of Ideology* (1989), Zizek refers to the Lacanian concept of enjoyment, *joissance,* to clarify how the logic of exclusion operates in such discourses as racism (or class bias). The directionality of exclusiveness is not just from high to low. My studies of low-income parents and adolescents indicate that people in low positions engage in various forms of resistance to being stigmatized and excluded. One form is inventing an alternative scale for gauging social value. They assert that, unlike wealthy people, they are not snobs, selfish, or full of themselves. Epithets such as good students, preppie, and respectable ones are imbued with derision and cynicism. Counterculture and anti-intellectual sentiments result in high achievers being called nerds or geeks. Misbehaving youth and even low achievers may be seen as cool. Negative terms become semantically positive, as in black adolescents use of "bad" for things they like and value. Nevertheless, consistent with ideas of hegemony, those in low positions also internalize the dominant class's degrading categorization of them and tacitly consent to being in the stigmatizing and demoralizing low placements to which they are relegated by those in power.

Unification ideological modes emerge as central to within-class solidarity and *fragmentation* operations are essential to between-class divisions. Regardless of individual differences, those within a social category are felt to be basically similar and those without a social category are in all ways dissimilar. Perhaps the greater the disparities in societal rewards, the more actors attempt to establish clear distinctions and solidify their position in the acceptable side of the binary. High and low positions are interdependent and juxtaposed. The sense of worthiness of one group is based on confirming the unworthiness of Others. Stallybrass and White (1986) use the term *demonization* for the process of fixing categories of exclusion in which the top is dependent on the low and claim "what is socially peripheral is often symbolically central" in human thinking (p. 128). Similarly, in *Playing in the Dark,* Morrison (1993) describes how insiders and outsiders are constructed and reified as the natural or essential result of group characteristics.

Sometimes notable distinctions exist in language, accent, skin color, or other physical traits, so group affiliation can be readily identified. Other times, groups seem so similar that those tangent to group formation are unable to see differences between them. Suburban people may not be cognizant of gang symbols, teachers may be unaware of cliques, Americans might not be able to tell a German Jew from a German Gentile or a Palestinian from an Israeli; yet insiders are acutely aware of distinctions and see them as extremely significant. In terms of visual rhetoric, groups may adopt dress codes or hairstyles that make their allegiance visible. If signs of group affiliation are not apparent, parties are left to search for evidence of membership status. In Hillsdale, youth and parents identify members of middle and lower classes by visible appearance (e.g., whether their clothes come from K-Mart or The Gap; confident body language) as well as invisible evidence of status (their elementary feeder school attendance, parental occupation, or home addresses). Each of these markers provides strong and meaningful evidence of class status. Once this information is known, division-producing processes intensify; individuals gravitate toward those they believe to be like themselves and avoid those considered to be Others.

Before I describe mothers' narratives about poor people, it is important to remind readers that 11 of the 20 mothers had attended private schools for at least part of their school careers, 7 had gone to suburban schools, and the

2 who went to class-comprehensive schools had been in high tracks. Hence, none had experienced a class-heterogeneous education. Furthermore, in their current circumstances, with the exception of a few with contacts through their careers, mothers did not interact with low-income people. All lived in class-segregated suburbs or a "university ghetto" south of campus.

Consistent with theories of the "new middle class" in modern society (Bourdieu, 1984; Gouldner, 1979; Wright, 1989), school achievement figured prominently in mothers' definitions of themselves. They spoke of their own education with nostalgia and pride. School was an arena in which they had distinguished themselves and established self-efficacy. Lynn "was a good student with confidence in myself and my success"; Rachel was "gifted and talented." Using a *reification* ideological mode, intelligence was constructed as the essence of positive identity; achievement and attainment were its signifiers: high tracks, good grades, and going to schools with affluent enrollments marked children and mothers as smart. Rather than being stratified along a continuum, like social class, intelligence was referred to in binaries (educated/ignorant; smart/slow). Using *symbolization of unity* and *expurgation of Other,* mothers conveyed that members of their class were substantially brighter than the poor. Because academic success was equated with general merit, a central function of schooling was to establish their children's worth.

Mothers' self-definitions extended to and incorporated their offsprings' success. Their children were "high achievers," "successful in school," "engaged in activities," "good students with *natural* ability who went beyond expectations," "disciplined and stimulated to learn," and "academically oriented." They were in gifted and talented, accelerated, and honors classes as well as in leadership positions. As Nicholls (1989) found with children, success for mothers was measured by superiority over others. Furthermore, a source of mothers' positive identity was attributing their children's achievement to their child rearing. Inevitably, *narrativization* figured in detailing the time, effort, and money devoted to ensuring children's success. Sally, a teacher at a low-income school, elaborated:

> People who value education put a price on it. They provide a home environment that encourages education by providing books, monitoring television watching, conversation at dinner tables. These increase kids' common knowledge of culture. If you don't have these, then you have differences. The family has a tremendous responsibility. Schools can do only so much and they are limited in every way—financial and otherwise. It's important for kids to have a lot of stimulation and we provided that: books, traveling in this country and Europe, talking about things. We did not expect school to do everything.

Using *differentiation* and *symbolization of unity* strategies, parents' achievement-supporting actions were given as reasons for their children's accomplishments. Dana's son "had a reasonable education, but we supplemented it at home." The inverse of seeing themselves as factors in their children's success, of course, was the implicit criticism *(expurgation)* of parents whose children do not do well in school. In an ethnography of an elite private school, Peshkin (2001) noted that students and their parents felt they deserved the privileges they had (p. 95). Again, the implication is that Others are not entitled to high-quality schools.

Using the symbolic construction, *rationalization,* when participants' children were not high achievers, mothers were bereft of standard status markers, so they (re)established children's worth by invoking situational factors (bad starts in school, ill health, divergent interests, parental divorce, drug problems). Lilly recalled: "Our daughter missed much school between first and fifth grade because she was sick and couldn't participate in tracking. She was like the stereotypic lower-class kid who was not tracked or in the gifted and talented program." Others launched into accounts of their children's being slighted or misjudged. Lynn complained:

> At Beauford Elementary I had to contact my son's teachers about ability groups. In the middle of the year, he was grouped and was not put into the highest class and I was in a dilemma because I don't believe in ability grouping, but there was a negative impact on him because his social studies teacher called him stupid. I then went to school and asked to transfer him to the other class. My husband even[3] complained after the principal manipulated us into withdrawing the request and also our statements about how unhappy he was. He stayed in that class and we couldn't do anything more. We should have taken him out of that school. I blame myself for that. He was really excluded from the advanced classes and was unhappy, so I'm happy he is included in them now, but I still don't believe in such programs.

The reason for Lynn's feeling that school personnel were biased against them was not addressed, yet such versions of school relations enabled mothers to believe that their children were smart when they did not do well in school or were not put in the highest track placements.

NARRATING THE OTHER AS UNDESIRABLE AND CONTAMINATING

Undoubtedly there were elements of truth in mothers' descriptions, yet *narrativization* was apparent in their versions of low-income people. Fully ensconced in the tradition of cultural deficit story telling, they perseverated on poor children's low ability, violence, emotional disturbance, and substance abuse. They attributed such children's problems to dysfunctional families, chaotic lives, broken homes, or to parents' alcoholism, their own drug addiction, and not caring about learning. Dana, a teacher, declared that "poor people are not able to provide a good home environment for their children." Using Myrdal's (1962) concept of the "undeserving poor," Gans (1996) claims the poor are "repugnant to mainstream norms" (p. 93) and that the fear of the underclass in the United States reflects feelings of being personally threatened (p. 90).

In this study, although mothers conveyed a sympathy for poor children, they certainly felt compelled to distinguish themselves from lower classes by *differentiation* and *expurgation of the other* ideological strategies. Margaret said: "Children at that school are poor and from multiproblem families. I don't want my children to go to school with children with too many emotional problems because they draw attention away from *ordinary* kids." When asked about her concerns about the current state of education, Finley animatedly expounded:

> Education has been drained of any excitement and adventure. It has become boring. There are a lot of mediocre teachers. I guess a major strength is children of all backgrounds (rich, poor, in between) go to school together and learn the same thing. They keep doing this, which is good, but they also try to lower the requirements in order to accommodate everyone.

Because Finley's children went to Beauford, a predominantly high-income school, her sense of them being in a mixed school and of lowering requirements to accommodate others is puzzling—it seems to be imagined rather than based on real circumstances.

With no substantiation from observation, theories about poor people were narrated as if mothers were the authentic authors.[4] Phoebe gave a classic rendition of deficit theory:

> Low-income kids are not usually exposed to books, printed material, and language use before school, so they are not prepared when they start school. Also, noise, crowdedness, and economic insecurity undermine a child's psychological growth before he goes to school. Most parents of whatever class have positive feelings about kids' experiences in elementary school. Only later, in high school, when school impinges on family life (more homework, longer day) so that the child can't do as many chores around the house—then the family is tested about the value of education.

Phoebe described Others with glib conviction that her ideas were true yet provided no actual sources for her knowledge. She had attended private elementary and secondary schools and an Ivy League university, her children had gone to high-income elementary schools, and she had never worked in a public agency where she would have contact with Others. Reasons for "lack of exposure to language use" and "noise and crowdedness undermining psychological growth" remained unnamed and unexplained (*passive* and *nominal*). Furthermore, Phoebe's stories were not internally consistent: Low-income youth were said to be distracted from school work by household chores; however, her accounts of impoverished lives left little space for chores for family members ("crowded into small homes") and spare time for parents ("don't work") to do chores themselves. Phoebe did not appear to notice that details of her story were inconsistent.

Wright (1993) notes that middle-class people presume that those of lower socioeconomic levels are less intelligent and less motivated to do well in school. The belief that poor people do not value education—a *differentiation* symbolic construction—reverberated through mothers' narratives: "kids don't see school as important," "getting good grades does not matter for them," "they don't value education," "they have modest aspirations." Catherine explained: "Some kids from low-income groups don't have ability and those who have ability with more encouragement and nourishment could use it more effectively, but they don't get it from their family." In my interviews with low-income adolescents (1993), many claimed wealthier students taunted them with "stupid," "dumb," or "retard." Yet, neither the affluent adolescents in that study nor the mothers in this one used such crude terminology. They did, however, continuously communicate that low-income students were less advanced academically and less intellectually competent than people of their class. Kalra (1995) claims that since the founding of the country, the upper classes have maintained the existence of differing abilities and talents to justify wage discrepancies, (p. 88).

Bourdieu (1984) observes that affluent people assume poor people prefer the lifestyles to which lack of funds condemn them. Similarly, Stallybrass and White (1986) maintain that "the bourgeois observer sees self-willed degradation in the slums" (p. 135). Attributing school class distinctions to low-income parents and students' intentions and deliberate choices—and not to societal conditions or even genetic heritage—diverts attention away from high-income people's school and life advantages. "Blaming the victim" rationale for Others' conditions allows high-status people to avoid the guilt that might/should be associated with the awareness that Others' disadvantages result from their own advantages, hence are unfair. Consistent with Thompson's *legitimation,* privilege and segregation were justified by discrediting the Other and veiling class bias and privilege. *Naturalized* and *eternalized* traits became the cause of, and justification for, the very obvious social class discrepancies in Hillsdale schools. Poor people were a negation of self and a referent in *legitimizing* status: compared to the poor, the middle class was smart, moral, and hardworking, and thus deserving of superior rank, exclusive conditions, and a larger or better share of community resources.[5]

INVISIBILITY OF BETWEEN-CLASS COMMONALITIES

Mothers recited tales about their own and poor people's lives that seemed congruent and overlapping. Yet, illustrating *differentiation* ideological strategies, mutuality and similarity were not part of mothers' story lines. Lack of time and energy for children were frequently cited as extenuating circumstances of poverty (and rationale for low achievement). Margaret said: "Poor kids can't get the same education because the low-income parent has so many problems they have no energy to provide anything or care for the education of the child. A high-income parent has the leisure and finances to provide extracurricular activities." Lilly believed: "Middle class parents have more time. They play with kids, buy toys, etc." Yet, most mothers fretted about the stress of meeting the demands of both professional and personal lives, of balancing career and family. Many claimed they felt guilty about not spending more time with their children. Some confessed that such parental problems as divorce, or other family-related distractions, interfered with their parenting and, consequently, their children's adjustment and achievement. Yet, unlike their sense that such distractions were permanent problems in Others, they conveyed that their own difficulties or children's flaws were temporary and not an essential part of their nature. None chose to say, "*All of us, regardless of class,* are confronted by similar issues in modern life"—an admission that would fracture the important image of class distinction. The equality implicit in seeing/naming commonality with Others was not the way the class-distinguishing game was played by participants in the study.

Constructions of the other class often involved selective forgetting of the characteristics of respondents' own children. Reynolds complained her sons "feel school was a waste of time" and "do not value education." Yet, using *displacement* strategies to justify her preference for class-homogeneous schools, Reynolds said: "I don't want them to go where kids do not value learning. Kids learn from each other—they must go where kids are inquisitive and parents value education. If parents value education and learning, that will influence the kid." Jeanne fretted about her sons' substance abuse but said that mixed schools would introduce low-income drug users to *ordinary* schools. *Expurgation of the other* and *displacement* strategies allowed the poor to be a complex of undesirable traits that mothers did not recognize in themselves or their offspring. Gupta (2000) examines the "root metaphors that govern interaction between people" (p. 19) and "dictate how to pursue a 'good life' in terms of manners, dispositions, and habits that are to be cultivated to *separate* oneself from others" (p. 59, italics in original). In terms of national identities, Harvey (2000) argues that people's spatial imaginaries relate to the geographical areas they occupy. Certainly, children conceptualize each other according to the differentiated placements to which they are relegated in school or the location of family residence.

DISTINGUISHING SCHOOLS

After being shown a list of high- and low-income schools, mothers were asked if they had heard of them, knew their location, knew students at them, and would want their children to attend them (Table 3.2). Respondents knew the locations of high-income schools and could name children of friends and colleagues who went to them. Most knew the locations of low-income schools; however, few knew children enrolled at them.

SPATIAL AND PSYCHOLOGICAL ISOLATION OF SOCIAL CLASSES

Social distance was evident in mothers' inability to name children who attended low-income schools (*nominalization, passivization*). Lack of knowledge about students and circumstances at low-income schools corresponded to the very evident class segregation in Hillsdale. Narratives revealed that mothers moved in social circles that were physically, socially, and psychologically segregated from low-income people. Because Hillsdale is a relatively small town, the well-entrenched social class isolation is strange and disconcerting. Although some mothers had contact through jobs,[6] such interactions were likely to have been circumscribed by traditions of separation of providers and consumers of services or co-workers of different ranks—situations in which interaction may be congenial but limited to formal work settings. Cicourel (1993) maintains that people interacting in

Table 3.2

Mothers' Evaluations of High- and Low-Income Schools

	Heard Of	Know Location	Know Students	Own Child Could Attend
Beauford	20	20	17	13
Eastside	20	20	17	19
Kinder	20	19	14	17
Richards	20	20	16	16
Downing*	19	18	6	3
Hillview*	19	16	3	4
Southside*	18	17	7	3
Westside*	18	14	3	2

* Low-income schools.

daily life do not always remind each other of the other's power—or lack thereof—in direct terms; the dominant resist displays of power (p. 217).

Not surprisingly, class segregation surfaced as a deliberate choice. Sally volunteered: "My husband and I liked Eastside Elementary best. That's why we bought our house—it's in the Eastside district." Martina confessed her family had looked at a "neat older home on the west side" but considered her children's education and bought a house on the east side instead. Schneider, Teske, and Marschall (2000) claim that "American parents have used their residential location decisions as a way to choose their children's schools" (p. 8). Moreover, Tooley (1999) maintains that this parental choice (for buying homes in the areas with the best schools) has been "within a heavily regulated *state provided and funded schooling system* (p. 9, italics in original).

With little knowledge about low-income schools and seemingly only fuzzy awareness of the class-bound nature of their choices, illustrating *standardization,* mothers readily judged schools with high-income clientele to be best. Catherine declared: "Kinder is one of the top three schools in town. The quality of teaching is good—it's an academic school—really the best of local schools." Evelyn felt: "Richards and Kinder are crowded but excellent. They have the reputation of being the best schools in town." Regardless of their perceptions of differences in curriculum or atmosphere among the four affluent schools in Hillsdale, for the most part, mothers rated them as good schools that would be acceptable for their children. A few parents who did not want their children to go to another high-income school said they had "heard" they "were crowded," "kids were snobbish," "the environment was too competitive," or "discipline was not good."A mother of children who went to Beauford did not like Eastside because "the climate was too progressive" and it enrolled "too many children of international students who did not speak English."

The reasons for rejecting low-income schools for their children or evaluating them as "poor" varied somewhat; however, most mothers narrated versions of lack of academic push. In a *rationalization* vein, Evelyn, a former Downing teacher, claimed: "Westside and Downing are in economically depressed areas and so are not demanding." Another teacher, Sally, claimed: "Mainly low-income students go to those schools, so their standards are lower." A high school teacher, Dana, concurred: "Less rigorous standards are commensurate with the needs of slower students." Thus, they acknowledged difference but indicated it was due to circumstantial rather than inequity factors. A similar pattern—that a good school is not necessarily one with superior facilities but one with the right students—was observed by Jencks (1972).

REASSURING MYTHS ABOUT SCHOOL EQUIVALENCY

Consistent with Thompson's *euphemization* and *nominalization,* all mothers except three were evasive about school social class distinctions or seemed to defensively rate low-income schools as good. In spite of perceiving high-income schools as best and the only ones appropriate for their children, eight mothers stated that all community schools were equivalent, four said low-income schools were inferior because of the nature or quality of the student body, and five "did not know." Although noncommital about rating low-income schools in response to this question, all mothers made numerous qualitative judgments about schools at other times in the interview. After declaring Hillview and other low-income schools as off-limits for her children, Rachel asserted: "Hillview is one of the real neighborhood schools—no better or worse than other schools." Phoebe claimed ignorance: "I don't know anything about those schools. I imagine the people who go there think they're good schools. I wouldn't really know." Those who rejected low-income schools on the grounds that they knew nothing about them did not use the same criterion to refrain from judging the high-income schools their children did not attend. Mothers vacillated in discussing whether there were qualitative distinctions between schools with predominantly high- or low-income enrollments. In response to direct questioning about disparities, some indicated that all schools in Hillsdale were the same, that there were no class distinctions between local schools, but then at other points in the interview described class and neighborhood differences. Thus, *euphemism* and *nominalization* were somewhat ephemeral—used at convenient times and dismissed at others.

At another point in the interview, mothers were asked if class bias existed in Hillsdale schools. Twelve said there was no discrimination, six were not sure, and two felt there was bias in the system. In spite of rating the four affluent schools as the "top schools" and claiming the other schools were "economically depressed," so she would not want her children to attend these inferior schools, Jeanne judged:

> I think all kids in town get an equivalent education. Low-income people may feel that a physically attractive school may mean quality education, but my experience is that quality comes from individual teachers. The quality of education for low-income children is a question of motivation: students and parents are not motivated.

Later Jeanne elaborated:

> Class has a degree of influence, but less in this country than in others. In my experience, class background has no effect and makes no difference. Curriculum and diversity are not affected by wealth but by wanting it and getting it.

My social background has no effect on schooling, except I sent one to a private school because of the kind of structure and wealth of choices that were available. He was not motivated to make the best of what was available in public schools.

Jeanne either did not recognize or did not acknowledge that most parents could not afford private schools for their children.

In terms of a stage 3 question about class desegregation at the end of the interview, a few responded that schools "already were mixed." Dana, a high school teacher, said: "Schools already have a class mixture—it may not be 50–50, but low-income kids are there in all schools just the same." When asked about the equivalency of Hillsdale schools, Dana "did not know." Dismissing the idea of inequities, Sally, another teacher, maintained:

I believe that in this school corporation all children get an equal education. Even in low-income areas, students get the same or at least similar opportunities to what children get at Kinder or Eastside. I think low-income parents feel the same way.

Yet, at a later point, Sally admitted:

Low-income parents may get upset when they know what programs their children are missing out on. My speculation is that low-income parents would want their kids to go to schools with high-income kids because they get a better deal in those schools—although that is not true because here all schools get good equipment and excellent teachers—it is not just that high-income schools have a better deal.

Sally quickly added: "They could have better dialogues if they really want to know what is going on. It is not social class but individual parents' attitudes that dictates their relationship with school personnel." Teachers were among the first to eliminate low-income schools for their children but also were intent on maintaining that all Hillsdale schools were roughly equivalent. So, too, Bingham, Haubrich, White, and Zipp (1990) found that teachers who rated the inner-city schools where they teach as good admitted they would not send their own children to them. Such schools apparently were only good for Other people's children.

In contrast to the somewhat defensive reaction of some mothers when asked about school inequities, in the debriefing that concluded her interview, Bryn said with insight and humility:

Some questions made me uncomfortable. There are inherent contradictions about the way I and others feel. I like to think that income does not make a difference in terms of educational opportunities, yet in the back of my mind I wonder if it is true. In some obvious ways it is not true that income does not make any difference.

RATIONALIZING SEGREGATED SCHOOLING

Illustrating Thompson's *fragmentation* and *dissimulation* modes of ideological operation, regarding the social composition of classrooms and schools, a constellation of versions of "meeting the needs of diverse students" veiled mothers' desire to have their children in advanced placements and quality (class-pure or not-too-mixed) schools. Children's "not being challenged" was a *euphemism* for their not being separated into advanced or accelerated tracks. Versions of this complaint included "boredom and lack of stimulation for gifted kids," "teachers teach to the common denominator and don't address the needs of advanced students," "lowered requirements to accommodate everyone," "a lot more time has to be spent on basics for average kids and less on enrichment for gifted kids," "unfortunately the teacher has to gear toward the average student and that means that the bright ones have to be slowed down and get bored," "lack of academic push for my kids, who are smart but not motivated to work on their own," and "teachers having to spend time on troublemakers who do not care about school, which means they neglect the ones that are there to learn." There was a consensus that class-heterogeneous schools would undermine the quality of their children's education. For example, Phoebe stressed the value of social integration but was ambivalent about any mechanism to accomplish it:

> A strength of public education is its ambition to serve all the student populations. A weakness is that it can't. When kids are together, the emphasis on skills is overblown and the content is shrunk. I think there can be content that we can all agree upon that is very basic and important. School would be an ideal place if we had all perfect students. But they aren't and all students should not respond similarly—they are different and respond differently. Schools need to have the flexibility to meet the needs of all students and that is difficult when kids vary too widely.

At a later point, Phoebe said:

> The biggest problem is finding new ways of dealing with the large population of kids whose backgrounds are not the same. Schools have lost flexibility and individualization. I'm in favor of a school with pluralism—a healthy mix—but no one group should be dominant. Since kids are different, bright and average kids should not be in the same classes.

Dana stated: "It is good for my kids to be in a mixed school but also have demanding academic standards. It is difficult to have both." So, too, Margaret expounded:

> Since teachers have to deal with more problems with low-income kids, I would not want my children to be where a majority of emotionally disturbed kids are, so I would send my kid to a more separated school—mixed are okay as long as there are only a few low-income people.

Thus, poor children were seen not only as inferior, but, using *expurgation* strategies, they were also distracting and contaminating—an impediment or threat.

Believing it would disadvantage their children to attend schools with predominantly low-income and clearly even substantially mixed enrollments, the possibility that attending school with mostly low-income children also might have an unfavorable impact on poor children was not mentioned. Mothers were so class encapsulated and so focused on their children that they did not consider the repercussions of class-segregated schools for poor children. Perhaps they felt poor children deserved to be together, whereas their children did not deserve to be with them. Negative images of the poor combined with a pervasive urge for children's personal success drove mothers to favor segregated and stratified policies and practices. Another explanation might be that mothers wanted to remain distant and not know about Others because real knowledge about Others might necessitate a change of perspective and a loss of legitimation for segregation and advantage. Watt (1994) argues that a motive for social segregation is that the conviction about Others' inferiority is easier to maintain if "contrary evidence is kept at considerable distance" (p. 217).

BEING ALLOWED TO NARRATE VERSUS BEING FORCED TO STATE A POSITION

Interviews culminated with two scenarios that forced mothers to make a commitment to specific positions phrased as to whether they would support school board action to (1) ban tracking and ability grouping and (2) redistrict to achieve social class balance in all schools. These forced-choice questions came after the first and second stages of the interview that allowed interviewees to express general opinions about education or social class. Instead of the open-ended questions in which mothers could narrate their versions of school issues and express their own concerns, the interview format changed so that they could not hedge and evade issues; hence, *euphemization, passivization,* and *narrativization* were less possible.

In terms of liberal ideals generally and the gist of the interview specifically, the right answers to the stage 3 questions were obvious. There were two types of reactions: mothers made a conservative choice, usually accompanied by an angry or defensive outburst, or they gave a compliant liberal answer followed by qualifying statements in which they reneged on their initial liberal stand. Two mothers curtly denied that current grouping or zoning patterns corresponded to class. Four defiantly stood their ground to oppose redistricting, then appended narratives (*rationalization, narrativization*) to deflect the finality of their choice and redeem the liberal image that was lost in their initial illiberal admission. Fourteen wavered, skirted around a direct choice, or glibly gave compliant liberal responses. Those who gave a politically correct answer that supported redistricting to achieve class balance eventually returned to telling why this "good idea" would not work and why compromise was necessary. One way to interpret responses to this scenario is that only four were candid in explicitly asserting their preference for class-pure schools. Of these, Leili seemed least bothered by stating her preference for segregated schooling:

> I just want my children to be with children from educated families who are motivated and have values and goals. I don't want my kids to be a model for other children and feel the gap. I would prefer my children to go to schools separated by social class. I don't want mixed schools. My opinions differ from other people's since I value education a lot.

Unlike mothers who rationalized that low-income constituencies preferred "their own schools," Leili admitted: "I think low-income parents prefer mixed schools because they want to pull up their kids and have them strive for the better. But I think they need to start at home and prepare their children for school." Leili immigrated to the United States as an adult, although she was upper middle class in her country of origin.

In responding to the item about the ban on tracking, eight mothers were vociferously opposed, four were evasive or noncommital, two supported in "principle" and "theory," and six claimed to be "very supportive." Again, either a flat tone of defiance or angry objection followed the "wrong answer" of supporting tracks. Avoiding a direct answer, Ann Marie snapped: "Social class wouldn't affect ability grouping because a child is judged by standardized tests." Reynolds complained: "Answering questions like these are rather hazy. You have ideal situations and real situations." Also diverting a direct response, Finley flared: "You can't make education better for poor kids. Education is there, and the way the system is set up does not deny low-income kids any more than it denies high-income kids. Do not blame the system!" Peggy was definitive: "In terms of education offered, all schools have teachers with energy and quality. Schools can't compensate for home disadvantage."

Phoebe's explanations about class differences, and her eventual testiness about detracking and redistricting, are fairly representative of the response sequence. Phoebe gave her version of low-income people and schools:

> Schools in low-income neighborhoods provide support for academics, but not to the same extent as high-income schools. Some are in depressed parts of the county where there are not high achievers. Low SES [socioeconomic status] kids have more failings; low-income schools have more problem kids and underachievers. The cause is double-edged. One is the conditions that cause families to be low-income, to be excluded from the mainstream. Then they are not prepared for school. Social conditions don't allow exposure to books, and there is crowdedness, noise. There is a lack of academic culture in these families. Then schools fail to deal with disrupted families and kids. They need a different approach. The family needs to be educated in order to help the kid. Perhaps the best approach is to get both parents and kids to go to school simultaneously—but that is expensive and you would also have to persuade them that it is worth it.

In speaking out against redistricting, Phoebe claimed:

> I am in favor of schools with pluralism (a healthy mix), but no one group should be dominant. Bright students should not be in the same class with slower students. I suspect low-income parents might want their kids not to associate with higher-income kids because they feel intimidated. I believe low-income parents want their kids to attend schools that are largely drawing from the same background—they don't feel comfortable with other families.

After this reply, when a request for her own opinion about detracking was repeated, Phoebe said: "It would not work. Both teachers and students would end up frustrated." When told that studies of heterogeneous grouping showed benefits for low-achieving students and little effect on the academic progress of high achievers, Phoebe flatly and firmly announced:

> I would challenge that information. I have seen much evidence of the opposite. I have not seen any situation where a high achiever was not frustrated when placed with low achievers, unless a teacher can individualize instruction, but I have not seen that.

Clearly embarrassed at having spoken against integration, Phoebe politely protested having been put in a position of having to make nonliberal admissions. When asked to comment on the study questions at the end of her interview, Phoebe suspiciously ventured: "I wonder why you are doing it?"

Only three mothers consistently admitted that social class bias existed in Hillsdale. One of these, Lynn, responded to detracking and redistricting, with:

> Mixing works if class size is small—otherwise it won't when you have a wide range of abilities (which is connected to social class). Otherwise teachers spend a disproportionate amount of time with students who are struggling and the advanced students suffer. I have mixed feelings about gifted and talented programs, although my son has benefitted from them.

Unlike most mothers, Lynn made no pretense of deferring to the sentiments of low-income parents for separated schools; instead, she said:

> Making low-income kids feel good about their abilities would make schools generally successful. I sent my kid to a mixed school but I am not sure if I would now. If it were really mixed but not where the majority are low-class. Low-income parents would want their kids in a class-mixed school. They see the difference in resources.

Another rationale given for opposing desegregation was the importance of neighborhood schools and problems with busing. Yet it is fairly obvious that local school enrollment patterns in Hillsdale are gerrymandered to retain class homogeneity. When new affluent subdivisions or subsidized housing complexes are built, children are districted to schools consistent with their social class status even if it means being bused past closer schools. It would be difficult for residents not to be unaware of this phenomenon. Nevertheless, Catherine reasoned:

> Like many parents in this area, we want a neighborhood school. I don't like the idea of busing. These bus rides are not good for kids. I know the idea of mixing different socioeconomic groups is good, but I don't like the practice. I like the schools to be close by.

THE DISSONANCE BETWEEN CLASS EPISTEMOLOGY AND LIBERAL IDENTITY

On one level, mothers espoused the liberal support for integrated, inclusive education that is associated with the middle class. They saw themselves, and wanted to be perceived by others, as compassionate and just. Dana declared: "Because of the presence of the university, Hillsdale is unique—things are different here. There is more emphasis on education and it is more open-minded than other parts of the state. People value not discriminating against others, including poor children." Jeanne claimed: "My colleagues and friends tend to have the same liberal attitudes that I do." Mothers represented themselves—seemingly even to themselves—as liberals who liked inclusive schooling, yet it was clear that they preferred conservative practices; that is, they harbored the illiberal desire for separated and advantaged status for their children.

Thompson's (1990) ideological operations and strategies of symbolic construction were productive in shedding light on the ways ideology works to establish and sustain a liberal image and to disguise self-interested educational choices. A resoundingly strong pattern of response was for mothers to initially state a liberal view and then reject it as they moved on to practical (self-interested, class-partial) reasons why the liberal approach was not feasible. By prefacing their remarks with ideals, mothers may have felt they could then dismiss them with impunity; that is, without damage to their valued liberal image. Indeed, they voluntarily distinguished the ideal from the real with "under ideal circumstances," "in the best possible world," "it would be nice if," and "in principle." Karla said: "Theoretically, school is designed to make people aware of themselves; for my children, to make them better people, better citizens. To pass on the culture of the Western world and get a good job."

Narratives concluded with caveats that ideals were impractical or impossible given the nature of local students, circumstantial constraints, or conditions of the times. This is consistent with Cicourel's (1993) claim that people rationalize power imbalance on grounds of temporary, necessary contingencies. After waxing eloquently on liberal schooling (equity, integration), even such mothers as Lynn and Lilly, who consistently acknowledged class bias, ended on an individualist note about their children's best interests. Lynn said: "When you live in a materialistic world, you must have skills appreciated in the market." Lilly felt school was "to improve your standard of living so you earn a good income and have opportunity to do what you like to do."

Euphemisms woven into narratives softened mothers' critical tone. Constraints were mentioned when mothers talked about poor people's flaws. Regarding low-income parents' educational aspirations for children, Catherine put diminished goals in the context of necessity: "It is more important for them to have their kids be earning in a job than to continue their education." Relatedly, to varying degrees, conservative possibilities in the narratives were edited out by *displacement* and *passitivization*. Mothers appeared to refrain from expressing certain views and embellished on others in order to project a liberal and caring image.

Another indication that certain verbalizations served mainly to maintain a liberal identity was the dispassion of politically correct replies compared to the intense, emotional descriptions of offsprings' difficulties. Evidence that liberal talk was used rhetorically appeared even in respondents who were attuned to the benefits of affluent status in dealing with school personnel[7] ("many teachers emerge from lower-income backgrounds, but as teachers they identify with the middle class and encourage middle-class students,"; "teachers reward and reinforce a child whose parents they are comfortable with,"; "high-income people are not intimidated to go in and talk to teachers or administrators,"; "high-income kids are treated differently because the school knows their parents are watching"). Such brief generalized observations were made calmly; however, when mothers were able to divert the focus to their children, their speeches were animated and even impassioned. A final representation of ideology's role in the narratives was resistance when liberal rhetoric (*euphemization, passivization, narrativization*) was not possible. When the format changed so that Thompson's strategies were less possible, some mothers were annoyed and others might have even been described as whiney.

Although mothers generally played down their competitive aspirations for offspring, it was clear their utmost concern was their children's success in school. In chapter 4, I focus more specifically on this aspect of mothers' desires for their children. Relevant to this chapter is mothers' conviction that their children's success required retaining and strengthening stratified and segregated schooling. Nevertheless, when directly asked to express conservative views, they were dismayed and defensive. Such internal contradictions in their narratives and their emotional reactions to "being put on the spot" indicated that they felt the need to conceal their (real) elitist educational desires. This narrative sequence (i.e., establishing self as liberal, stating conservative realities) revealed (1) multiple and contradictory levels of thought; (2) the image-producing and -maintaining role of narrative; (3) a very present sense of personal distinction between real and ideal; and (4) the need to disguise, *conceal,* deny, or contextually frame self-interested desires for their own children's schooling.

THE INVISIBILITY OF CLASS PRIVILEGE AND PERSONAL POWER

These affluent mothers, powerful members of the community[8] in terms of their impact on the nature of local schooling, appeared unaware of the extent of their power and influence or their children's advantages. They explained away or rationalized class-related material or faculty differences in local schools. It was convenient not to notice inequities. Yet, when inconsistencies in their statements or illiberal views became visible and their progressive image was threatened, such as when mothers were asked to endorse or reject the ideals of inclusive schools/classrooms, mothers were anxious, unhappy, and defensive. In debriefing at the end of her interview, Margaret complained: "The interview was hard for me—you asked a lot of searching questions. I thought the focus would be on my goals for education. I am not interested in social class." Jeanne felt: "Some of the questions were too general. I had a problem with the method. I could see there was a goal, a direction in the questions, but differences in income are misleading in terms of social class perceptions." Peggy said: "I am interested in the topic, but it was hard to come to grip with general questions. It was easier to deal with more specific questions." Yet, like most mothers, Peggy was more befuddled and bothered by specific, forced-choice questions. Less upset, Sally said: "Tough questions. Thought-provoking." Karla's response concurred: "Very thought-provoking, demanding trying to clarify some things in my mind."

In debriefing, some mothers said that being asked to see things from low-income parents' perspective was disconcerting. Perhaps a sign of psychological (class) insularity—*nominalization* and *passivization* of Others—was their difficulty in responding to a question about low-income parents' preferences for the class composition of schools. Thirteen were noncommittal, four believed low-income parents would prefer integrated schools, and three felt that they would be "more comfortable with their own kind." As Martina, a former teacher and now a homemaker, said:

> It is an advantage to have schools that are largely low-income. If low-income children are a minority in a school, then their opportunities are limited. If they don't feel different—like when they're in a low-income school[9]—they will explore more and participate in activities.

Mothers were confident in describing characteristics of different classes. Intellectualizing about the implications of class status was something they had learned to do and could do readily. Being asked to identify with the position of Others, however, may have brought Others' humanity to the foreground, creating an emotionally near experience that made them uneasy. Consistent with Thompson's *nominalization, passivization,* and *dissimulation,* class bias mostly was denied, distanced, and diminished in importance. That being asked to see schooling from Others' point of view was unsettling to mothers indicates a certain level of consciousness about the inequities from which their class benefits. During debriefing, with genuine humility, Evelyn said: "One disturbing thing was having to think about how low-income parents feel."

The extent of mothers' awareness of contradictions in their attitudes toward their own class and Others can only be surmised. Similarly, the level of conscious awareness of their own advantages is not clear. It seems that rather than being intentionally misleading or Machiavellian, mothers were mostly unaware of the inconsistencies between their liberal verbalizations and their deeper conservative self/class interests. Perhaps maneuvering the schism between the conflicting perspectives was so practiced that discrepancies were no longer evident to them. Delpit (1988) claims that powerful people are unaware of or are unwilling to acknowledge their power, whereas those without power are cognizant of Others' power (pp. 282–283). In studies of local low-income parents and adolescents, I found that they continually complained that students from affluent families ("rich people," "respectable ones," "to-do's," "influential people") had better school circumstances and were treated better in local schools. Yet the blatant inequities that they and I have observed over the years seem not to be as apparent (nor as bothersome) to their high-income counterparts. Dickstein (1996) writes about "diminished sympathy for the poor" and "willed ignorance" of their lives (p. 19). Peshkin (2001) claims that groups "do not plan to do injustice to other children but it happens as an artifact of privilege" (p. xiii).

Consistent with Goffman (1959, 1963), Baumeister (1996) claims that the desire to think well of oneself is a fundamental and pervasive motivation of human psychological functioning. From this framework, it might be surmised that mothers repress the self-serving sentiments that would cause guilt if recognized. Similarly, McAdams (1997) claims that the self seeks temporal coherence. These theories about the importance of self-image (in this case, as liberal regarding class relations and generous to less fortunate Others) provide an explanation for mothers being upset when they were confronted with the possibility of their own class privilege. Rhetorical mechanisms or *mystifying ideologies* that allow inequities, discriminatory practices, and class advantages to remain invisible appear to play a symbolically mediating role in preserving positive social identity (Ricoeur, 1986, pp. xvi–xix). Ideology allows the dissonance aroused by a clash between desired liberal identity and class interest to be allayed. When mothers were asked to breach the conventions of narrating about Others that depend on *dissimulation* and *legitimation ideological operations,* they were confused and upset. Hence, when the liberal screen was penetrated so that elitism or privilege was insinuated, mothers were defensive. Watt (1994) claims that lack of awareness of advantage is convenient. That mothers balk at openly stating elitist preferences attests to the probability that "consciousness[10] of the real status of stories has not been totally repressed" (p. 189) and their hostility to exposure in the forced-choice scenarios.

WOMEN'S ROLE IN REPRODUCING SOCIAL CLASS INEQUITIES

Each gender has "systemic connections to capitalist economic exploitation" but also distinct patterns of participation in the vertical class system (Connell, 1987, p. 94).[11] Men of the middle class "exercise influence on events, products, and people as they conceive, advise, hire, promote, judge, select, and allocate the most valued resources in advanced industrial societies" (Lamont, 1992, p. xxiii). Women's domestic position is heavily overlaid with work that produces status for the family; thus, they have a significant role in the cultural reproduction of the middle class (Atkinson, 1985; Collins, 1992). The old middle class reproduced itself through strongly framed cultural systems; the new middle class is characterized by weaker boundaries and women as agents of cultural reproduction (Hennessy, 1993). Hollway (1989) conjectures that because of their marginalized status and the competing discourses associated with that status, women's subjectivities are complex. Morrow and Torres (1994) regret the undertheoretization of the links between economic structures and the subjectivities and status of ethnic and gender subcultures. The concept of nonsynchrony highlights differences in interests, needs, desires, and identities that separate groups (McCarthy, 1993, p. 337). Acker (1989) claims that teachers (mothers) are complex figures positioned between powerful adults (males) and children—a conflicted standing that mirrors Wright's (1985) ideas about a contradictory middle class.

To some extent, mothers in this study expressed the caring, socially inclusive views associated with women (Belenky, Clinchy, Goldberg, & Tarule, 1986; Gilligan, 1982; Noddings, 1992). However, it appears that their role in maintaining family status is pushing their children and pushing for their children in schools. Clearly, there was a tension in being asked to care about other people's children when it seemed to them to threaten their own children's well-being. Gender role distinctions may be blurred in modern society; however, consistent with the findings of other studies, it is women who negotiate family status within modern institutions (Atkinson, 1985; Collins, 1992; Connell, 1987, 1998; Fraser, 1989). Although somewhat attracted to inclusive school ideals, mothers were intent on securing the circumstances likely to have the best outcomes for their children. Thinking of themselves as benevolent and socially inclusive, nevertheless, mothers supported conservative school agendas that result in social class hierarchies within schools.

In explaining why schools have turned away from social justice and equity (and toward conservative social agendas) in the past two decades, David (1993) points to the trend toward a "parentocracy," in which children's education is increasingly dependent on mothers' actions. David, as well as Useem (1992), Lareau (1989), and Biklen (1995), maintain that mothers, rather than fathers, are the ones who are informed about local schools and interact with personnel regarding their children. Useem (1992) notes the propensity of educated mothers to be integrated into school functions and information networks so that they are knowledgeable about school affairs. They exert considerable influence on school practice by pressuring school personnel to put their preferences into effect (Oakes & Guiton, 1995; Olson, 1983; Sieber, 1982; Thomas & Moran, 1992; Wells & Serna, 1996). The informational resources, attitude of advocacy, and critical examination of school practices that affluent mothers bring to parent–teacher interactions are powerful in shaping their children's schooling (Lareau, 1989, p. 175).

Unfortunately, the reality is that as high-income mothers intervene with school personnel in decisions made regarding their own children, they affect other people's children as well. As high tracks are created to accommodate the preferences of affluent parents, low-income children are relegated to low tracks. As affluent people vote to retain the practice of having local property taxes finance schools, disparities between schools in high- and low-income areas increasingly widen. Furthermore, in noting who middle-class people petition to implement their school ideals, it must be recognized that school personnel also are middle class and their decisions are based on that class standpoint (Tyack & Hansot, 1982). Consequently, the middle class determines the nature of public education for their children and, simultaneously, even if inadvertently, for children of other classes. Therefore, the nature of their thinking and their requests must be carefully scrutinized, and requests that impede equitable education must be denied.

This chapter documents how middle-class mothers—perceived as liberals who believe in integrated and inclusive education—prefer segregated and stratified schools that benefit middle-class students.[12] My findings are consistent with Roth's (1992) claim that stratified school structures and outcomes are intentional products of middle-class desire. For this reason, it is necessary to challenge the exemplary status attributed to middle-class parents' educational values and goals, support for education, and involvement with schools by scholars (Epstein, 1990; Epstein & Scott-Jones, 1992), journalists (Will, 2002), and the general public.

In conclusion, in spite of considerable variation in mothers' responses, several patterns of "meaning in the service of power" surfaced. Mothers (1) continuously made binary class distinctions; (2) located themselves and their children in the top half of that binary; (3) perceived a need for class segregation in schools; (4) indicated that their own identity formation was based on their children's school status; (5) revealed that their own class advantage is mostly invisible to them; (6) depended on a variety of ideological operations to veil their class advantage; and (7) displayed a dissonance between their class epistemology and desired liberal identity.

CRITIQUING THE SUBJECT

Some qualitative researchers recommend that informants' narratives be taken at face value and that the researcher's role is to be a vehicle for participants to tell their own stories in their own ways. Such common methods as member checks have participants verify not only what they said in interviews but comment on how what they said was interpreted. Researchers may allow participants to delete things they said that they retrospectively wish they had not (see Silverman, 2000). In my studies of low-income parents and adolescents, because I knew they had been silenced, I took the approach of validating their voices and felt that one of my purposes was to bring their messages to those in control of schools.

In the case of low-income participants, my studies had some comforting or therapeutic value in that I reassured participants that their perceptions that schools were biased against them were generally accurate and hence that their bitterness was justified. These studies had catalytic value in that I helped low-income participants see members of affluent classes in a less positive light (as not necessarily smarter and more worthy of school advantage) and attempted to persuade parents to speak up and insist that their children not be put in the embarrassing and detrimental school placements they complained about. In a later study (Brantlinger, 1993), I encouraged adolescents to be more assertive in making their feelings known to school personnel. In contrast to studies directed at historically oppressed people, when I turn the scholarly gaze upward and look at elites, I cannot validate their flawed and distorted claims about Others or their self-perceptions as more worthy than people of lower classes. Granted, *elite* is a relative term and perhaps not legitimately used to describe middle-class mothers. However, such mothers have the power to determine the nature of schools not only for their own children but also for the children of other classes.

4

Conflicted Pedagogical and Curricular Perspectives of Middle-Class Mothers

Progressive educational philosophies, associated with the names of Francis Parker, G. Stanley Hall, and John Dewey, among others, date back a century and have waxed and waned as prominent school reform discourses. Debates among advocates for different types of pedagogies persist on university campuses, in educational and popular journals, and at the community and school levels. Although the complexity of pedagogical and curricular preferences is recognized—hence the difficulty of classifying them—for purposes of the arguments put forth in this chapter, I cluster advocates into two camps: conservatives and progressives. Conservatives favor a technical or classical education in which knowledge is predetermined and aligned with subject matter disciplines, which are further sequenced into linear grade levels. There are fairly rigid boundaries between subject area disciplines and also within ranked levels of achievement within subjects. The knowledge base is supposedly[1] of Western European origin and therefore monocultural and assimilationist in perspective. For conservatives, the task of schooling is the transmission of traditional academic content through didactic pedagogy from a knowledgeable person (teacher) to one who knows less (student). Successful learners are to learn and retain prescribed subject content and literacy skills and demonstrate their knowledge and skills on standardized tests. Freire (1989) refers to this as the "banking concept" of education. Excellence is enforced through the top-down control of accountability standards and mandated competitive evaluation.[2] Conservatives want to preserve the status quo—or return to a time perceived as being closer to conservative ideals— so their goals are to enhance students' skills and credentials to prepare them for a place in a preexisting, hierarchically stratified postschool life.

Progressive education is defined in a number of ways, so I spell out my own criteria. Progressives recommend loosely framed, child-centered, problem-oriented, interdisciplinary, and multicultural educational forms. Advocates for progressive pedagogy are constructivists who believe that students naturally construct knowledge and acquire competencies and skills as they need or want them when provided with a stimulating learning environment. Learning takes place in different ways for particular children because they each select what is meaningful to them from phenomena in their surroundings. The role of teachers is not to directly deliver information in a pedantic style but rather to facilitate intellectual, social, and affective growth by bringing interesting and diverse realms of knowledge into the classroom (or taking children to interesting sites outside classrooms) and by acknowledging and building on students' own prior knowledge and skills. The content to be learned is multifaceted, broad, and dynamic. Because it is understood that children learn in various ways at different rates, and diversity is expected and valued, curriculum is developed so as to be accessible and relevant to students' achievement levels and learning styles. Evaluation is flexible and individualized; it measures students' personal accomplishments and does not make comparisons between them. Ranking systems in schools are to be diminished or eliminated. In addition to developing student competencies for assuming (horizontally) diverse, multiple, and satisfying roles in post-school life, progressives' agendas include structuring schools as model moral, inclusive communities that allow students to practice the behaviors necessary to take an active part in a democratic society and to shape their own futures according to their ideals. An ethics of social reciprocity is fostered.

Various educational theorists have conjectured about which groups favor conservative and which progressive education. Some of these scholars are discussed in more depth later in this chapter, but it is generally believed that political conservatives and lower-income people favor conservative forms of curriculum. The presumed proponents of progressive schooling are middle class, and college educated. In chapter 3, I addressed mothers' resistance to socially inclusive schools. In this chapter I examine their ideas about curriculum and pedagogy—about the nature of learning and what is to be learned.

THE STATUS OF PROGRESSIVE PEDAGOGICAL PRACTICE

My mapping of educational characteristics of schools and classrooms constructs a neat dichotomy between progressive and conservative camps. Yet, in actual school circumstances, a pure progressive or conservative situation would probably be rare. Similarly, there is little consensus about the actual dominance of either pedagogy in practice. Members of one camp typically accuse the other of having control—and of messing up. According to hooks

(1994), conservative pedagogy reigns: "most students experience classrooms in which prevailing pedagogical models" are based on the assumption that "knowledge can be deposited, stored, and used at a later date" and are "coercively hierarchical," with the teacher as the "privileged transmitter of knowledge" (p. 85). In contrast, conservatives contend that the quality of public schooling has declined in recent decades due to the prevalence of liberal (progressive) agendas (see review by Daniels, 1995).

Although she probably would not call herself a conservative, Delpit (1988, 1995) argues both that progressive pedagogies prevail and that they are preferred by school professionals and middle-class parents because they advantage children of their class. According to Delpit, liberals believe it is against principles of student freedom and autonomy to be explicit about rules or expectations. She argues that middle-class students who already know the rules and substance of the culture of power do well when progressive practices are in effect, whereas poor and minority children need direct instruction in all aspects of dominant culture to succeed; that is, they need conservative pedagogy. Delpit attributes the lesser achievement of subordinate children partly to the practice of progressive forms of schooling.

Delpit's theories are interesting and provocative, yet two of her assumptions must be questioned. First, her assertion that progressive pedagogy prevails in public education does not seem to be valid. Second, her assumption that middle-class parents prefer progressive pedagogy may not be correct. This study was not designed to disprove Delpit's sense that progressive education is widespread. Nevertheless, based on my personal observations in local schools and conversations with colleagues here and elsewhere, I generally agree with those who maintain that progressive ideals have rarely been realized to any large extent in the everyday practices of public education (see Daniels, 1995; Fullan, 1993; Goodlad, 1992; hooks, 1990; Lien, 2001; Oakes, Gamoran, & Page, 1992; Sarason, 1990; Weiss, 1995). In spite of the ubiquitous and enduring discussions among educators and scholars about the value and effects of progressive projects, public education remains remarkably conservative. Delpit may have correctly characterized the teachers she observed as having a progressive approach, yet she generalized their sentiments to the middle class more broadly without actually studying the attitudes of middle-class parents. In this chapter I detail how my study of middle-class parents casts doubt on Delpit's second assumption by providing evidence that at least some middle-class people actually have negative or ambivalent feelings about progressive schooling, especially regarding its value for their own children. I also show how these parents communicate their conviction that low-income children need a narrow and watered (or dummied)-down basic skills curriculum.

Some evidence about the particularistic prevalence of progressive education according to the income level of constituencies comes from Anyon's (1980) study of schools serving students from different social classes. She found that progressive education was in place in high- but not in low-income schools. Advancing the idea of a hidden, disempowering curriculum for low-income students, Anyon documented the connections between everyday classroom activities and unequally structured economic relations. In her study of five schools—two "working class," one "middle (mixed) class," one "affluent professional," one "executive elite" (p. 83), Anyon found class distinctions not only in the availability of classroom resources (i.e., the higher the income levels of families, the better and more abundant the materials) but also in the nature of instruction and schoolwork. Working-class students were assigned mechanical tasks that involved rote learning. They had little opportunity for choice or decision making. They often had worksheets rather than texts. In the (lower-income) middle-class school, although the lessons were based on texts, good grades still depended on "right" answers. Conservative pedagogy predominated in the three schools with lower-status students. In contrast, creative activity independently carried out by students was evident in the affluent professional school. Students were to express themselves and apply ideas. Among the executive elite students at the fifth school, the development of analytical intellectual powers was valued and encouraged.

Anyon showed qualitative school differences that corresponded to the social class status of their enrolled pupils. The affluent schools were "good schools" in that they provided a "top academic quality" that allowed students to "achieve[3] and excel," yet also were characterized by a negative "individualistic and narcissistic orientation" (p. 74). These two affluent schools were segregated (exclusive) schools, which, according to my criteria, could not be judged as entirely progressive. Their pedagogy contained the constructivist, problem-based, and student-centered aspects of progressive education, but the social class-homogeneous nature of their enrollment precluded any realization of school as a model of a moral, inclusive, and democratic community. Affluent students might learn to collaborate with each other but would get little experience (or, for that matter, develop little if any incentive) to cross class lines in social interactions or become sensitive to the nature and needs of other social classes. Perhaps it is overreaching common notions of progressive schooling to insist that segregated schools cannot be considered progressive, yet, for me, social integration along with constructivist practices, student choice, self-determination, and individualized evaluation are all essential components of progressive *democratic* education. And, as chapter 3 illustrated, it was the threat to social exclusiveness that was perceived as a great disadvantage by mothers.

PEDAGOGICAL PREFERENCES OF LOW-INCOME PARENTS

Anyon (1980) documented the distinctive conditions at schools that served children of various classes. Although I have observed broadly in the community and in local schools for 34 years, the focus of my actual research has been more on the attitudes, feelings, and opinions of various constituencies in Hillsdale. I often have made the case that unique perspectives are embedded in each social class position. Admittedly, everyone's thinking is complex, changing, and multifaceted. Therefore, it is not surprising that the evidence related to distinctive mindsets of members of different social classes is ambiguous and often contradictory. Some sociologists would concur with Delpit's hypothesis that low-income parents prefer conservative schooling; however, they offer different reasons than access to the culture of power for explaining poor people's preferences. Illustrating that differential class-tied socialization takes place in various homes and schools, and emphasizing the impact of such differentials on human outlook, Bernstein (1973), Bourdieu (1977), Kohn (1969), and Kohn and Slomczynski (1990) claim that working and lower classes support conservative educational practice because it corresponds to their work and home circumstances. However, these authors would emphatically reject Delpit's idea that conservative curriculum enhances poor children's education or empowers them. Indeed, they would be likely to maintain that this lesser curriculum further diminishes poor children's chances for social mobility precisely because it denies them access to the culture of power.

Before I begin to show how the assumption that middle-class people favor progressive schooling is flawed, I turn to my own past studies to claim that there is also little validity to the broad-based assumption that low-income people prefer conservative pedagogy (e.g., workbooks, rote learning, pedantic teaching styles) or approve of the separated arrangements (e.g., compensatory programming, special education, vocational education, remedial tracks) that have been instituted primarily (or presumably) in their behalf. In my studies, low-income parents (1) preferred schools with diverse student enrollments (1985a); (2) envied the enriched, interesting, and accelerated curriculum that they felt was available at high-income schools or in high tracks (1985b); (3) were bothered that more self-determination, choice, independence, and respect were afforded to affluent pupils than to their children by school personnel (1985b); (4) had high hopes and dreams for the educational and occupational futures of their offspring—they did acknowledge that realizing such aspirations was unlikely (1985c, 1986a); and (5) resented, but rarely officially resisted, the separated and stigmatizing settings and practices inflicted upon their children in public schools (1986b). Regardless of low-income parents' concerns about or wishes for their children's schooling, class inequities continue to exist in schools across the country (Kozol, 1991; Orfield, 2000; Yeo & Kanpol, 1999).

Although low-income parents did refer to many of the ideals of progressive education it is important for me to admit that many seemed particularly concerned that their offspring acquire literacy proficiencies. They rarely mentioned either a broad knowledge base or effective expressive or analytical skills as educational goals for their children. One reason for this could be the emphasis on test scores that usually show children in their schools to be at the bottom of highly publicized district-wide rankings. Perhaps these parents felt that a focus on basic facts and skills would improve their children's scores. Although I found a clear emphasis on certain aspects of conservative pedagogy and outcomes on the part of working-class and poor parents in my study, in this chapter I show that these parents are not alone in their emphasis on skills, facts, and standardized knowledge.

REASONS FOR THE LACK OF SUCCESS OF PROGRESSIVE SCHOOL REFORM

Although they differ on their reasons for this assertion, there is a consensus among Bernstein, Kohn, and Delpit that the middle classes prefer progressive pedagogies for their children. They also concur that progressive practices benefit middle-class students and imply that middle-class parents and students believe this to be true. Yet, combining this assumption with the fact that it is the educated middle class that wields the power to shape public institutions in capitalist societies, and especially schools (Bourdieu, 1977; Bowles & Gintis, 1976; Gouldner, 1979; Gramsci, 1929–1935/1971; Wright, 1989), it is surprising that progressive practices are not more prevalent. With the purported support from powerful constituencies, the supposed failure of progressive reform is puzzling.

There are several plausible reasons for the lack of success of progressive school reform: (1) conservatives block progressive agendas for schooling; (2) conservative practices are easier for teachers to implement than progressive practices; (3) traditional conservative practices are naturally self-sustaining; (4) the current logic of control mitigates against progressive schooling; and (5) progressive schooling has few supporters among influential classes. I briefly address the logic and viability of each of the first four arguments before I move on to show how the results of my study of high-income parents indicate that reason 5—that progressive school reform is not really endorsed by powerful parents—may at least partly account for its failure. In later chapters that focus on school personnel, who are also members of the middle class, further evidence of the lack of middle-class support for progressive schooling is provided.

CONSERVATIVE (ELITE, CAPITALIST) CONTROL OF PUBLIC SCHOOL CURRICULUM

There are reasons to reject hypotheses that elites with conservative philosophies block progressive educational agendas. First, although there have been convincing descriptions of big business and state control over curriculum through domination of textbook companies (Apple, 1992, 2001; Giroux, 1992; Metcalf, 2002), there is no apparent reason why big business could not profit from materials used in progressive forms of schooling as much as from conservative ones.[4] Second, although private enterprise management of public schools looms as a possibility, presently schools are mainly in the hands of public (college-educated, middle-class) officials. Recent press releases report that some private companies have abandoned attempts to manage public schools; that there may not be enough money in public schooling to entice capitalist interest. Third, attempts to divert public funds to finance private (choice) schools (Mintrom, 2000) have, as yet, been mostly unsuccessful (see Cookson, 1992). Fourth, because their children rarely attend public schools, or at least public schools with class-heterogeneous enrollments (Peshkin, 2001; Powell, 1996), elites would seem to have few personal stakes and therefore little interest in public schooling as long as it demands limited financial resources from them and produces a complacent workforce. Moreover, and at the same time, with the exception of not being socially inclusive, elite academies come closer to realizing progressive ideals than public schools (Peshkin, 2001). They tend to be family and child centered because of the power wielded by wealthy children and the entitlement (social capital) felt by influential parents. These schools are enriched to accommodate and incorporate the wealth of experiences—the cultural capital—of students. Finally, children of most elite families have secure financial prospects, so parents do not have to worry about their offsprings' competitive edge on tests and other ranking systems in a time of economic uncertainty for others. Also, for them, academic achievement and attainment may not have the same meaning and importance for adult status and material outcomes as it does for the educated middle class or the lower ranks of the middle class.

EASE OF IMPLEMENTING CONSERVATIVE PEDAGOGY (AND DIFFICULTY OF PROGRESSIVE APPROACHES)

A credible explanation for the ubiquity of conservative school practice is the ease in using it compared to putting progressive forms of schooling into effect. A conservative curriculum consists of texts, tests, workbooks, and worksheets that are commercially available and designed for convenient use by teachers. Group control is easier to maintain when schoolwork is routine and predictable and children can be kept on task by manipulating external rewards or threatening penalties for noncompliance. Evaluation is "objective" and clear: standardized measures show that students either have or do not have the skills and knowledge offered through the predefined curriculum. In contrast, the child-centered, evolving nature of progressive practices necessitates continual alertness, flexibility, creativity, and energy expenditure on the part of both students and school personnel—a tenuous and tedious vigil, especially for those not schooled in progressive ways themselves (see Iran-Nejad, 1990; Iran-Nejad, McKeachie, & Berliner, 1990). Regardless of ideals and intentions, it is easy for school personnel to slip back to comfortable and readily accessible instructional forms, especially when their own evaluation is based on students' scores on standardized tests (see McGill-Franzen & Allington, 1993; McNeil, 2000a; Neill, 2000). Logic informs us that progressive forms of education take more planning and skill on the part of teachers. When teachers' work conditions are difficult in the best of circumstances at high-income schools and deplorable at the schools low-income children attend (Bowes, 2001; Orfield, 2000), the time and energy required to fulfill progressive ideals may simply not be there (Lien, 2001).

SELF-SUSTAINING NATURE OF TRADITIONAL INSTITUTIONAL FORMS

There is certainly validity to arguments that schooling is affected by tradition and that conservative practices are self-perpetuating (Britzman, 1991; Meyer & Zucker, 1989; Tyack & Cuban, 1995). Making substantial, lasting changes in schools is difficult because of the durable and resistant thinking of educators and the public (Goodlad, 1992; Sarason, 1990). According to Gardner (1991): "Deeply entrenched, persistent scripts, conceptions, and stereotypes" (habits of mind) that students and teachers bring to school-based learning resist being refashioned or eradicated (p. 5). Conservative content is familiar. People are schooled to see known forms of education as natural and eternal. Even historians see schools as "permanent, stable, and fixed features of the social landscape subject to tinkering but not transformation" (Finkelstein, 1992, p. 273). Discussing the "grammar of schooling," Tyack and Tobin (1994) note: "What legitimates institutions like schools or churches is the maintenance of ceremonial categories and processes, whether the third grade or high mass" (p. 478), and "the hold of the cultural construction of what constitutes a real school is so powerful that teachers and others habitually adapt reform to local circumstances" (p. 479).

CONTROL LOGIC MITIGATES AGAINST PROGRESSIVE REFORM

Going beyond the notion of self-sustaining rituals, Howe (1994) argues that such school improvement initiatives as *Nation at Risk* and *America 2000* incorporate a conception of education that is grounded in the utilitarian principle that if high standards and rigorous assessments are applied to all students, then the economic health and leadership of the country will be restored. Goodson (1994) makes similar claims about British reforms: "Rhetorically, the national curriculum is presented as a part of the project of economic regeneration, but behind this broad objective two other projects can be discerned: the reconstitution of older class-based British 'traditional subjects' and a reassertion of the ideology of nation-state interest in mass education" (p. 96). Drawing from Noddings's (1992) ideas about the ideology of control, Howe writes: "Spurred and reinforced by 20th century positivist social science and the associated technocratic solutions to political problems, the impulse for control runs deep in United States education" (p. 28). Further, Howe claims that the currently touted "content standards in core academics" are not coherently related to democratic educational aims but actually crowd out the political goal of fostering democratic character and citizenship (p. 31).

Control mentality is very much part of the standards and accountability movement—a movement that has been increasing in force in all parts of the world during the past decade. This movement has had a large conservative impact on school practice, and the high-stakes testing bandwagon that it has spawned has had a chilling effect on school climate. Neill (2000) calls high stakes "a bad reflection of even the better parts of standards" and claims that it causes (1) a narrowing of curriculum through the elimination of curricular depth because tests cover only general factual knowledge; (2) increased student dropout or push-out rates; (3) a weakening of the constructive purposes of tests; (4) speeded-up or intensified mechanistic school work; (5) bureaucratized, centralized power; (6) disempowered teachers; (7) alienated students; and (8) standardized minds.

ABSENCE OF SUPPORT FOR PROGRESSIVE PEDAGOGY

Elite domination, difficulty of implementing progressive pedagogies, absence of progressive traditions that would serve as models, and the current control mentality in the standards and accountability movement surely influence the nature of public schooling. Nevertheless, it is necessary to examine the impact of the fifth consideration: the absence of actual constituents' support for progressive schooling among those who most influence public schooling; that is, the educated middle class. Although not unrelated to the other four influences, this possibility may have the greatest explanatory power in the puzzle regarding the lack of success of progressive school reform in gaining a foothold in public education.

UNDERSTANDING PEDAGOGICAL PREFERENCES OF THE MIDDLE CLASS

The progressive position is broadly associated with college-educated members of the middle class—or those Anyon (1980) refers to as "affluent professionals." The actual pedagogical preferences of this group, however, seem not to have been studied. Researchers usually attribute positive views about education to middle-class individuals as they focus on the problems and risks of low-income groups (see Delamont, 1989; Valencia, 1997; Wright, 1993). So, without scrutiny, the presumed enlightened perspective and active participation of the middle class become the ideal for all classes. As I report on the curricular and pedagogical preferences of interviewed mothers, it is necessary to reiterate that each of the mothers had unique opinions and concerns, yet common strands of thinking surfaced and themes could be identified as generally present in participants' narratives. While I acknowledge a myriad of differences among mothers and occasionally include idiosyncratic perspectives, I mainly focus on their commonalities in this chapter.

SELF-REPRESENTATION AS PROGRESSIVES

Narratives revealed that mothers perceived themselves (and others of their class) not only as liberals but also as people who valued progressive forms of education. Like scholars, these lay educational philosophers conveyed that their progressive outlook was typical of, and unique to, the middle class. Karla conjectured:

> My guess is that low-income parents are more concerned with their kids getting a high school diploma and finding a job than going to college—than broadening horizons. They are less interested in the education of girls. High-income people emphasize high academic achievement and going to college for both sexes. Low-income parents deemphasize arts and music.

Just as researchers (e.g., Bernstein, 1973; Bourdieu, 1977, 1984; Epstein, 1990; Kohn, 1969) distinguish the standards and values of middle-class people from those of low-income people, so did respondents in this study.

So, when talking broadly about their preferences for educational practices, mothers initially verbalized progressive ideals: "let children have choices," "flexibility and individualization," "creativity and independence," "learn at their own pace and not by a certain time that school requires," "get to know the full range of children," and "learn all kinds of things, not just academics." They also criticized present practice from a progressive standpoint: "school stifles creative imagination," "the natural curiosity of my kids is systematically dampened by busy work and boring assignments," "they are lectured to," "they are not given opportunity to work with ideas." A preliminary inspection of interview transcripts revealed that the majority of participants expressed a variety of sentiments that on the surface seemed to favor progressive schooling.

THE PREVALENCE OF CONSERVATIVE DESIRES

Progressive status seemed important to mothers' self-image. Although narratives consistently opened with expressions of support for progressive ideals for education, such sentiments were quite fleeting; they were glibly expressed, then qualified, then contradicted and rejected. Gleaning the narratives as a whole, it was clear that conservative ideas dominated. These desires surfaced in six contexts: (1) discussions of the purposes of education; (2) analyses of the strengths and weaknesses of public education; (3) expression of concern about local educational practices; (4) rationale supplied for preferences for certain local schools; (5) comparisons of their offsprings' education with their own; (6) descriptions of ideal educational outcomes.

Purposes of Education   In venturing opinions about the purposes of education, mothers vacillated between progressive and conservative values. Interspersed with "expand their body of knowledge," "develop creative imagination," "prepare for dealing with situations in life," and "get kids to analyze things from a different perspective" were constant reiterations of children's need to master subject-area content and acquire academic skills (e.g., "master basic skills," "know material," "they must focus on the basics," "really get to know the subject matter well" "developing academically as much as they can," "provided the basic tools"). Phoebe explained:

> School was founded and instituted because it was thought that certain basic knowledge was important for citizens. School experience should be academic and can't deal with social problems—it should be for the basic skills and academics.

Dana clarified: "School should provide the basics so children can learn on their own. They have to have a foundation to help them achieve what they want to achieve in the future." Catherine reiterated: "Schools should teach kids basic skills: verbal, mathematical, scientific, methods of inquiry. And, I hope schools teach kids morals, the basic principles that civilized human beings should live by." This emphasis on school's role in preparing their offspring for higher education and jobs certainly was linked to a concern about their children's futures. Reynolds felt: "Schools should teach the fundamentals of education and prepare them for college and productive jobs." Lynn said: "When you live in a materialistic world, you have to have skills that are appreciated in the market." For Bryn, education was meant to "improve your standard of living so that you earn a good income and have opportunity to do what you like to do."

Evaluations of Contemporary Public Education   Mothers were concerned about the quality of contemporary education. They complained about "low standards," "assignments too limited," "schools needing to be academically more rigid," "too much free time," "kids not stretched enough," and "poor study habits." Finley said:

> The history textbooks are disappointing because of excluding religious reference or major wars. We moved from Michigan where my children were in Catholic schools and had a lot of reading and a good curriculum in literature. The whole thing was based on reading—I was very satisfied with that system. We miss the structure.

Mothers were wary of variations from standard academic curriculum, heterogeneous grouping arrangements, and opportunity for student choice and self-determination. Many complained that such "fads" as cooperative grouping, critical thinking or problem-solving approaches, and special non-academic projects were deflecting attention away from the subject-matter focus. Reynolds confided:

> I know that some students thrive in open-type classrooms, but my boys need much more structure to learn. They are not particularly self-motivated students. We were glad when our neighborhood was districted to Richards because the principal there is a traditional academic man who demands a good deal of accountability from teachers in terms of classroom structure.

Although they criticized "monotonous routines" and "boring reading materials and workbooks," mothers were also wary of such alternatives as cooperative grouping. As Lynn complained:

> My son's social studies teacher organizes his class around group work, and my husband and I believe that our son spends a lot of time waiting for others to get organized when he could progress faster on his own. Although our son might disagree, we think that he would learn more with a more traditional textbook-oriented approach.

Concern about Local Schools   As a newcomer to Hillsdale, Finley was disgruntled about the quality of local schools and spent much of her interview complaining about them:

> Teachers are wasting their time asking children what they think about things rather than giving them information—once in a while it is okay. I would prefer to put more factual information for students to use. Part of teaching is to help students find or form a basis for opinion. The questioning approach is not that great. Teaching is better than class discussions. I know from my own

studies that education fashion in this country changes every 20 years. They can't settle on what is a good education. They keep stirring the pot. Whatever the situation is at the moment, someone will try to change it.

Mothers were skeptical about innovative programs that were not specifically academic and school based. Jeanne felt:

Winter Intensive is a waste of time. Some of the choices have educational value, but, of course, those aren't the ones that my kids choose. One did bicycle repair and the other did rock climbing.

Winter Intensive was a 3-week period between semesters in which students took part in such thematic all-day classes as spelunking, quilting, karate, winter camping, and film studies. They also could choose to be involved in service learning projects such as construction for Habitat for Humanity or work in day care centers, shelters, or community kitchens. In spite of the enthusiasm for the Winter Intensive program among students and teachers, the school board canceled it after 2 years in response to parental expressions of dissatisfaction mainly based on the sense that it was a distraction from the true academic purposes of education.

Reasons for Preferring Certain Local Schools   Mothers were shown a list of high- and low-income schools, and were asked to rate the quality of each and identify the schools that would be appropriate for their children to attend as well as the reasons for their particular school choices. Preferences for conservative pedagogy surfaced in mothers' rationale for liking some schools more than others. Catherine judged:

Kinder [high-income school] is one of the top three elementary schools in town. We felt that Eastside [high-income school] was creative but too unstructured. At Kinder the quality of teaching is good. It's an academic school. Really the best of local schools.

Phoebe viewed Eastside differently—she felt that it did have an academic push:

There are a lot of professional people's children at Eastside and teachers recognize that these children are more advanced and must be challenged, so they push our children to achieve at higher levels. My third-grade son was working in a fifth-grade math workbook last year. I don't particularly like Richards, Beauford, and Kinder. They are yuppie schools. At Eastside there were low-income married students [international students] from university housing, so it meant the enrollment was more diverse, but that did not mean a lack of support for academic achievement.

As noted in chapter 3, the most salient criticism of low-income schools was mothers' perception that they had "low standards" and "lacked academic push." An underlying worry apparent in discussions of heterogeneous schools was that meeting the needs of other people's children would undermine the rigor of their own children's education. "Rigor" seemed to be a code word for being pushed or being placed in settings with higher levels of academic subject matter content. Mothers trusted that affluent schools would provide the best (most advanced and rigorous) academic environment and were content with the social class-homogeneous milieu.

Mothers' Comparisons of Children's Education with Their Own   In contrasting their children's education with their own, 18 mothers felt their own had been better in most ways. There were few complaints about their own education among the 11 mothers who had attended private schools and 7 who attended affluent suburban schools. Again, these mothers spoke of rigor and academic push as positive aspects of these elite settings. Details of the characteristics and quality of their own education again revealed mothers' approval of conservative structures and practices. They valued "rigor," "basic skills and academics," "basic knowledge," "solid academic curriculum," "structure," "old literature," "classical education," "tough curriculum," "the best of private education," "discipline," "Western civilization," "high academic standards," "ability to compete with kids all over the world," "more rigid academics," "high standards," "strong work ethic," "a basic subject-area education that prepared me for advanced education," "a good preparation for college," and "an education that allowed me to excel in college."

Many were nostalgic about their own schooling, few mentioned any dissatisfaction with it, and most claimed that they wished their own children's school circumstances were more like their own. In speaking about her own K–12 private school education, Phoebe said: "It was narrow but quality. It was old-fashioned, but what was taught was well done. Theirs has not been as rigorous and the quality of some of the teaching is poor." Sally went to boarding school and "got a classical education only available in the best prep schools in the East. There was nothing bad about it."

As a high school science teacher, when asked to compare her education to that of her own children, Dana's clarification also seemed to reflect what she was experiencing as a teacher:

> I grew up in the era of the space race when there was support for education in math and science. I was pushed academically—and that was a positive thing. Looking back, I think that the push was valuable. With my children there has not been enough homework, not enough push. Children then did what you asked them; they were cooperative, curious, they did their homework on time, and didn't talk back. I wanted to learn and would go beyond what was taught.

Similarly, Finley said:

> There is no comparison. Mine was private education and theirs is public. We were supposed to be self-disciplined, polite, and responsible. I had to do assignments. That is not true anymore. Today's kids won't go beyond the requirement.[5]

Some mothers who felt their own education was better expressed disappointment that accelerated or advanced academic (magnet) public or private schools had not been available locally for their children. School was an arena where mothers had established personal efficacy through traditional, conservative educational practices. Lynn had been "a good student" in Catholic schools that were "rigorous" and "rigidly academic." Perhaps because of their sense of their own success in traditional schools, they preferred conservative forms of schooling for their children.

Descriptions of Ideal Education Outcomes   In documenting offsprings' (and personal) school success (and superiority), mothers mentioned their own and their children's participation in "gifted and talented programs," "accelerated tracks," and "honors courses." Members of their families were described as "high achievers," "higher than average in academic success," "above average in learning ability," "disciplined and stimulated to learn," "successful in school," "very active in activities," "in leadership positions," "good students with natural ability who went beyond expectations," and "academically oriented." Clearly, such educational accomplishments were status markers strongly linked to establishing a desirable and respected personal identity as being a cut above others intellectually. Peshkin (2001) notes that elite academies often select teachers with degrees other than teacher education because they want them to have advanced work in their subject areas (p. 39).

Consistent with theories about the new middle class in modern technological society (Bourdieu, 1984; Gouldner, 1979; Wright, 1989), academic and intellectual competencies provide the underpinnings for positive identity. School achievement and attainment signify intelligence; hence, high tracks, good grades, and advanced degrees are valued. Because academic success is reified to mean general merit, a central function of schooling appears to be to establish worth. According to Wexler (1992), children's school success is part of status competition among parents who "worry about downward movement for high achievers" (p. 55).

INCONSISTENCIES BETWEEN VERBALIZED IDEALS AND REAL DESIRES

Again, as discussed in chapter 3, a resoundingly strong pattern in mothers' narratives was an initial verbalization of progressive ideals and a subsequent qualification or rejection of those ideals; that is, a progressive preface preceded conservative choices. Ideals were given, but there were always practical— usually local or temporary—reasons why the ideals would not work. Skepticism about progressive pedagogy countered original progressive sentiments. Indeed, it seems that these internally contradictory messages in the responses provide the strongest evidence of the generally conservative nature of mothers' pedagogical desires. Although mothers represented themselves—seemingly even to themselves—as liberals who favored progressive forms of schooling, it became clear that they really felt conservative pedagogical forms had been best for themselves and would be best for their children.

Many mothers categorized their own progressive statements as theoretical and used such terms and phrases as "ideally," "under ideal circumstances," "in the best of possible worlds," "it would be nice if," and "in theory." As Margaret said: "Theoretically, school is designed to make people aware of themselves; for my children to make them better people, better citizens. To pass on the culture of the Western world," but then she added with emphasis: "And, to get a good job." Mothers often concluded their own progressive statements by adding that they were based on impractical or impossible ideals given the constraints of local circumstances or particular conditions of the times. Mothers clearly wanted to avoid a pushy, selfish, or elitist image. Yet children's school success surfaced as foremost on their minds. Similar to the findings of Ames and Archer (1987), these mothers' pragmatic desires were for academic push and measurable achievement in a curriculum that has clear-cut status definers.

The progressive narrative introduction served the function of establishing the participants' status as a liberal. Once a progressive image was set, mothers could reject "theoretical" progressive school alternatives by naming "realistic" constraints supposedly without damage to the valued image. They could then make conservative statements that meshed with their actual desires for their children's schooling. This pattern mirrors the use of qualifiers that often preface racist statements (e.g., "I'm not a racist, but . . ." or "Some of my best friends are black—or Jewish or gay—but . . ."). Inevitably, mothers' discourses about schools terminated with their advocating rigorously academic, tightly sequenced, subject-bound, highly evaluated, Western civilization–oriented curricula.

Educational capital advantages members of the middle class and establishes boundaries between middle and other classes (Bourdieu, 1984; Brown, 1995; Gouldner, 1979; Wright, 1989, 1994). By situating the participants of this study within the confines of an intellectual and education-controlling class in modern technological society, the finding that middle-class mothers prefer conservative pedagogy for their children, although contrary to common thought, does make sense; that is, mothers prefer forms of schooling that advantage their children.

THE STABILITY OF CONSERVATIVE PEDAGOGICAL PREFERENCES

My research did not track pedagogical preferences longitudinally; however, it seems reasonable to conjecture about the impact of economic downturn on perspectives. During the 1950s and 1960s, a time of relative economic growth and prosperity, educated middle class Americans seemed to endorse progressive, inclusive forms of schooling.[6] School segregation was litigated and desegregation was enforced. Although much of compensatory education is segregated, stratifying, and based on assumptions of inferiority in certain populations—thus, ultimately cannot be considered progressive or democratic—at least middle classes voted for money to be spent in behalf of others.[7] At the same time, affirmative action policies and practices were initiated. The advent of multicultural and bilingual education meant that the official middle-class and European-centered curriculum was supplemented by the subcultural knowledge of groups that had traditionally been excluded from or marginalized in American schools and society. A sense that all could prosper, or that others could join in the prosperity without the life chances of the middle class being threatened, seemed to have prevailed.

Yet the progressive reforms that originated in the 1960s potentially could undermine the basis for social hierarchy that was integral to schooling (Shapiro, 1993). The diversification of curriculum that would occur if the personal knowledge of those who had been excluded from or silenced in schools was to be incorporated into the official school knowledge could erode the traditional separation of school experiences from everyday life. It is these school-from-life distinctions that sustain elitist (and middle-class) notions of "being educated." Extending the curriculum means that cultural capital—the "source and product of middle class advantage in transmitting the division of labor to offspring"—is threatened by devaluation (Shapiro, p. 291). For cultural capital to have value, its availability must be controlled (Shapiro & Purpel, 1993). Morrow and Torres (1994) argue that when the number of people is in excess of available positions, some exclusionary practice grounded in a process of signification occurs. For instance, sexist ideology justifies differential treatment of women in the labor market and racist ideology establishes the basis for exclusionary practices in a variety of institutional settings (p. 56). de la Luz Reyes (1997) writes of the continuing expectation at the university level that diverse individuals conform to monolithic, homophobic, and Eurocentric scholarship.

In explicating the implications of economic trajectory, Wright (1989) argues that perspective is different if people believe there is a high probability of upward rather than downward mobility. Plank and Boyd (1994) claim that recent school politics with its "obsessive concern with failures of the educational system" has resulted in a "propensity to embark on a flight from democracy in the search for solutions" (p. 264). Lasch (1984) observes that the central value in American culture—competition—began to center less on a desire to excel and more on a struggle to avoid defeat, an attitude that results in a cautious hoarding of resources. Lasch argues that the desire of the middle class for their children's retention of a major share of resources is the impetus behind their conservative educational choices. Lasch (1995) eventually proclaimed that selfishness of elites was destroying American democracy.

According to Piven and Cloward (1979), it has never been possible to compel concessions from dominant groups to sustain oppositional organizations over a prolonged period of time. It might be reasonable to conjecture that in prosperous times the progressive ideals and progressive self-image of the middle class are fairly congruent with their personal desires for schooling. In times of economic stagnation or decline, however, their ideals/image and personal self-interests diverge. According to Brock (1999), it has always been possible to see education as a commodity, a service to be paid for or exchanged with, and for some the economic function has been paramount (p. 7). Although education is to contribute to personal and national economic growth, it does have other political, custodial, and humanitarian functions.

Mothers spoke of progressive ideals with seeming conviction, yet a perusal of narratives revealed the preponderance of conservative preferences. This finding challenges Delpit's (1995) premise—and that of other scholars and lay individuals—that members of advantaged social classes value intellectually flexible, self-directed learning. In fact, mothers in this study would be likely to agree with Delpit's (1988) choice of conservative forms of schooling for marginalized students. However, they would also maintain that an open-ended, nonexplicit curriculum is not suitable for their own children—that they need direct and systematic instruction in the culture of power in order to continue to excel over children of lower classes and to compete with children of their own class.

The assumption that progressive education is the ideal of the college-educated middle class has been challenged previously. Apple (1992) argues that struggles over curriculum are between two factions of the middle class—one supporting a "visible," subject-centered, tightly controlled pedagogy and the other an "invisible," child-centered, more loosely controlled pedagogy (p. 135). Yet conservative preferences may be even more prevalent than Apple surmises. Indeed, if the findings of this study are similar elsewhere, Apple's latter group may be distinguished by progressive rhetoric rather than progressive ideals. This study would tend to confirm Popkewitz's (1991) contention that liberal[8] and New Right agendas appear to be in ideological conflict but are based on similar assumptions and have similar implications.

5

Positions and Outlooks of Teachers at Different Schools

School personnel with considerable experience in the Hillsdale district were purposefully selected for this study because (1) they would be likely to be informed about schools and (2) they might have the security and confidence to be candid in expressing their views. A list of personnel in the district was obtained from the central administration and a cross-section was chosen to represent (1) schools located in higher- and lower-income neighborhoods; (2) a grade-level distribution from elementary through high school; and (3) teaching and administrative ranks. The school-based experience of participants ranged from 3 years to 41 years. Two had taught fewer than 5 years: an itinerant teacher had taught art at various high- and low-income schools and a secondary social studies teacher had attended Hillsdale schools. Twenty-two teachers and eight administrators were interviewed (see Table 2.2).

The most salient distinctions between the backgrounds of interviewed mothers and school personnel were that the former largely came from out of state, were offspring of college-educated parents, had attended suburban and/or private elementary and secondary schools, and had gone to Ivy League universities or prestigious liberal arts colleges (see Table 2.1); the latter had grown up in rural areas and small towns within the state, were first-generation college, and had attended public universities or small religious colleges that mainly drew from local populations. I believe that these demographic differences align with unique positions in a social class hierarchy and therefore correlate with their distinctive standpoints and the power they held relative to one another to set school policy and influence school practice.

For purposes of analysis and theory building in this book, I usually compress what I know is a multileveled social class system into a binary of high and low classes. In this chapter, I introduce a more complex system that somewhat corresponds to the second and third of the five class levels delineated by Anyon (1980): (1) affluent professional and (2) average middle (white-collar workers with salaries commensurate with the working class). According to this breakdown, 11 teachers and 4 administrators might be considered to be average middle class because of their families' employment and educational backgrounds and, at least with teachers, current family income. I refer to this subset as "*in the middle.*" In contrast, mothers in this study were equivalent to the affluent professional class both because of their current educational and financial status and the educational attainment heritage of their parents/families, hence their long-term affiliation with and allegiance to an affluent professional (upper middle) class.

School personnel were not specifically queried about their current social class status or parents' occupations; nevertheless, they volunteered information about family members' occupational or financial status either currently or when they were growing up, and they continuously referred to their class affiliations, often in the context of who they were similar to and how they differed from people of other classes. This information turned out to be pertinent to the study.[1]

Twenty-two of the 30 school personnel claimed that they and/or their siblings were first in their family to attend college. Eight directly used the term "poor" to describe their parents' monetary status. As Alice[2] said: "We were poor when I was growing up, but then everyone else in my town was low-income so that it did not make much difference. I did not feel deprived or inferior to anyone." Two additional interviewees talked about their families as "struggling to make ends meet" and "being financially burdened." Still another said, "My parents were farmers, but they always had to do extra work to make a go of it." One (i.e., the 12th to mention financial constraints) said to "save money" his father gave him haircuts. He recalled being so embarrassed about the way he looked that he started wearing caps—a habit he continues today.

Eight school personnel were offspring of college-educated parents. Three elementary school teachers were daughters of retired school administrators and another of a local doctor. An additional four, who were not raised in Hillsdale, reported that their parents were professionals. The six women were married to men employed in profession fields or business, hence were similarly positioned to the affluent mothers who taught in Hillsdale. Thus, it is not surprising that their interviews were much like those of the high-income mothers in terms of how they described social contacts, residential neighborhoods, children's educational careers, impressions of local schools, and sentiments about students of different social classes.

Two administrators and six teachers who had similar demographic characteristics to high-income mothers are called "*already there.*" Five additional teachers and two administrators shared most demographic traits with *in-the-middle* personnel; however, because their outlooks on schooling were similar to the *already there* group, I call them "*upward strivers.*" An assistant superintendent confessed that as a child he was ashamed that his father was a school janitor. He praised teachers for "encouraging me anyway," noting he had been a "good student—both academically able and well behaved," which he felt accounted for the "kindness" of teachers and administrators. He, as well as six others whom I call "*upward strivers,*" claimed lowly origins but reiterated the theme of having been recognized in school as bright and hardworking. *Upward strivers* conveyed that they were self-made people in a world that was mostly fair in recognizing merit. And, unlike the *in-the-middle* but like the *already there* interviewees, five *upward strivers* were fairly defensive about implications that the local system might not provide an equal education for all children. Although *upward strivers* identified largely with affluent, educated people, *already there* personnel and mothers might see them as class imposters because of their local (lowly) origins and cultural styles.

In addition to distinctive social class origins and present status, the *already there, upward-striving,* and *in-the-middle* status of teachers mainly corresponded to the income level of schools where they worked (or track assignments at secondary schools). In conjecturing about possible reasons for this correspondence and the consistencies in within- and between-group narratives, it is possible that (1) school personnel sorted themselves when they sought and accepted jobs at schools that were similar to the ones they had attended in their youth (i.e., that matched their own class background) and were comfortable for them; or (2) they were selected by the personnel director and building administrators according to their educational outlooks, histories, and current cultural styles. In the next section, I address the nature of these groups' self-descriptions and the distinctive lens through which they viewed schools and students.

As one who has been informed and influenced by a postmodernist recognition of the dynamic, multifaceted, and multilevel nature of human thinking, I know that dividing and subdividing study participants in this bounded manner is risky (see Eisenhart, 2001). Yet, after multiple readings of the interview transcripts and considering participants' narratives in relation to their demographic characteristics, I did find substantial internal consistency within clusters of responses that made it seem reasonable to designate these as somewhat unique groups. Thus, I name the groups and speak of group outlooks, although I also note personal idiosyncracies in participants' responses whenever relevant.

CONSTELLATIONS OF RESPONSES: SEEING THE WORLD THROUGH A PARTICULAR LENS

School personnel were asked whether they had been proud of something during their schooling. Fifteen (eight *already there* and seven *upward striving*) focused on having been strong students. They mentioned academic honors (salutatorian, valedictorian, honor roll, dean's list, earning a 4.0 GPA) and advanced track placements. They won spelling bees, placed first in science fairs, and were leaders in extracurricular activities. A daughter of a retired administrator was not specific about any one achievement but announced in a matter-of-fact manner that she "always was a leader in school, a favorite of many teachers," adding: "everyone in my family and my teachers expected me to do well." *Already there* and *upward striving* emphasized that school was a venue for establishing personal success (superiority).

The 15 *in-the-middle* professionals (11 teachers, 4 administrators) were humble about their academic and leadership history. Teachers admitted: "I did not always get the best grades"; "I never made the honor roll, but I got an award for attendance"; "I was a pretty average student." One judged that she "had not been an outstanding student but was steady and got the required work done." A central administrator recalled "struggling in school, but I did graduate." Although a teacher's sense was that nobody had encouraged him to go to college, as a veteran he took advantage of the GI bill and got his teaching certificate. When asked what he had been proud of, he smiled woefully as he admitted: "that I got through college when nobody thought I would." One said that although she had "never been a top student," she "had not caused anyone any trouble and tried as hard as I could." Others claimed they had "been well behaved" and some contrasted themselves—and sometimes their whole generation—with today's problematic students.

In-the-middle teachers and administrators mainly focused on social aspects of their school days: "I always got along with teachers"; "I was a polite child who did well socially—I earned the respect of teachers and peers"; "I was a kid who liked to please." One teacher said: "I am proud that I had a good disposition and was a pleasant child" and confessed that "the most important thing about school was being with my friends at recess." Another called herself "a person who stood behind the scenes rather than one who stood out," noting, "I liked it that way." When asked what she had been proud of, a teacher pondered the question a while, then ventured: "I don't think I ever did anything different than anyone else." This *in-the-middle* subset generally described less-distinguished personal academic and school leadership accomplishments. As they mentioned social rather than academic strengths, they conveyed that school was a place to be with others.

Similar to high-income mothers, the *already there* and *upward-striving* teachers spoke about high educational and occupational aspirations for their own children and bragged, or worried, about their offsprings' achievement and school status. In contrast, *in-the-middle* teachers did not dwell on the accomplishments or academic prowess of their children. Some who were parents of adult children volunteered that certain of their children had not gone to college or had not completed college. They talked about sons and daughters in the military or in working-class or nonprofessional white-collar jobs. Some spoke of this lesser attainment as something they were somewhat bothered about, but more often they seemed satisfied that their children had stable lives, secure employment, and especially that they lived locally, so they could keep in contact with their families. Although these demographics were not officially collected, *in-the-middle* teachers volunteered that their spouses were not college educated and did not have professional careers. Some women were single parents with one salary to support their families.

DISTINCTIONS IN TEACHERS' IDEAS ABOUT THE PURPOSE OF SCHOOL

Recall that when asked about the purpose of school, affluent mothers mostly mentioned academics. If they referred to civic or social purposes, they did so briefly and went on to speak of the advanced or accelerated academic needs of their children as they complained about how these needs were not met. *Already there* and *upward-striving* teachers (and mothers who were teachers) were not as likely to complain about local schools as mothers in other professions; still they distinguished their academic strengths by contrasting them to the lesser academic achievement of individuals at low- or mixed-income schools.

Whereas high-income parents and *already there* school personnel dwelled on the need for advanced academic achievement, *in-the-middle* teachers and administrators stressed the social, civic, and nonacademic personal objectives of schooling. Three exceptions included rather modest academic goals: (1) "get kids to think," (2) "have children learn, think, expand knowledge," and "encourage sound knowledge of 3 Rs to foster social adjustment and self-confidence." Two gave a version of "help children reach their potential," with both adding that they did not mean only academic potential. The social or civic purposes they provided included "teach children to be responsible citizens," "help children understand people in authority so they can be reasonable," "for students to become enthusiastic and caring people," "prepare children for the future—change them as persons," "prepare them for life—to enjoy life and live life to the fullest," "prepare good citizens who are productive and healthy (not just to impart skills but attitudes as well)," "to enable a child to get along in society and be a contributor," "to help a child be a successful person," "prepare the child to face the world and be patriotic," "teach man's concern for fellow man," "teach them to strive to do their best," "teach them to get along with friends," "make individuals realize their full potential and overcome limits inflicted on them," "prepare students to face society—which is pretty tough these days," and "prepare them to make informed choices and to continue their educations." These responses were more child centered than the individual achievement-oriented replies of mothers and the *already there* and *upward-striving* teachers.

It might be hypothesized that group differences result from *in-the-middle* teachers spending their days in the dynamic and often conflicted social environment of the classroom with the humanity of their students not only ever present but also constantly in need of being shaped. Nevertheless, based on my own observations—and the opinions of some knowledgeable informants in this study—*already there* teachers are also surrounded by students who are more unruly and antisocial than children at low-income schools. So, it seems that *already there* teachers would be attuned to social goals. Perhaps the best explanation is that the difference in response is related to the nature of the pressures put on them by parents of children who attend their schools and by administrators who reinforce parental perspectives. Another explanation is that *in-the-middle* teachers did not see competitively high academic achievement as either possible for their students or as a likely avenue to social mobility for them.

As an educator who falls squarely within the progressive education camp, I would tend to agree with the social and civic purposes of schooling named by *in-the-middle* teachers. However, when this perspective is unique to teachers with low-income student populations, it must be seen as problematic. Such expressed purposes and goals are likely to correlate with less academic push of pupils than would follow from achievement-oriented perspectives. When I observe at Head Start, I am bothered that their curriculum is not as academically or intellectually oriented as private preschools. Distinctive program orientations and expectations for pupils surely figure into the differential readiness status of their respective pupils when they go on to kindergarten. I also am troubled to see that the skills orientation and pedantic pedagogy of some low-income schools contrasts with the enriched and interesting curriculum and respectful pedagogy of those in affluent neighborhoods. In the long run, such distinctive orientations can account for the eventual class-related achievement disparities.

On the other hand, given the nature of working-class jobs and the personal attributes needed for them, these teachers may be realistically aiming at—and valuing—more relevant attributes for their pupils. Yet, in a country with low minimum wages and no wage caps, significant salary disparities exist between individuals with different levels of educational attainment; that is, postschool jobs and thus material outcomes are related to educational capital. Thus, distinctions in the education offered to students from different social classes must be judged to be unacceptable. School-related factors affect the perpetuation of class-related inequities. If salaries in this country were equal, then disparate academic achievement outcomes would be less important. In the meantime, because all families and children do not have access to the same material goods and status, it is important to focus on the social mobility possibilities of poor and working-class children by making sure that they are provided with an equal education.

TEACHERS' "IDEAL" STUDENTS

Portrayals of preferred students were again fairly internally coherent and consistent for each group. *Already there* and *upward strivers'* ideal student had such traits as "intellectual curiosity," "drive," "high standards," and "high aspirations." Keeping in mind that most mentioned several attributes, 12 *in-the-middle* teachers first listed a version of "well behaved," including someone "who gets along with others," "is happy," and "with high self-esteem." With more academic focus, the first responses of the other 3 were "enthusiastic about learning," "has a good work ethic," and "curious." Other attributes were "interested in ideas," "alert," "willing to try new things," "eager," "energetic," "responsive," "sits up and listens," "respectful," "good attitude," "good disposition," "good sport," "contributes in class," "good attention span," "motivated," "takes part in discussions," "doesn't complain," "has small-town values," "average," "has no learning problems," and "has concerned parents." *In-the-middle* teachers' ideal students conformed to institutional routines and got along with peers and teachers. Many descriptors had to do with feedback from students that teachers were interesting, respected, competent, and well liked. A high school teacher who taught general tracks felt: "An ideal student would be willing to try some new things, to sort of wrestle with the ideas; who would be willing to persevere, discipline themselves. You know, put some real effort into their work, to try to develop their own skills." Joan, a Hillview teacher who called her students "ordinary," stated:

> In terms of ideal student, I could never really say that any one of them is ideal, because some of the ones I liked the best were the worst rascals I ever had. I really like working with the children with problems. I would rather work in the kind of school I work in where kids do come from upset backgrounds as to work in the "elite" schools.

Joan came out strongly for inclusion, heterogeneous grouping, and class desegregation of schools, saying: "People look down on Hillview, Southside, and Westside, but especially Downing, because it is closest to the Projects—and the kids and their parents know it!" In terms of the purpose of schooling, Joan said: "Well, hopefully, it would be to help kids have a chance—to go out and find a useful place in society, which I'm not so sure we do, but I at least make a stab at it. It's not easy. Getting along in society is pretty tough these days."

Many *in-the-middle* teachers mentioned that ideal students "do not need to be very intelligent" or "high achievers." One said that an ideal student was "one who is not in the highest academic bracket but is a B student who is all round—academics alone don't make a student." Descriptions corresponded to teachers' images of themselves as students and perhaps even their educational and vocational desires for their offspring.[3] So, demographically clustered teachers sorted into fairly distinctive realms in terms of their ideas about the purpose of school and the ideal student.

One reason for the correlations between teacher demographics and responses might be that these long-term teachers had been socialized by their distinctive working environments, so their outlooks had come to match those of their colleagues as well as the goals and aspirations of students at their schools and their students' parents. To conjecture further, it seems that it is this status of *in-the-middle* school personnel—combined family income in the moderate range, residence in a modest part of town or rural area, their own children primarily attending mixed-income schools, their own working-class and moderate middle-class backgrounds, and satisfaction with security and stability for their children and spouses—that leads me to conclude they rank lower on the social class status hierarchy than high-income mothers and the *already there* and *upward-striving* teachers who taught in high- or mixed-income schools.

TEACHERS' CONCERNS ABOUT CURRENT TRENDS IN SCHOOLING

Interviews were launched with a request that teachers talk about current education. Like parents, most focused on concerns. An idiosyncratic but interesting response was from a Beauford (high-income school) teacher, Betty, who was the oldest person interviewed in the study. Born and raised in Hillsdale, her father had been local superintendent of schools at one time. Betty observed:

> I used to be concerned about patriotism in Hillsdale. I'm a patriot. I am glad that now it is becoming more in vogue to be a patriot. I had the feeling in the sixties and early part of the seventies when a group of people—a great number—seemed to want to downgrade the United States and said how much better other countries were, and yet they sure didn't want to leave here. Some of them were teachers in this district![4]

When comparing *in-the-middle* school personnel's responses with those of affluent mothers, distinctions were profound. Mothers were obsessed with "the decline in school quality"—a decline that they felt would affect their children's future in facing what they feared would be an increasingly competitive world. Only two (*already there*) teachers addressed a decline in schools' quality (i.e., "low quality of education," "schools should raise standards"). Both had children in high school at the time of the study. These teachers' pattern of responses closely resembled those of mothers. Not surprisingly, most other teachers' initial responses centered around the quality of students and families. Some complained that due to the multitude and intensity of such problems, they were "forced into counseling, but aren't trained for that role" or "must focus attention on AIDS, sex, and drug education instead of academics." Although 21 named some form(s) of student or family deficit in their initial reply, teachers at high-income schools spoke of problems that were of a somewhat different nature than teachers at low-income schools (see Table 5.1).

Table 5.1

Teachers' Ideas about What Is Wrong with Current Education

Teachers at High-Income Schools and Secondary Schools	Teachers at Low-Income Schools
Too little home life	Bad influences in the home
Family breakup	Family breakup
Little contact with mothers	Kids' and parents' attitudes toward learning Poverty in the home
Too much time in day care or extended day programs	Number of at-risk kids with whom we have to deal
Kids have a "me" orientation	Attitudes toward work, effort, learning, discipline
Kids want to get by with the least work possible	Home problems that are reflected in school
Student behaviors	Number of students with family problems
Number of students who won't behave	In-between children not eligible for special ed.
Student attitudes	Decline in home standards
Parents putting too much pressure on kids and teachers	Reaching at-risk kids
Drugs, alcohol, gangs, at-risk students, number of dropouts	Home environments with physical and mental abuse
Absentee parents	Broken homes
Broken homes	Uncaring parents
Kids too concerned about clothes and material goods	Kids who don't care about learning

Mothers talked about flaws in Other people's children as justification for separated schools, whereas deficit narratives by *already there* teachers were offered as rationale for why they were glad not to teach at westside schools. Although they also saw flaws in the affluent students at their schools, for the most part, they emphasized the behaviors and attitudes of a problematic few and not of the whole student body. *In-the-middle* teachers' deficit talk often was some expression of sadness about the plight of some students and/or worries about the pressures of their work conditions when so many children lived in difficult conditions. Joan, a conscientious Hillview teacher, reiterated despair at not meeting students' needs:

> Teachers are expected to be too many things, I mean, you're supposed to be a mother, nurse, teacher, savior, advisor, counselor, doctor, nurse. You name it and you're supposed to be it. And I don't think teachers can be all those things successfully all the time. They can only do them partially.

In-the-middle teachers usually were empathetic to the impoverished conditions of families and gave examples of particular cases of "dysfunction" in families (e.g., when a parent lost a job, was incarcerated, was terribly poor, was disabled, had a substance abuse problem, had abused their children). They were less likely to engage in generalized victim blaming or cultural deprivation narratives. Thus, teachers who were exposed to low-income families generally were more likely to see them as diverse and as thwarted by various societal (structural) conditions; that is, their stories were informed by actual contacts and not just by geographical imaginaries.[5]

The most prevalent initial concern listed by *already there* teachers was that societal decline or increasing complexity of modern life had repercussions for children and ultimately for teachers and schools: "television has a bad influence—kids stay up too late and nobody reads to them or encourages them to read anymore," "negative influences of the media," "the rapid pace of life affects relations," "there are too many distractions out there, kids can't concentrate on their school work," "trying to reach kids who have too much stuff going on in their lives," and "there is no incentive to read anymore, everything is handed to them on television."

NAMING THEIR OWN AND OTHER PEOPLE'S CHILDREN

A great deal can be learned about social life from the names and labels used by various people for themselves and others (see Table 5.2). Although similarities can be noted in the lists, it is important to acknowledge that teachers tended to see distinctions among the children at their school and schools with similar students but referred to children at schools at the other end of the social class spectrum as homogeneous; they saw the trees, not the forest,

Table 5.2

Names Used to Refer to High- and Low-Income Students

Names for High-Income Students

Used by *Already There* Teachers	Used by *In-the-Middle* Teachers
People with ambition	Spoiled bunch (at Kinder)
The stars	Kids who are pressured
Spark plugs	Higher-up ones
Super-motivated kids	Well-to-do kids
Ones with superior intellect	Upper edge
Those with top intelligence	Their kids
Advanced student	Yuppies from the east side
Higher students	Snobs
Superior intellect	Ones who think they are better than everybody else
Eastsiders	Cliquey and nasty kids
Our kids	Spark plugs
High side	High intelligence bunch
Upper strata	Kids with pushy parents
Kids from the best families in Hillsdale	Kids whose parents pressure them too much
Ones with the better background	Kids who are very competitive
Doctors' children	
Professors' kids	
Upper-edge families and children	

Names for Low-Income Students

Kid for whom it's a battle to survive	Poor children with lots of problems
Kids who break your heart	Children who break your heart
Low-ability children	Kids who learn differently
Different-ability children	Kids from low conducive-to-learning homes
Kids who aren't smart	Students who are good at working with their hands
Extreme bottom	Kids who fall through the cracks
Ragamuffin	Ones who have given up already
Ones who break your heart	Kids with low skills
The bad boys and girls	Kids from SES deprived backgrounds
Angry, at-risk kids	Our kids (used by most)

(Continued)

Table 5.2

Names Used to Refer to High- and Low-Income Students (*Continued*)

Names for Low-Income Students

Used by *Already There* Teachers	Used by *In-the-Middle* Teachers
Naughty boys	Ones with no hope
Grits (used by several)	Ones who have given up on learning
Grits (I'm quoting the kids)	Kids without confidence in learning
Westsiders	Scruffy people
West-side poor white	West-side kids
Some skewed downward	Our kids
Low students	Just ordinary run-of-the mill kids
Lower end of society	Children whose parents struggle to survive
Lower-class students	Children from broken homes
Lower spectrum of social class	Children with single mothers
Kids with poor role models	Children with no male role models
Blue-collar workers	Class goats
Kids who are on free lunch— who have textbooks paid	
Kids with parents who are on food stamps	

at their own schools, and the forest, not the trees, at other schools. Louise, a Hillview teacher, called certain low-income children "scruffy" but others "kids that break your heart" when she spoke about the problems children at her school endured because of family poverty; whereas Nancy, a Beauford teacher, called the whole Hillview enrollment "angry, at-risk kids."

Several patterns can be discerned in the names used. One is that children were referred to by family attributes (e.g., high-income parents' occupation, low-income parents' marital status). Most importantly, both *already there* and *in-the-middle* teachers equated high-income status with advanced achievement and high intelligence and low-income status with low skills and behavior problems. Some *in-the-middle* teachers made a point of denying the correlation. Louise caught herself making the assumption of class and intelligence correspondence, then cautioned: "But we can't equate low income with low ability necessarily, and sometimes it's hard not to get caught up in thinking of the two as the same. And high income does not necessarily equate with high ability either." Nevertheless, there was considerable evidence that even *in-the-middle* teachers assumed that students at low-income schools were less intelligent or at least less achievement oriented. What is equally important is that many communicated that they also saw themselves as less intelligent than teachers, parents, and children at the east-side schools.

Some *in-the-middle* teachers talked about bright children as the exception in their schools. A Bluffton Elementary (mixed but predominantly lower-middle-class school) teacher told of her puzzlement about a high-achieving student and her indecision about how to react to him:

> I have one low-income boy who I really think is qualified for gifted and talented classes if the parents were interested in that sort of thing. He's the kid who no one would ever suspect of being gifted. In fact, I couldn't figure him out. When we did our testing, he was high in so many things that showed up on the state achievement test that I got out my sheets on gifted and talented and was just mortified, really. I did not realize there were so many areas he just fit right in and I was really missing the boat with him.

When asked to clarify her mention of the possibility that his parents were not interested in his being in a gifted and talented program, she continued:

> No [they would not block his attendance], I find that if their [low-income parents] children qualify they don't usually stand in their way. Sometimes they are real borderline and these parents don't know it and don't push it [for a gifted and talented placement]. It's not that they're dumb people—in fact, just the opposite. It is because of their background—they don't know what is available. My kids are at a disadvantage [in terms of access to advanced programs] because of their lack of background. There are gaps in vocabulary. Even IQ test scores are affected by experience.

As she described parent inattention to children's intelligence, she alluded to her own tendency to ignore these capabilities and her uncertainty about how to deal with high achievers at her school.

TEACHERS' ACCEPTANCE OR REJECTION OF CLASS STEREOTYPES, STRATIFICATION, AND INEQUITIES

In one way or another, allusions to class distinctions in Hillsdale schools surfaced in all of the interviews. Claire, an *in-the-middle* teacher at a rural school (Ushville), recalled her schooling:

> When I went to Eastside Elementary for a while, I was probably underprivileged in a privileged setting. I lacked background. But when I moved to the west side, I was the richest girl in the school. I was the smartest, most knowledgeable girl in the school and yet I had just moved 2 miles. I remember a sixth-grade teacher who talked to me as an equal. I also went to a country

school where there were all kinds of kids, some from hovels, rural kids. I had a sense of being able to accomplish things, that my education meant I could be like better people around me. Socioeconomic grouping took place then in junior high school—this lasted through seventh and eighth grades. We were grouped by our previous elementary school. I was from the west side and was grouped accordingly—though I didn't quite fit because my parents weren't quite west siders. There is a certain amount of prejudice toward poor kids— if a kid comes in and his clothes are totally dirty and he hasn't washed in a while, well, that affects peer relationships.

In discussing access to quality education, Claire focused on the community rather than schools as she asserted: "There are programs available at the university, but I find kids that come from poor families do not sign up because they don't have the money to pay the fee or transportation is not available." Claire went on to discuss the influence of social class on her daughters' education:

Our family hasn't chosen to live in affluent areas, so my children went to Hillview and Bluffton, but they were naturally drawn to able people who had some ambition; they were not drawn to scruffy people. Our home also provided much support. They were good little girls who did what the teacher said. There was some negative interaction with aggressive poor kids. [When asked to clarify, she said:] Well, then my girls' teachers would think: "Now where can we put Antoinette (black student) so she won't disturb others?" And, they would put her next to my daughter. [Was your daughter bothered by that?] No, my children had no out-group feelings. But I was bothered about them using my daughter to control other kids' behaviors.

As this quotation illustrates, class was not the only category of social affiliation. Yet the population of Hillsdale is predominantly white, and race was not directly addressed in the study and rarely was mentioned by interviewees. One exception, Louise, a Hillview teacher, named "conflicts with minorities" first when asked about current school problems. In describing her adult daughter's early education, Louise related:

She went through busing in Louisville public schools and it was horrible. She lost one year of school because of that. Total disruption, total chaos for one year of school because the blacks were bused into her white school. So she went through a year of that and it was a very traumatic experience for her. Not because she was with mixed groups of children; it was because of the animosity kids had for each other because they were forced into it. It was a horrible experience. I don't know if that turned her off to school or not, but she didn't have a good year. I don't think many kids learned much that year.

At the time of the interviews, Downing had the highest percentage of African American students (7–10%) and Hillview the second highest (5–7%), and both were often characterized as the worst schools by teachers who did not teach at them. Louise judged Downing to be "unacceptable," adding: "I don't want my name linked to any of this, but I also would not want her attending Eastside because of what I hear is a tremendous population of foreign students, of non-English-speaking students." In spite of expressing negative racial sentiments, Louise showed a great deal of loyalty to Hillview and considerable understanding of low-income students who attended there.

Data on families eligible for free lunch at each school are published annually in the local newspaper. This statistic shows the high concentration of family poverty in particular schools in the district. The realtors' guide routinely includes the school attendance zones for housing in affluent suburbs but not in neighborhoods zoned to low-income schools. Teachers were aware of the predominant social class of students enrolled at their schools, but some defensively claimed their schools had a social class mix ("kids from both ends," "top to bottom of socioeconomic ladder," "whole spectrum of social classes," "rich students and poor students"). Kinder is the only school that has no low-income residential areas in its catchment zone, so other schools do have some mix. Betty, a Beauford teacher, was able to say: "Our school is located in one of the better parts of Hillsdale." Yet, in discussing the possibility of school desegregation in Hillsdale, she said: "I think schools are already mixed." A more realistic appraisal came from Louise: "I know there is a small group of low economic kids at Beauford, but there's mostly the other side of the coin—the rich ones. I also know that there is real snobbishness there; they look down their nose at poor kids. . . . I'm wearing my designer clothes and you aren't—that type of thing."

As might be expected, teachers' perceptions of their students and their students' families varied according to their own demographic characteristics. Although there was some overlap in the responses, what they chose to notice in social class relations and resource discrepancies was related to who they were and where they taught. *In-the-middle* teachers often mentioned social class bias among school personnel, parents, and students as well as discrimination in the practices and structures of schools; that is, they showed greater insight into the nature of the social class politics of Hillsdale. They were also more likely than their *already there* counterparts to express empathy for poor students and their parents. Howard, an itinerant physical education teacher, compared the two schools where he taught that year:

> Every day that I come to Hillview, I see teachers busting their tail ends to help these kids, you know, to teach them. It's a no-frills education. I don't

think the creative aspect is there as it might be at other schools. I came from kind of a poor background, so I can identify with these kids. I think that is why teaching at this school is easy for me because I have empathy for kids who don't have the same things as other children. At Lexington [mixed income], the facilities are better—but I am not sure that matters. I went to school for a time in a one-room schoolhouse. But there is a better library at Lexington and it has science labs, which they don't have at Hillview. I know they get different stuff at different schools in this corporation. Maybe that's the way it is all over the world—I don't know.

Howard went on to conjecture:

By and large, the people from lower-income families trust the corporation more than people with more education and more money. You could go over to the east side, say Richards, where my wife teaches, and its not unusual for a parent to come in in August and demand—not ask but demand—a certain teacher. And these people have more money, more education. They're trying to guide their child through life so they take the path of least resistance. They have this idea that "if I can make an ideal situation for my child, perhaps he can have a really good education." It's almost like it's a setup. And my view about that is that you should take your child to school and let him find his way. I think here at Hillview that some teachers feel like the parents don't care. I prefer to think that they trust what we're doing. I think that at Richards and Beauford there is more competition for parents and children. That's a real difference. And parents have money to spend for extra things for their kids like sports and music camps. Now that affects the kids' education even if its not taking place at the school.

Some *in-the-middle* teachers used negative stereotypes ironically. Louise recalled her initial dismay at being assigned to teach at Hillview with "dummies from the west side." Joan, another Hillview teacher, fondly described her class as she talked about the importance of her job and the reason she liked to teach at her particular school: "Picture a mass of humanity wiggling all over but ready for some kind of direction." *In-the-middle* teachers appeared to identify with their students. As she discussed her students' feelings, Maureen, a Southside teacher, recalled her own negative experiences "as a poor child" with "teachers who didn't listen or treat me with respect—who looked down on me": "Higher-class parents encourage their children to avoid/minimize contact with lower class." Praising Southside parents, she said:

All parents here probably want something good for their children. I think that lower-class parents want their children to have a better life than they have had—like a nicer home, more education, a better job. Mine did. They were proud that I did well in school and became a teacher. I suppose that upper-class parents' kids may be expected to maintain the status quo—to be like their parents.

A Bluffton teacher, Alice, wavered in that she first typecast students according to their social class status but then caught herself doing this and denied the usual stereotypes:

> The lower-class child always has, often times, a chip on their shoulder be-cause they do feel inferior. And they want to be a part of . . . want to fit in, but, you know, sometimes the kids don't want somebody with tennis shoes from K-Mart. It's a real prestigious thing now, you know—they look at the coats the kids have on, and they know who's on who's Little League team, and a lot of the children from lower socioeconomic backgrounds don't have those advantages. Now they don't get to be taken to Little League, they don't have soccer practice after school, a lot of them go home from school and they're on their own. But I don't want you to think that all poor children are going to be coming from a low conducive home. That's not true because my family—I was very poor. Yet, my parents, as I look back, gave me the most important things without much money. I have a little boy this year from a broken home situation, the mother didn't graduate from high school—he's a very bright little boy. Academically he's very good in math. And I'm trying to inspire him and the mother for them to go on. I hope he can go on because he would do well. A lot of it is the money. Education is an expense.

One of a few teachers to target schools or classrooms as sources of student problems, Alice said: "A child could be in an unruly classroom and that would just be a wipe-out year." Alice observed with concern that "the wealthier kids are in higher-ability-level classes, at least at Bluffton." Because Alice talked at length about social class, it is important to give her ideas space here:

> I am very concerned about the fact of labeling children. For instance, gifted and talented, which I think comes from a kind of separatist idea about an elite society. They seem to think that a core of individuals need methods that to some degree do not work for the "average" child—if there is such a thing. I really personally don't like the gifted and talented program. I think if a teacher is on the ball, she can give those children experiences in a regular classroom, and that kind of program is really . . . giving those children a false impression of themselves. They may have a lot of money, but they still may be just as sick as someone else that is poor. I think every child is gifted in some way.
>
> And, by the same token, you have the LD [learning disabled] child, and so forth. There needs to be a lot of care to keep LD kids in contact with regular kids and not isolating them. For them to be only with other children that also

have special problems all day, now I have a problem with that. I know a lot of teachers that do not like these children mainstreamed, but I really see a harm that comes by sticking a label on them and sending them off by themselves, because children do learn good things from each other. I have heard some people say some cruel things about some of our poorer, less intelligent kids. In terms of inclusion, too many of them are left in there [self-contained special education classes] when they should be either partially mainstreamed or at some time taken out. I really will have to say now as a parent—I had a daughter with perceptual problems—and I would have to think a long, long, long time before I would let any of my children go into a special program like that. Now, I'm not speaking as an educator but as a parent.

Alice again spoke from the position of a parent as she discussed her daughter's experience with tracking as well as her own opposition to it:

My daughter tracked herself into college-bound classes in high school and I had two teachers call very unhappy because she was in there, saying that if she, if we would allow her to go into a different track, as hard as she worked, she'd make straight *A*s—she was only making *B*s and *C*s. They thought my husband and I were forcing her to do this. We talked to her and she said to us: "I really have trouble with reading—you know how hard I have to work to read. But I can listen to the discussions, I can hear the teacher talking, and I get so much sense out of it that when I read it the second time, it begins to click. I won't get it if I go back into those other courses, and I'm determined to go to college. Don't you dare take me out of that track!" So we'd write the teachers a nice little note saying that we had not put her in there, and it was Jill Ann's decision, and so forth. I think kids are kept out that might be very successful if the opportunity was ever given to them. But they never—because of social, economic—never go against the doors. They are not going to take that chance—the chance of being told no, of being turned down.

Bryk, Lee, and Holland (1993) claim that the "shopping mall" approach of contemporary public high schools results in increased stratification because some minority groups disproportionately choose nonacademic courses. Addressing differences in family expectations, Alice explained:

Affluent parents have extremely high expectations, sometimes to the place of being unrealistic, even to the place of . . . of the parents doing the work. For instance, one mother was quite upset because the teacher was having the child edit and she said, "Well, my child will always have a computer or a word processor so that . . ." The middle- to lower-income parents, for the most part, just really seem warm and they welcome any personal attention, any praise, any improvement at all, any good perks you can give them. The problem is that extracurricular programs cost money. There are funds for scholarships, but a lot of people have their pride and will not call the administration building. I wouldn't do it. I imagine most people wouldn't. In terms of access to programs, it's the teacher's responsibility to let them know because a parent is not going to call a superintendent's office and ask. Now, with your affluent one—no doors are barred. But with someone with less confidence and with less interaction with that kind of individual [professionals], then they hesitate. The teacher has to reach out to them more, do more calling. The parent that has more money and more social skills is going to call me.

In terms of material differences between schools, Alice maintained: "After Superintendent Dieken came, there's equality of materials and so forth. But there are some schools that have a lot more because they got it before the equalization started." Speaking about peer relations, Alice hypothesized: "I think they seek their own. Especially when they get into middle school and high school, if they know their house is not as nice, say, they will get self-conscious about it. That's just like it's always been. That's what it was like when I was in school. It hasn't changed."

Alice was one of a few teachers who discussed how she worked with children who had academic difficulties:

This year is a difficult year for me. I have lots of children behind academically. A lot of these parents from the lower . . . they have the desire for their children to be successful, but they do not have the skills or knowledge of how to get the child turned around. They don't know how to set aside study time at home. I've done a lot this year. I've taught parents how to set up a study time at home, and how to say no, and how to not be manipulated by their child, and set timers 45 minutes . . . basic homework skills for parents.

Corey also discussed her approach to reaching certain students: "Remedial students are inhibited and afraid to try new things, even in art. I try to be looney with them—loosen them up so they have fun and trust me. It is important that this kind of child feel accepted by teachers and peers."

When asked if she liked teaching at Bluffton or whether she would prefer to teach at another Hillsdale school, Alice responded:

I've always felt that I could go into any school and teach. I'm sure that there are some teachers that because of their background might be more comfortable say either with the affluent or less affluent. My husband taught at Beauford for a while when it was a junior high school, and, of course, he was from a poor family and had never traveled. These professors and what have you came in and . . . he was a social studies teacher . . . and when he sent home a circular for volunteers, at first it was very intimidating for him. Some of the kids would come in who had stayed a year in, say, Africa, and he told me, "I read all the books, but that is not the same as having been to Africa." But he realized there could be sharing, that he could learn from these kids and parents, and so finally within a couple of years he began to relax about it. Now my husband teaches history at high school, and he said now that they started the gifted and talented there, that the other kids don't have the challenge and something to reach for. Now he feels that his classes are plodding along and a lot of that energy, that questioning skill, that vroom has disappeared because the minds that would question everything have gone. A lot of it is that the other kids feel that they've been left behind.

Alice showed considerable insight into how lower-income children, parents, and teachers are intimidated by their more affluent counterparts. Yet, in debriefing, the insightful and caring Alice apologized: "I'm just sorry that I'm not able to be more articulate. I know I have a tendency to ramble and pull in experiences I've had—it's one of my downfalls."

A Hillview teacher, Bernice, was another interviewee to volunteer information about how she dealt with social class and achievement differences among students:

I make sure that no one thinks/acts like they are better than anyone else. A teacher has to be a warm, dedicated, kind, strong-willed, qualified person. I think that there is a lot of time wasted in school. I teach; I don't mess around. I do give time for play and relaxation—that's proper. But I think some teachers fall into a pattern or just kind of getting lax—and nobody seems to push them. I like to set high expectations, and that doesn't mean I'm a slave driver. You have to get their attention, especially, say, if they're worried that their mother and dad were going to kill each other last night—then you have to get their attention, distract them from home problems, distract them from thinking they're not as smart as somebody else. And I like to see teachers keep up-to-date. Like I'm the computer coordinator for my building because nobody else will do it, and I'm the second oldest teacher in the building. I tell you another thing I disagree with is grading on the curve where you have everything from A to F for kids—I think that is totally unfair!

Bernice mentioned a lack of academic push at Hillview. None of the teachers at affluent schools made such critical observations of colleagues.

A Bluffton (*upward-striving*) teacher discussed how she dealt with peer rejection, yet her solution seemed simplistic and unrealistic:

The teacher has to do some social work and teach acceptance of people. Work on their social skills. I had one boy in my class that by Christmas it was very obvious he did not have as much as other children in my class. So I contacted his parents and told them that I thought this was adding to his problems. They made sure he had a good Christmas and he's been more accepted. You don't teach school anymore; you do a multitude of things. It would really be wonderful to have more upper-edge students at this school. Last year we had a tremendous fifth grade, but this year academically our high side is very meager.

This teacher communicated her sense that poor parents really did have the resources to make material intervention possible and that this could change their son's stigmatized image.

Already there and *upward-striving* teachers mostly discussed local schools as fair and equitable. Showing her isolation, Marsha, a Kinder teacher, falsely assumed that schools with low-income populations received more funds than schools in affluent neighborhoods. Signs that they assumed lower-income children and parents were innately or culturally inferior were woven into their responses. Such teachers indulged in narratives that closely resembled those of affluent mothers. Nancy, who had always taught at Beauford, related a classic deficit narrative:

A big difference exists between middle-class and poor parents. College parents are interested in their kids. They are always willing to come in, have talks with their kid. Most lower-class parents don't get involved at all. They don't really care. Then poor kids get a poor foundation in elementary school; they don't get the same start as higher-income students get. If they don't pick up basic skills, they're stuck, and it becomes impossible to catch up. The best-achieving kids are professional people's kids, and more higher-income kids are willing to get involved in extracurricular activities.

Here, Nancy inadvertently implies that school quality varies along social class lines, a phenomenon she vehemently denied at other times.

This study indicates that personal contact with low-income students seems to result in teachers having more realistic and less biased views of poor children's intellect, work ethic, and educational aspirations, and more concern about the material disparities among families and among schools. It might be assumed that such contact partly explains *in-the-middle* teachers' greater sensitivity to the needs of poor people and enhanced insight into the nature of social class influences on schooling. Yet Cheryl provided evidence that cross-class contact does not always result in empathy for low-income students or concern about inferior conditions at low-income schools. Married to a lawyer, Cheryl's extended family included teachers and administrators. Her two girls had attended Kinder, which she "loved." With an elementary teaching certificate, Cheryl began her career at Downing (low-income school), where she taught for 10 years. Open about "hating" her experience at Downing, Cheryl called its students "low-ability, angry, at-risk kids." Cheryl had earned a gifted and talented endorsement, which she volunteered she had sought as a ticket out of Downing.[6] Cheryl applied for and got a position in a school-wide gifted and talented program located at Eastside Elementary (high-income school).

Cheryl was opposed to the "fads of inclusion and detracking" because they "neglected kids" and did "not see how teachers could teach without ability grouping." Speaking of her daughter, Cheryl admitted: "Our kids are spoiled at Kinder. She was shocked when she got to Loring Middle School at the lack of materials—and at the other kids." Although Cheryl taught at Downing for a decade before her transfer, there was no consternation in her voice as she noted the vast material discrepancies between that low-income school and Eastside. Moreover, she glibly cited these advantages as being one of her reasons for preferring Kinder and Eastside to any of the low-income schools for herself as a teacher and for her daughters as students. Cheryl checked the two other high-income schools as acceptable for her girls but rated the rest of the Hillsdale elementary schools as unacceptable, explaining: "The expectations are higher at the schools I checked. At Kinder they run at least a semester to a year ahead [on achievement tests] of all others schools." Nevertheless, Cheryl claimed to be "for" mixed schools but qualified: "I want my kids to be pushed; they would not be pushed in some of those schools." In terms of the purpose of schooling, like other high-income mothers, Cheryl again focused solely on academic dimensions of schooling:

> An obvious one is kids getting the basics down for [state achievement exam] testing. Making sure you have the basics, and I want the kids to be prepared to make logical and adequate decisions for themselves. I think probably teaching the kids enough facts to be able to think through problems and express themselves in whatever field they want to, whether they pursue an advanced education or just pursue a vocation. Learning basic facts so they can earn a living.

Given her gifted and talented endorsement, it is curious that Cheryl focused so narrowly on skills. Professors of that certification sequence consistently emphasize creativity and enrichment rather than subject matter acceleration for high-achieving children. Yet, regardless of her specialized training, like other high-income mothers, Cheryl named academic push as most important. In contrast, Karl, an *upward-striving* Beauford teacher, was particularly attuned to class issues. Because of his insight into class inequities, his narratives were more like *in-the-middle* teachers; however, he consistently stated academic purposes for schools and frequently spoke about his own academic strengths as well as those of his children. Karl elaborated:

> We can see [class] difference in terms of the PTO [Parent–Teacher Organization]. The high-income parents are officers of the PTO, and so, from that

point of view, they set the tone for the school as far as what we're going to do. They decide and we do it. There's a lot of teacher choosing here. I know that the high-income parents tend to ask for certain teachers more than low-income parents. So if a teacher is popular, you might get a class that has more high-income kids in it. It's kind of like the squeaky wheel gets the grease. I think they do complain more, although the low-income parents are verbal. A lot of times they feel offended if something has happened to their child. And they're going to come up and fight about it. They're not as diplomatic.[7]

I think whether poor kids get a good education depends on the teacher. Maybe the teacher doesn't like poor kids—maybe she thinks they are all dumb. There is prejudice among the kids. It would be hard for me to believe it doesn't exist here. It would be kind of idyllic if it didn't. I don't know how long you've lived in Hillsdale, but there's actually a considerable bias on the east side of town towards the west side of town. Some people just will not shop, just virtually will not go over on that west side of town—it's the other side of the tracks literally. Well, there's getting to be a bias—I hear kids saying things like, "Oooh, he's a grit," which means he comes from what they consider a lower-class background, is not aspiring to do the type of things they do, he's just not as sophisticated, and all of that. We're tending to just judge people. It's really a prejudice, so I think kids are not as likely as in the past to pick friends from different so-called social groups. They're more likely to stay in their own group now. I think that there are teachers at certain schools that are closely matched with their students, which is unfortunate.[8]

In discussing the comparative quality of high- and low-income schools, Karl said:

The west-side schools are not considered to be as good. Now, Southside has definitely improved, it has widened its borders and so a new population is coming in, and I think it's enrollment is more rounded than it used to be. There is a lot of class division in this town and it's sort of set up—I mean these neighborhoods are set up by the realtors, the developers, the businessmen, they plan these neighborhoods. It's like advertising—you target neighborhoods for a certain market—and it has succeeded wonderfully in creating a segmented society now. Parents make a big difference. Parents at Beauford and Richards, well, if they don't do as much as the next person, they feel a little guilt trip, so they do more. It becomes like a self-fulfilling prophecy. I think that the teachers, knowing this is the situation, feel like, "well that's the way it's going to be." It can be very depressing how we've divided up society—and I don't think that it's just Hillsdale. I'm not keen on social stratification, as you've probably already guessed. There is no question that schools are unequal. When a school has a certain reputation, good programs will tend to go there. Everybody wants success, so they'll go to a place where they feel like they'll get more, and then it tends to split things even further apart. Some schools go in a positive direction, create more opportunities, then they get the lion's share, and the ones that don't have that reputation, we just sort of forget about them. The parents at this school, you better believe you have to please them; otherwise, when they start yelling, start getting on the phone, there's going to be some action downtown, you know, at the administration building—faster than if some west-side parent complains. When the Beauford PTO raises four or five thousand dollars and decides to spend it on computers, well, the school system is not going to turn that down.

In response to the forced-choice questions about redistricting to achieve a social class balance and detracking in Hillsdale schools, Karl replied:

Redistricting would be an upheaval. I think redistricting so that each school would end up with a variety of students would be front-page news! If you do a lot of ability grouping, then . . . I once taught in a junior high where we had well-to-do farm kids and Mexican American migrant workers mixed together— what a wild combination that was. And there were really strong feelings between those groups. By separating them, you were setting up almost open warfare.

In debriefing, Karl queried:

I am curious what you found in interviews with other teachers. I wouldn't be surprised if my opinions were in the minority. I have the feeling that most teachers [he teaches at Beauford] tend to go along with this social stratification that we're seeing in our society and are quite comfortable with it. I know that outstanding students come from poor backgrounds, but I don't think everybody recognizes that.

When asked about his reaction to the interview, Karl said, "Well we've hit on a lot of areas that I really wanted to talk about, so it was a good thing."

Regarding her opinion about school equity, a Downing teacher, Audrey, was aware that Superintendent Dieken had changed some longstanding discriminatory policies. She elaborated:

In terms of building, equipment, and materials, well, we used to have a book rental policy in the system where you got a percentage back of the amount of money your kids paid in. And so, at Downing, say we could collect 50% of our book rental. So that meant we got 50%, where say at Beauford they got 98%. But that was changed under Dr. Dieken. So, theoretically, all the schools get the same amount of money for supplies. There may be a difference now in that those schools who had more money at the beginning have a stockpile of materials. So you may see a difference there. Also PTO support is different at the schools. One thing that proves discriminatory is homework. If you have someone at home who helps you do it, that's a big factor in success in school, and I don't think teachers can do anything about it. Teacher discrimination is another big factor.

FEELINGS ABOUT THE NECESSITY OF ABILITY GROUPING AND TRACKING[9]

Teachers' views of tracking and ability grouping were highly correlated with their *already there* or *in-the-middle* status. An assistant superintendent in charge of secondary curriculum, classified as *in the middle* because of his rural origins and educational philosophy, asserted that:

> Every kid could succeed in more heterogeneous grouping. It's a real challenge, but I am more and more convinced that we can succeed, but we need to do it right. We need to develop our teachers so they can do it. Tracking is a problem because it turns us into a selecting and sorting kind of school instead of a teaching and learning school. We need to develop an attitude that says: "You are here, and regardless of your differences, I'm going to teach you." We put kids in boxes here in Hillsdale, but it is not just here—kids in boxes is a national issue!

In discussing his first years in an administration position, an *already there* middle school principal conveyed that he accepted tracking as inevitable: " I was soon made aware of affluent parents' preferences to have their children in high tracks with excellent teachers." This principal—undoubtedly in charge of making teachers' course assignments—did not mention the criteria he used; however, the implications of his statement are clear. A widespread assumption that came through in interviews with secondary teachers and affluent mothers was that the "best" teachers taught high tracks. Furthermore, most were vehement that this was the way it should be. This principal was evasive when asked about the typical class status of students in high or low tracks, but his actual awareness of the pattern of low income/low tracks came out in a number of ways.

The two high schools and two junior high schools had class-heterogeneous enrollments because they were located on the north and south sides of town, thus cut across the east and west income-level divisions in Hillsdale. Nevertheless, extensive tracking at all four schools resulted in an obvious social class resegregation of students. There had been an attempt to heterogeneously group social studies classes; however, by the time students' schedules were set for their tracked English, math, science, and foreign-language sections, there was no possibility of mixing in social studies sections. An *already there* high school teacher who taught mostly high but some general tracks responded to the tracking item with:

> We intuitively track for math and science. In English I need to have only one kind of kid to serve them well. Students themselves have said that they don't

want to be mixed. We should not segregate by social class. Kids are selected by SATs and not by address, but higher-class kids have higher SATs. A lower-class kid is not likely to be selected for high tracks, but a kid can move up if he wants to. If we mixed, I would want to make sure that the truly gifted and truly special ed. kid received appropriate alternatives. Bright kids do need to be taught that the world is filled with many kinds of people.

This teacher finally announced his real feelings: "The superintendent doesn't believe in tracking. I have never heard that detracking succeeds. It wouldn't work here. If you don't track by ability, some students don't receive alternatives—the extremes don't get alternatives."

Other secondary teachers implied that instituting heterogeneous classes was a good but improbable plan. A teacher who mainly taught honors and advanced placement sections said: "There are no disadvantages to mixing, but there are challenges. People like to be around people that are the same as themselves. At least that is what I see around here." Later, when asked if he was concerned about the number of low-income students in special education placements and low tracks, he blandly observed: "I think we need to make sure we don't segregate those kids." Yet he thought inclusion was "impractical, unrealistic." In contrast, another high school teacher, Esther, was disturbed that "special education and low tracks are dumping grounds for poor white kids." Secondary teachers conveyed that tracking was popular with the influential parents of high-track students and that it was too entrenched in Hillsdale schools to be changed. Secondary teachers did not appear to be interested in talking about detracking, perhaps because they recalled what happened a few years earlier when Superintendent Rockenweil tried to institute it.

Most *already there* and *upward-striving* teachers at elementary schools expressed some support for heterogeneous groups, but like affluent mothers, then provided what they felt would be compelling evidence about why it would not work. Again, as with high-income mothers, when teachers openly opposed heterogeneous grouping arrangements, they often did so in an annoyed tone of voice. An *upward-striving* Bluffton teacher vehemently voiced negative sentiments:

> I definitely don't agree with mixing ability groups. I am against inclusion. There are some children that I could not handle in my class, like the special education child that needs a lot of restraint, the mentally impaired child that needs a lot of physical care. They need to be taken out. You need grouping where a child feels they are achieving.[10]

When asked if students' social class status affected track or group placement, she wavered: "I don't think social class influences tracking at all. . . . I, really . . . unless you're in a school that's definitely an elitist school, and then it might, but . . . I don't think that we've got any around here that are totally that." Nancy, a Beauford teacher, asserted:

> As an educator, I can't understand how the teacher can be asked to work with all of them. Reading groups help the teacher organize. I would only teach that way [without tracks] if I had to, but I would feel we were neglecting kids. We'd have to teach to the middle of the road and couldn't challenge some[11] or would be over the heads of others. So, it would be dissatisfactory for the kids.

When asked if social class might influence ability group or track placement, Nancy responded:

> I do not think that social class is a big factor because if a child demonstrates ability, it doesn't matter what their background is or how they dress—if they can do it, great, let's put them in that class. That's the feeling at Beauford. Let's arrange it. Opportunity is there. The kid can grab hold of it if they want to. Some just sit in the low groups[12]—maybe I'm contradicting myself—but that's where you need ability grouping. The advanced need the challenge. It is frustrating for the middle performers to go too fast. Tracking can be detrimental, so you have to do it careful. You're not just doing it because you think it's neat to have smart kids together, or the dumb kids together, or whatever.

Then Nancy challenged the idea that the board of school trustees might make the decision:

> Well, the decision about it [ability grouping] should be left to individual schools because they know their kids best. The principal should make the decision. I think the higher ability are most affected—they're in the classroom, but you're spending time with children who have a harder time learning. I think it [mixed groups] can be used if they are used judiciously.

Betty, another Beauford teacher, simply announced: "I have reading groups and everybody seems happy." When asked about the class correspondence, she questioned: "All kids in a class can't be in the top reading group. How would a teacher handle it without groups?" Then added, "I don't like the labels, though; the labels follow you." When an *upward-striving* Beauford[13] teacher, Karl, was asked if class background of students made a difference in track placement, he hesitated and then admitted: "I'd say it might have some influence—it shouldn't, but it might." Another *upward-striving* teacher, Marsha, volunteered:

> I like to teach the just average middle-class kids because, frankly, they're the easiest—with a few upper-strata thrown in, maybe some lower. Maybe in

smaller groups in a friendlier setting we can teach them to get along with each other better. I would bend over backwards to keep them from discriminating against others.

The implication was that this was not likely to happen at Kinder. An Eastside teacher stated her opinion: "Well, you know, we have reading groups mainly because it's easier. Well, I think that the top intelligence [students] needs to recognize that they are the top and can do more. And you have to do it subtly—and that's hard to do." When asked about whether the social class status made a difference in who made it into which group, she answered:

> Well, of course, let's face it. You'd like to think that it doesn't, but the ones with the better background are more apt to be in a higher intelligence group, and some poor little kid who it's a battle to survive, well, school is one of his lesser things to cope with to just live everyday.

Teachers at low-income schools were less inclined to support tracking and ability grouping. Some told of having used homogeneous grouping previously but had given it up because of its negative impact on students. A Hillview teacher, Bernice, talked about her opposition:

> I have never agreed with tracking in elementary. Having taught a lower-ability group for many, many years, I found it gives them very few models to follow. They don't even understand how much better other kids are doing. They've been with the same class for 3 years in a row. All they see is what's going on in that same class and your top student maybe couldn't even make it in another class. Whereas if they had been mixed all along, they might see you've got to do these things to be accepted or to get along in this world. I have a lot of intelligent parents who want their kids moved out of tracking because they see that it's dragging their kids down too because there are so many discipline problems when you get a low track. So, I'd rather see them mixed and regrouped for subjects. At least be in contact with the group at least half of the day. In my class now, I keep telling them, "You can do this. You're just as smart as any of these other kids. It's just that you don't really care whether you do it or not." And yet they really do care, but its just a pattern they've gotten into. It just like they've felt that they couldn't do the work. So when they kind of get that feeling about their whole life, it's pretty hard to overcome. Some individuals do rise above it.

When asked about group and social class status correlations, Bernice responded:

> Oftentimes the high reading levels will be from higher-income families. So, when you track by reading you will not have much if any relationships between those students because they're in different classrooms throughout the

day. I'm not saying that's always 100% true. But there's a large percentage of the low SES group that are the low readers. It depends on the individual. There could be a dedicated low-economic-income child with high ability and high achievement, but, overall, through the years, oftentimes it's the low-achieving kids that are low-income.

Louise related her experience with ability grouping and why she now resisted homogeneous class arrangements or tracking:

A large percentage of Hillview children come from, well, homes that have a lot of problems. Some have problems learning too. One year I took the poorer students and put them together because I thought I could work with them more. That did not work out. Because my poor students needed the higher students to look up to. The teacher that had the better students found that she did not have students that could do a lot more with their hands or who had a lot of ideas. And we found we needed all of them. We needed all ladders of children to have a really well-rounded class to work with.

Joan, a Hillview teacher who was consistently oriented to social class issues even in the neutral stage 1 questions, conjectured about the effects of social class conditions and reiterated her opposition to tracking:

Poor people get beaten down so much they lose their aspirations. They sometimes start out with them, and pretty soon it gets so . . . well, it's a losing battle, so why bother? I hear that from the kids too: "Why should I try?" Especially the ones in low groups—they say, "I'm never going to get anyplace anyways." That's why I don't like tracking.

In debriefing, Joan apologized for "getting so worked up." When asked if other teachers felt the same way, she said that she did not know because she "was kind of a loner" and did not spend much time in the teachers' room because she had "too much work to do" and because she "didn't like to hear some teachers put the Hillview kids down."

Some teachers did not separate their attitudes toward tracking as a teacher from their own children's experiences with tracking. As Audrey, a Downing teacher, said:

We don't track at Downing, but most teachers have ability groups in their classrooms. I notice that sometimes there is a difference in kids' social class background in terms of where they get placed. Once when my son was put in a low group at Richards, I talked the teacher into putting him in the middle group, and then we worked with him so he wouldn't fall behind. That's what a lot of middle-class parents do, I think. They complain when their kids get put in low groups. At least, that's what we did. Our son was upset about being in a low group and that provided him with the incentive to agree to extra work sessions with me and my husband after school.

To summarize, four *already there* teachers approved of ability grouping and tracking; the other four, like affluent mothers, claimed to support de-tracking but gave multiple reasons why it would not work. It seemed that they could so easily speak in support of heterogeneous grouping because they were sure it was not going to happen. Teachers at low- and mixed-income schools mostly endorsed heterogeneous grouping arrangements. This may be partly due to their exposure to the philosophies of inclusion. Low-income schools traditionally had housed special education classes, and even though disability-identified students mainly stayed in their home schools after the adoption of inclusion, low-income schools still had a higher percentage of classified students. Mainly due to local building-based teacher initiative, Hillview, Southside, and Westside Elementary Schools had been in the forefront of the inclusion movement. Additionally, most *in-the-middle* teachers were more attuned to seeing homogeneous arrangements through the eyes of students who ended up in them. Again, there was less parental pressure for hierarchy creation at the schools in working-class and low-income neighborhoods.

TEACHERS' IDEAS ABOUT THE POSSIBILITY OF SCHOOL-WIDE DESEGREGATION

In addition to the forced-choice item about homogeneous grouping that was asked at the end of the interview (stage 3), school personnel were asked if they would support a school board decision to redistrict to achieve social class balance in Hillsdale schools. Similar to affluent mothers, most *already there* and *upward-striving* school personnel indicated that social classes should ideally be integrated through school desegregation and heterogeneous grouping within mixed schools but then went on to say why it would not work. Some staunchly maintained that schools already were mixed. A few openly opposed redistricting.

Nancy, a Beauford teacher who had been proud of "holding various offices in her sorority in college," was vehement that "all Hillsdale schools already are mixed." When asked if all schools were of similar quality, she promptly replied, "I hope so." When probed, she continued to maintain that there was "not much local social class discrimination in Hillsdale like there is in other places." Yet, in listing acceptable schools for her own children, she initially named only Eastside and Kinder, adding that she would not want them to attend Beauford because she taught there. She then sharply changed directions and added: "Really any school in Hillsdale would be all right." Earlier she had spoken enthusiastically about the quality of Beauford's teaching staff and the support of interested and talented neighborhood parents. She bragged about the school's high test scores and gave "excellent teachers" credit for them. At another point, she noted that "families—not teachers—were responsible" for lower achievement at other schools. Although gregarious and expansive in responding to the neutral (stage 1) part of the interviews, Nancy answered questions about social class equity in the district (stage 2), and especially the forced-choice items about detracking and redistricting (stage 3), in a perfunctory, evasive, and annoyed manner. She seemed relieved when the interview was over and claimed in a rather stiff, offhand manner in debriefing that she had "no problem" with the interview.

Already there teachers showed little interest in discussing class desegregation, perhaps because they knew it would be impossible given the sentiments of the influential parents they had come to know so well. Marsha, a Kinder teacher, said: "Kids need to learn that not everybody is like them and to live with others who are different, but they would have to change their attitudes. It would be desirable to rezone, but I don't know how we would ever do it." Marsha brought up her opposition to inclusion several times in the interview, for example, she said: "A disadvantage with mixing all kids, like in doing inclusion, is that children would not get the individualized attention they need." Her reply was couched to make it seem that her opposition to mixing was due to concern about children with disabilities or lower-income children rather than that she might not want them to be in her class.

When asked about integrating students from high- and low-income schools, an Eastside teacher glibly recalled: "We tried that. We had kids come to the Gifted and Talented Program at Eastside from Westside Elementary and it did not work. They were never integrated and they always seemed like loners." This teacher did not mention that anything had been done to make the Westside students feel welcomed; in fact, her tone implied that the social failure was due to a personality flaw or some deficit on the part of the Westside students.

Some *in-the-middle* teachers talked passionately about the ideals of integration, with many mentioning its importance to democratic schooling. They named the benefits of desegregation for the high-income children; of their "getting a taste of the real world" and "learning that others did not have their same advantages." A Westside teacher said:

> There should be a variety. When you get a group—even if they are all high-income with high-achievement orientations—you've got problems when they're too much alike. They need to recognize differences, learn to be a little more human. If everybody's like you, boy you get cliquey and nasty. It is a big mistake not to put a variety of people together—that's what life is all

about. Yes, mix neighborhoods, mix teachers from those various schools. But you wouldn't want teachers who had been at Beauford (high-income) and were used to that population to then suddenly get a big influx of Westside Elementary (low-income) types. That would be asking for disaster. I wouldn't be in favor of busing kids from the east side over here and kids from the west side over there. With busing, that's just people trying too hard. It should come naturally. With busing, adult opposition will carry over to the children. They'll bring it to school. It's better to happen naturally like when children from the east side move in here and try to blend right in. It would be easier for them to blend in if Eastsiders came over here than for our kids to go over there. But if kids are left alone, things are going to work out. It's when adults start meddling it's a problem.

This teacher's use of "naturally" is curious as is her conjecture that high-income families might move into the west-side neighborhood. When she spoke of the advantages of mixing, she equated low-income students with lower achievers:

I think mixing might be good. Kids might have other kids as models; they might be inspired by better-ability kids. If you don't have the spark plugs in your class, the performance of everybody goes down. If you have a few good students, people participating, then everybody does better.

Although *in-the-middle* teachers claimed to favor heterogeneous schools and classrooms, with resignation they conveyed that the likelihood of this happening in Hillsdale was remote. A principal at a low-income school addressed the issue with considerable feeling:

You ought to have all strata together. There ought to be from the highest to the lowest in every school and it ought to be equal all the way around. But the trouble with that is you have to bus kids, and I hate busing! Another disadvantage would also be that you have to make sure that you had a faculty that could deal with all kinds, because it's sometimes not easy. Teachers at some of those [high-income] schools could not handle our kids. And getting those parents to accept it would be a difficult thing. I mean it's just like if you took Kinder and took half of those kids from there and bused them here and half from here and bused them to Kinder. I'm sure those parents over there would be up in arms. I don't think the parents in this area would care. They might care later about their children having to face the social pressures that they'd have to face, but I know it would be a bigger outcry from over there.

This principal used the example of Kinder, which was on the opposite side of town, while Eastside, Richards, and Rogers were to the east but also were tangent to her school's catchment area. She was not alone in stating that class mixing was impractical because it would entail busing. Yet, over the years as new schools were built and others closed, elementary and middle school catchment zones were gerrymandered so that children consistently were assigned to attend school with others from their same class status. Hence, significant social class desegregation could occur without busing many more children. These experienced teachers should have been aware of this. Yet many who claimed to support desegregation mentioned busing both as a constraint and a rationale for opposition to system-wide desegregation.

The desegregation item brought to the surface *in-the-middle* teachers' knowledge that their schools were looked down on by affluent parents and their east-side colleagues, and aroused their resentment about east siders' smug sense of superiority. It also revealed their loyalty to the schools where they taught. Some were cynical about high-income parent opposition to any social class desegregation plan. Corey, an itinerant teacher who had taught at various schools, observed:

> There needs to be integration—that's something I feel strongly about. I'd like to see schools more integrated, but how do you do that? I mean, are we going to start busing in Hillsdale? How do you tell kids' parents that live in the Kinder district that their kids are going to start over at Downing? That's just not going to happen. But it'd be ideal. It would help kids at an earlier age accept people for abilities and not for what they have.

In-the-middle teachers were concerned that integration would not work because of insurmountable prejudices on the part of affluent children. Joan remarked: "I like mixed schools, but if you do it, you should never tell kids that they are 'different.' " These teachers spoke of the negative influence of high-income children's bias and even more about the prejudice of their parents. Yet, in the context of district-wide social class desegregation, none mentioned the impact of such attitudes on themselves as teachers; however, the teachers at low- or mixed-income schools conveyed their view throughout the interviews that parents in high-income school catchment zones were powerful people who were demanding and intimidating. They may be worried about the likelihood of bias against themselves as well as against their school's children.

SELECTING APPROPRIATE HILLSDALE SCHOOLS FOR OFFSPRING

Attitudes about the importance of the impact of social class on schooling emerged in force when teachers were requested to select acceptable schools for their offspring. *Already there* and *in-the-middle* personnel had quite distinctive responses to the task; however, some appeared not to be candid when they recognized that class bias would be evident in their choices.

Table 5.3

High-, Mixed-, and Low-Income Elementary Schools in Hillsdale

High-Income	Mixed	Rural	Low-Income
*Kinder	*Lexington	*Ushville	*Hillview
*Eastside	Farley	Brookton	*Southside
*Richards	*Bluffton		*Westside
*Beauford	Brightwater		*Downing

*Schools on the list that participants were to identify as acceptable or unacceptable.

Schools were presented in alphabetical order and were not grouped by income level as in Table 5.3.

Already there and *upward-striving* teachers who worked at high-income schools and whose children attended them inevitably listed those as favorite schools. A Kinder teacher said: "I prefer Kinder, Beauford, Richards, and Eastside, in that order, although none are unacceptable. I chose those schools because I know more about them and I am loyal to where I teach." Pointing to low-income schools, she added: "A lot of these schools are dilapidated. I wouldn't want them to go to Hillview—its on Pigeon Hill and the students would be rougher. I wouldn't want my children interacting with them." In spite of their prompt and clear preference for high-income schools, with the exception of a few who glibly identified only high-income schools as acceptable, most appeared to be uncomfortable and were evasive or noncommittal about the acceptability of low- and mixed-income Hillsdale schools. Throughout most of the interview, however, teachers elaborated about good and bad schools without hesitation.

Differences in material, building, and human resources often surfaced as a reason for preferring the high-income schools. In rejecting all low-income schools, an Eastside teacher conjectured: "This particular school [Westside] does not have children from a wide variety of backgrounds. In other schools I think they do. I think the low-income schools could have less funding, less qualified teachers, and less parental support." An Eastside teacher chose her school as "tops," saying it was "well equipped," but rejected Kinder because "it seems not to be flexible in terms of teaching styles." She refused to comment on other schools. In contrast, a Beauford teacher who liked her school because of "the good mix of kids" expressed definitive opinions and chose or rejected schools based on their social class composition:

> Westside is on the border of town and the expectations are much lower; you know, they have blue-collar factory workers' kids there mainly. My friend's

daughter went there and she ended up being virtually a teacher's aide and that frustrated her. There weren't enough spark plugs in the class to keep up a good atmosphere. Kinder has a pretty good mixture, basically a good school. Eastside would be considered pretty good, maybe with the exception of once in a while you run into some incredible situations where more kids than not cannot speak English well and it becomes difficult for teachers to make the progress you would like. Hillview and Downing both pull a lot from the same population as Westside. Unfortunately there's a lot of depressing home situations—drug problems, abuse problems, family instability. There are very angry, at-risk kids[14] there. Southside has definitely improved. It has a stereotype in Hillsdale, but I don't think that stereotype is nearly so true anymore. At those schools there would be much less encouragement of a child to do a top-notch job on their homework. It becomes a self-fulfilling prophecy—the teachers say, "Well, you know, that's the way it's going to be." It can be a very depressing situation all around because everyone is accepting the idea of low perfor-mance. Just like enthusiasm is contagious and negativeness or crankiness is a real downer—it does not turn people on. When a school has a good reputa-tion for good programs, good families will tend to want their children there. Everybody wants success. So they go to a place where they feel they'd get more response. So it tends to split things even further apart. When they're going in a positive direction, they get the lion's share—and the ones that don't have that reputation, we just sort of forget about them.

Nancy, a Beauford teacher, first expressed annoyance that "this ques-tion does not take school location—where you live—into account!" She then went on to elaborate:

Beauford is a good school—we're proud of it. I don't think any of them would be bad. Well, truthfully, I hate to say it because there is nothing wrong with any school—it's just that . . . well, there are more problems there [Downing], I think, of a different type than we have. And I'd just as soon not have to cope with them. Well, I sound like a snob, but I don't mean it that way at all. I wouldn't mind teaching there, but I'd just as soon my child didn't go there. I don't think I'd want them to go to Hillview either. Now, I mean it's not a bad school, and I wouldn't mind teaching there. It's nearly all completely . . . a lot of kids that break your heart. I've had friends that taught there, and they've had problems that I just didn't realize that people had in school today. A lot of people that are on welfare—and, that's not against anyone, but I mean that they are having a hard time making it. A lot of people from the poorer parts of Hillsdale, and I think they have problems that need help. But it's not a bad school—they have a lot of good programs there, a lot of wonderful teachers there.

An *upward-striving* Kinder teacher, Marsha, readily admitted that she would not want her own children to attend Downing, Southside, Westside, or Hillview, but then switched gears and said that she might "prefer to work with low-income children who appreciate you. It's just more rewarding and satisfying to work with the ragamuffin than the doctor's daughter!" When asked if she thought that other Kinder teachers felt that way, she laughed and said that she was "probably an exception. Most teachers are here at Kinder because they prefer to work with the best families in Hillsdale." Although Marsha's own children were grown, she checked high-income schools as appropriate for her children and consistently emphasized academic goals and purposes throughout her interview. Nevertheless, a number of times she alluded to not being appreciated by Kinder children and parents and feeling left out of the mainstream teacher social group at Kinder. Marsha, along with Karl at Beauford, were among the *upward-striving* teachers who appeared to straddle the somewhat precarious and unrewarding position of not feeling fully accepted at their high-income schools but still not wanting to be at low- or even mixed-income schools. Karl admitted that the principal hired him because there were no men at Beauford and she "wanted a man for disciplinary reasons." Marsha had transferred to Kinder when a kindergarten teacher retired and the kindergarten age enrollment had gone down in her previous mixed-income school. Karl and Marsha's self-reported ambiguous status at high-income schools meant that they might be dubbed "pseudos" or "wannabes"; they wanted to fit in but were not fully accepted by others. These two were aware of their marginal status and they also wavered philosophically between *in-the-middle* and *already there* clusters more than other *upward strivers* who were more confident about fitting in and about the validity, benefits, and fairness of meritocratic schooling.

Three *in-the-middle* teachers chose mixed-income schools for their children, shunning high- and low-income schools; four selected some low-income schools, including their own; two chose a couple at each income level; and two rejected only high-income schools. A Westside teacher liked her school because of its "caring principal" and "sense of community." Her son attended Hillview, about which she said: "I like the fact that he is exposed to children who do not have so much. He once told me, 'You can wear socks as gloves. If I lose my gloves, I'm just going to wear a pair of socks when it is cold out.' " She rejected Beauford and Kinder (asking that this be kept confidential): "They aren't as diverse. It is an artificial environment with kids similar to each other—a skewed population." Another Westside teacher chose her school for her children but shook her head negatively about others, occasionally saying, "maybe okay," then proclaimed: "Definitely not Kinder. My daughter went there for a while and the kids were a bunch of snobs."

Revealing her *in-the-middle* position, Joan rejected or accepted some low-income schools as well as some high-income schools as possibilities for her offspring:

I definitely would not want . . . Downing is unacceptable. Students from Downing transfer here, so I've been hearing things all the time. I hear bad vibes about Southside because there's not enough discipline, so I would rule that out. I like some things about Eastside. Of course, they're off on their own. From what I've seen of our faculty here at Hillview, we've got a lot of good going on here. Beauford has pretty good students. Westside—no. Kinder—no; it seems to be permeating prejudice against lower SES—we've always got a lot of that because we're on the west side of town and we're just trying to bring Hillview up so it doesn't have such a bad reputation because it's on the west side of town. There's a lot of east side/west side here in Hillsdale—there always has been in this town. Some teachers at the rich schools would not go to schools with low-income levels like Hillview or Downing, and, like, a lot of our teachers would not teach at a school like Kinder or Eastside simply because of that population—it's reverse prejudice. I have a friend whose kid is at Kinder and she wishes that she never put him in there. Those kids never have any contact with poor kids except maybe passing them on the street.

Joan repeatedly used Kinder as an example of an elitist or snob school.

A pecking order of acceptable low-income schools was evident as some *in-the-middle* teachers ruled out Downing, which not only draws from the oldest subsidized housing project in Hillsdale but has the largest African American population. Louise confessed: "At first I was annoyed at being put with dummies from the west side, but some new students [who were in the district because of west-side gentrification] have come to Hillview and they have balanced out the dummies a bit." When it came to selecting schools, Louise said:

I like Hillview because we have a wide range of economic levels of children. My second choice is Westside; it is a nice, well-rounded neighborhood school. I would be concerned about Eastside because of the tremendous population of non-English-speaking foreign students. Downing would be unacceptable—too many discipline problems and not enough time spent on academics. (I don't want my name linked to any of this.) Richards—no it is sort of an upper-class-type school situation too, like Kinder and Beauford, and I think it would be harder sometimes for just average children to fit in. I am very biased, so I hope this doesn't get out.[15] I have taught in quite a few of the schools and I definitely would not want Downing. Another thing, say with Downing, I think when they made up the school areas, for the school district around Downing they didn't water down the population enough. By that I mean they didn't bring in enough children of different socioeconomic backgrounds to help the ones that you know are really deprived. Well, what I mean really is that they didn't water it down enough so that it seems to be a concentration of low-income families with a few middle-income families sprinkled in. It used to be more diverse.

In-the-middle teachers described the prejudice they knew existed and the likely rejection of their schools by Eastsiders. Audrey, a Downing teacher who had taught at Southside, said: "I'd rather not have my own kids go to Southside or Downing." Apparently sensitive to the class bias of her choice, she said: "Don't put that in there!" Audrey then went on to observe:

> Although there are good faculty at Beauford and Eastside, I still would not want a child of mine to go there—and least of all Kinder because it's a snob school—kids and teachers. There is too much pressure there on the kids, too much for the parents, too much on the teachers, and the parents put too much pressure on the kid to succeed. I'd rather see a school that is a crosscut of everybody. Most people would say, oh, I don't want my kids to go to Downing because of the kids on the hill. Well, I've taught the kids on the hill and they've got their problems, but believe me, I love every one of them and I have some real problems with a lot of them. And I still enjoy seeing them, talking to them, hearing about them. If you interviewed parents on the east side, they'd say: "I'd rather my kids go to Kinder or Beauford or Eastside—I'd never have them go to Downing or Hillview." I'm sure that is the reaction you would have gotten.

Corey, an itinerant teacher who was single and childless, rated the schools at which she had taught, but refused to "pass judgment" on schools where she had not taught:

> I definitely would not send my child to Beauford or Kinder—definitely not Kinder—never, ever. Downing would be a good possibility because it has a good mix of children. At Eastside, the cultural environment is very, very strong. I'd want my child to be accepting and knowledgeable about other cultures and peoples. At Kinder, especially, I'd say the majority of students there are upper middle class. The students that I ran across there are more concerned about the way they dress, the activities that they do—they get to go to the lake, you know, on their parents' boat! I am being really catty here. Yeah, Kinder, it's the real status school. I'd just say that the children on the whole are a little bit too spoiled for my liking. Nothing is new to them either. I can say that from experience. In fact, I think there's more discipline problems there than at Downing—definitely more discipline problems there. Well, kids just think, hey, who are you to tell me that I can't do this? They have a real cocky attitude. I don't have anything to verify this, because I wasn't there at the time, but through the way rumors filter through the school system, I heard they had a lot of problems on the last day of school with the sixth graders being overly destructive—it got out of hand with practical jokes and pranks. I can see that happening. Whereas at Brookton [rural school] it was nothing but tears and hugs. At Brookton I feel like I really am an important part of the child's life and education and I know that the other teachers feel

that, whereas at Kinder I don't think you are as important. The teachers were snobs too. I felt shunned—an outcast—as a traveling art teacher. It's not just the kids.

Like Corey, other teachers answered questions about school quality and preference more in terms of where they would like to teach than where they would have their offspring attend. The age of teachers and the fact that many of their children were adults was probably a factor in this trend.

In-the-middle teachers who taught at mixed schools often rejected lower-income schools. After saying she would "not mind" Beauford or Kinder because her children had attended Beauford and many of her friends' children went to Kinder, a Bluffton teacher clarified:

> We are a school that mostly has working parents. Downing is made up of a lot of students who are from broken homes. At Richards it is sort of an upper-class school situation and I think it would be hard for just average children to fit in there. Bluffton is a good school, but at Bluffton there still is a big stigma from being on the west side.

Then this Bluffton teacher explained:

> The only ones I would quibble about are Hillview and Southside. Then, again, I would have to say that one of my best friends teaches at Southside and she's had wonderful kids in her classroom—and I don't think that kids should be totally protected. They ought to know what the rest of the world is like. But I know from here at Bluffton that the level of excellence is different at different schools because of the clientele you're teaching. At Eastside you could learn from the non-English-speaking—and that would be great. It would be great to have more integration in Hillsdale, but there would be such a problem with discontented parents that your teaching would really be hampered because of the discontent.

Just as with many teachers at low- and mixed-income schools, she was keenly aware of affluent people's prejudice against their schools. They also knew that mixed schools were lumped in with low-income schools as unacceptable because they did not have predominantly high-income enrollments nor were they located in the wealthier suburban areas of town.

Teachers at low-income schools were, of course, more aware of and more vociferous about disparities between schools according to their social class status. As Joan noted:

> It seems when you go into schools with the higher income levels you usually find the carpeted, air-conditioned classrooms. It's not supposed to be this way

as far as materials. Our schools, Westside, Southside, and Downing, have the lowest—we're going to be remodeled—but it's been a long time coming. The buildings are in need of more work.

Similarly, Audrey, a Downing teacher, acknowledged that her school might not provide a quality education because of resources:

Schools like Kinder and Beauford, you have more parents who want to come in and initiate areas of the curriculum that we don't always have over here. I think at Downing maybe our teachers are better because they're willing to work with low-income kids—they want to make a difference. Teachers are the key. I don't think it's the building. I don't necessarily think it's the students. You can have a class of rich kids in a room with a teacher and maybe she doesn't like rich kids. You can have a room full of poor kids and maybe the teacher doesn't like poor kids—maybe she thinks they are all dumb. I think teachers have a great amount of influence on the outcome or on the education the students receive. But we have problems here getting resources, like we cannot always collect book fees. We've had some people that don't like the mix here and transfer out to a school like Beauford. We were talking about our hill group—that's the Hilltop housing addition—now we get all those kids, and it would be nice to split that group up so that they don't take the same fights from home to school. That might be a disadvantage with Downing—the kids all stay together all the time.

When teachers at low-income schools spoke of material disparities that varied according to the social class status of local schools, their perceptions were correct. In a report I prepared for the Hillsdale school trustees, *What a Model Community Sweeps Under the Rug* (1984), I delineated numerous class-related disparities. In response to this report and complaints from Hillsdale activists, some inequities were remedied during Superintendent Dieken's administration. Low-income schools were remodeled and they received new playground equipment. The original Southside school was torn down and completely rebuilt on the grounds. The school's annual non-reusable supplies were distributed on a per capita rather than a funds-collected basis. Nevertheless, inequities remain. It might be assumed that low-income schools would have smaller class size, yet there is a longstanding pattern of the advantage going in the other direction: low-income schools consistently had the highest pupil-to-teacher ratios. A Hillview teacher informed me that she received $75 annually for non-reusable school supplies (paste, glue, crayons, markers, art paper), whereas teachers at Kinder received $750 per year. The Kinder Parent–Teacher Organization had supplemented the $75 per teacher district amount by $675.

In-the-middle teachers complained about advantaged circumstances at high-income schools (better pupil-to-teacher ratio, better building and grounds, better equipment and materials, more money available for incidental supplies, better libraries, and separate rooms for the art and music teachers) but still said they would not want to teach at "those" schools because they were "snob schools." After looking at the list for a long time, Joan finally said she might prefer Lexington or Bluffton because they "weren't too high-pressure schools" but did not have "a high percentage of children with real learning problems that would absorb the teachers' time and attention."

In chapters 3 and 4, I addressed the beliefs and actions of affluent mothers who negotiate and rationalize privileged school circumstances for their offspring. In this chapter, I documented that *already there* teachers were in an almost identical position to that of affluent mothers and shared outlooks on educational matters. Although *upward-striving* teachers did not always have the same high status as the *already there* school personnel and mothers, they aspired to their class position, their children benefitted from social class hierarchies, and their educational outlooks were similar to those with a family history of being in an affluent professional class. *In-the-middle* teachers ranked below these others in the social class hierarchy because they were first-generation college and mainly lived in modest areas of Hillsdale rather than in the affluent suburbs of other professionals in town. Their children attended mixed- or low-income elementary schools and were rarely in the highest tracks at the secondary level. From their reports, it was clear that neither *in-the-middle* teachers nor their offspring benefitted from school and town hierarchies in the same way and to the same extent as colleagues who taught in high-income schools. They were attuned to many class-based disparities in Hillsdale, but as chapter 6 will demonstrate, they tended to be silent about them.

6

Impact of Teacher Position on Divided Classes

A *lready there* school personnel knew that affluent Hillsdale school patrons negotiated school advantage and segregation, but most saw this as legitimate parental behavior. In contrast, *in-the-middle* teachers and administrators disapproved of their actions and were upset about disparities, favoritism, and elitism. The essence of any social class system is that resources flow to powerful constituencies, and an unequal distribution of material and status resources exist. Yet it is also the nature of the system for those on the losing end of the distribution to protest and resist the implicit hierarchies. After many close readings of interview transcripts and much pondering over teachers' narratives, I came to the conclusion that damaging repercussions for school equity arise not only from status and power differentials between affluent families and poor families but also from differentials within school personnel.

The lower position of *in-the-middle* teachers and administrators affects their insight into the class disparities in schools but also their sense of themselves, their willingness to publicly express concerns about unfairness, and the likelihood of their working to eliminate school disparities. With more confidence and feelings of entitlement, *in-the-middle* administrators and teachers might fight discrimination or at least speak up about it. *In-the-middle* teachers were aware of inequities and suffered because of them in their professional roles; they mostly did not benefit from them in their personal roles as parents. Although they were discreetly vocal about their observations of school discrimination in the interviews, they admitted that they remained passive and did not directly, or indirectly, confront bias in the system. Their compliance with class disparities was one of the bewildering and unsettling findings of my study.

Critical theorists have been accused of being reductionist in dichoto-mizing social classes. I, too, usually condense social class relations into a binary of high and low positions and maintain there are valid reasons for doing so. Yet, in understanding the perspectives of school professionals on equity, my interviews reveal the need for a more nuanced understanding of the complex class affiliations in Hillsdale. Although "middle class" and "teaching profes-sion" imply a homogeneity in status and perspective, in chapter 5 I enumer-ated various differences between three clusters of professionals: those who were *already there*, those *upward striving*, and those *in-the-middle*. In this chap-ter, I explore the impact of these within-class distinctions on the dynamics of social relations and on the continuing disparities in schools.

THE PASSIVITY OF IN-THE-MIDDLE TEACHERS

In commenting that *in-the-middle* personnel were aware of inequities and bothered by them, I also noted that none said that they did anything about them. This chapter centers on the nature and extent of their passivity, likely reasons for their silence, and the subsequent impact of their lack of activism. *Already there* school personnel were similar to affluent mothers in their outlook on the need for social class distinctions in classrooms and schools as well as in their confidence about the correctness of their opinions and descriptions of their assertiveness in dealing with school officials. Therefore, because their per-spective was covered in chapters 3 and 4, I focus less on them in this chapter.

In-the-middle teachers seem to be in the majority in the Hillsdale dis-trict; nevertheless, they have little voice in school politics. Ignored by afflu-ent people, they are also deliberately silent because they believe they must keep their opinions to themselves to keep their jobs. The unfortunate result of this hierarchical positioning among professionals is an interactional dynamic that interferes with the creation and protection of social equity. My timing for asserting this conclusion at the start of this chapter may seem mis-placed. Nevertheless, it is important for readers to have this explanation in mind as they peruse the report of interviews with *in-the-middle* personnel and my conclusion about their general political passivity.

FALLING INTO TEACHING

Already there school personnel alleged to have chosen teaching as a career because they "always loved children," "played teacher from kindergarten on," "liked to read and learn," or, in the case of secondary teachers, had an inter-est in subject matter. They described "outstanding" teachers who inspired them to enter the profession. Some *in-the-middle* teachers remembered con-sidering teaching when it was mentioned as a possibility by teachers. A sec-ondary teacher said: "I got good in math because a teacher picked me up by my bootstraps and made me do it. I got interested and then got good at it!

That's when I began to think that I could teach math." Another recalled having been unhappy at a large high school after attending a small elementary school and confided: "I think I would have to say that if it hadn't been for a core of teachers that I began to relate to at that high school, I don't think I would have stayed in school and gone on to college to become a teacher."

With overtones of resignation, many *in-the-middle* teachers admitted that teaching had been the logical, convenient, or perhaps only choice for them—the obvious and expected career path for first-generation college-bound students. Alice generalized: "You were considered an oddball if you went for anything besides teaching." Women had conformed to the expectations of relatives who felt teaching was an appropriate or achievable career for them. Some recalled that when they established themselves as decent students, their parents began to mention the possibility of their attending college specifically to become a teacher. Comparing her career opportunities to those of her children, Joan said: "My daughter has such a wide field that she can go into, where I was sort of limited. Now women are in so many other areas—other than teaching." Louise said: "When I went to college in the 1950s, most women only had teaching and nursing opportunities. I always wanted to be a teacher, so that wasn't a stumbling block, and there were a lot of avenues open for me to become . . ." She drifted off and changed the subject to: "It was a difficult burden for my parents to put me through college." Audrey recalled: "We were very, very poor, but my parents still helped me pay for college. They were happy I wanted to be a teacher. Teaching meant financial security to them and, I guess, to me." In contrast, Bernice complained that her working-class father had not encouraged her to go to college, but she "had always wanted to be a teacher," so put herself through. *In-the-middle* teachers had practical, modest career goals.

A few teachers discussed their impression that unmotivated teachers had always entered education for the wrong reasons and were still doing this. Louise, a 30-year veteran of teaching, complained:

> Some people are going into teaching because either they can't get into something else or they might not have been successful in some other field. They really should have a loving concern for children. Some teachers just grind out the mechanics and feel they were taught to teach a skill, trained to teach a subject area, and they don't want to get too personally involved with the individuals that they are teaching.

Although *in-the-middle* school personnel spoke of having drifted *passively* into teaching, none explicitly claimed they had been more interested in less accessible occupations or that teaching had been a second choice when other career dreams fell through.

It might seem that administrators, who had moved up the career ladder, might express greater ambitions, yet all eight narrated a version of having been satisfied with teaching but were almost inadvertently sidetracked into administration when a principal's job came up and they were persuaded to take it. Most became assistant principals before starting to take courses toward an administrator's license. They did not speak of teaching as a stepping stone to administration yet admitted that a monetary incentive had led them to agree to be administrators. None mentioned personal ambitions being fulfilled by their leadership position nor did they talk of grand visions for improving education or spearheading reforms. All did speak of a commitment to high standards, sound management, fairness to constituencies, and a willingness to take on responsibility for school governance.

STAYING ON THE JOB

In-the-middle teachers communicated that teaching was hard work, stressful, and often depressing. Some said they felt "exhausted" or "burned out." Yet, in spite of their dissatisfaction, none mentioned any intention of leaving the profession or finding other work. They tolerated their disenchantment, perhaps because their awareness of working conditions for others made them skeptical about finding jobs that would be easier or more lucrative. Job tenacity did not seem to be a deliberate choice, but teaching was a secure job in an unstable world. With the exception of two of the administrators who were interviewed, others had spent most of their careers in the local district. It is difficult to move from one district to another after earning a master's degree and accumulating teaching experience. In the state where Hillsdale is located, until about 15 years ago earning a master's degree within 5 years was required for teachers to continue teaching. Subsequently, under pressure from districts with financial constraints, the state overturned that legislation to follow a lifelong learning model in which teachers without master's degrees must earn a certain number of credit hours to retain their jobs. Rural and urban school districts are known to hire neophytes to avoid the expense of experienced teachers. Regardless of the constraints surrounding career change, after perusing the entire set of interview narratives, it seems reasonable to conclude that teachers were neither ambitious in terms of career advancement nor were they risk takers—most clung to their jobs and, as will be addressed later, refrained from saying or doing anything that they felt would put their jobs at risk.

THE IMPACT OF A SECOND-RATE SELF-IMAGE

In-the-middle teachers were confident about their teaching competencies, but they knew their schools were seen as second rate and they felt that others in the district looked down upon them as well. In the privacy of interviews, *in-the-middle* teachers and administrators accused the personnel, students, and parents at high-income schools of being snobs and elitists, and some passionately condemned them for negotiating to get higher status and exclusive school arrangements and more than their share of resources. These same teachers admitted, however, that they kept these opinions and resentments to themselves. Furthermore, after being critical of elites, they inevitably apologized for "being negative" or getting "worked up." The reverse side of portraying people at high-income schools as snobs and elitists is that these feelings reveal their sense of lesser status, of being *in the middle* between higher-status professionals and the poor and working-class residents of their schools' catchment zones. They were clearly in awe of, and intimidated by, more affluent people. Recall that they saw their own educational careers as mediocre—they described themselves as plodders who fit in and caused little or no trouble. This low self-image may partly explain their lack of self- and student advocacy.

Research indicates that people's sense of entitlement—or lack thereof—plays a role in determining how they act (Freire, 1973, 1985; Hunt, 2000). Revolutions happen when oppressed people begin to feel empowered. *In-the-middle* teachers felt downtrodden by the conditions of teaching and others' demands. They did not feel empowered enough to act on their sense of injustice. They were skeptical about the logic and motives of legislators, school board members, and affluent parents, yet they also obsequiously hinted that others were entitled to make demands or at least that they personally had no alternative except to comply with them.

THE IMPACT OF CRITICISM ON TEACHER MORALE

The 22 experienced teachers all showed an avid interest in discussing what occurred in their schools and hypothesizing about the state of education. *Already there* teachers were more likely to claim a continuing enthusiasm for teaching. Most were confident that they were good at what they did and that their teaching was effective and valued. In contrast to *already there* teachers, some *upward-striving* teachers spoke of not being respected by certain students, parents, administrators, or colleagues. Yet even teachers who claimed to receive nothing but praise from all sectors knew they were part of an under-valued and criticized profession—and resented it. *In-the-middle* teachers were sometimes quite emotional in vocalizing hurt feelings about the bad rap teachers got, whereas *already there* teachers seemed to dismiss such criticism as not applicable to them personally.

In-the-middle teachers generally felt they had a valuable impact on students, yet because of the bad press their schools had received as a result of developments in the standards and accountability movement, they felt humiliated by aspersions that cast them into being uncaring, lazy, or incompetent teachers. Working-class schools inevitably were rated as "unsatisfactory" in statewide assessments, and the schools' test score rank in the district and state were published in the local newspaper. These low rankings were seen as a condemnation of their teaching. Some teachers were tormented not only about their own bad image but that such public displays of inadequacies caused students and families to be demoralized. Then, too, "failing schools" were "put on probation," which meant they had to follow a set curriculum for months prior to the annual testing.

In-the-middle teachers and principals were disgruntled about their school's bad image in the community, depressed about their comparatively low test scores, and frustrated at having to comply with state-mandated remedies that they felt were unfair, unreasonable, and counterproductive. They complained that a "teach to the test" mentality pervaded the school climate the entire year. Certainly, *in-the-middle* teachers' anguish arose from the particular circumstances connected with teaching at low- and mixed-income schools. In contrast, announcements of school-by-school test results were seen as confirmation of outstanding teaching, smart students, and caring families for *already there* teachers.

Frustration due to the accountability and standards initiatives was compounded by concern about declining conditions for working-class families. A factory that was a major employer in the area had moved its operation to Mexico in the late 1990s. Another transglobal corporation had moved some of its divisions to third-world locations and had laid off a third of its local workers. Remaining workers were anxious about the future and agreed (with resentment) to forego raises with the hope of retaining their jobs.[1] Service industries (particularly motels—a major employer in this sports-oriented town) had learned that they could save money by firing local workers and replacing them with imported workers who would demand less money.[2] As a result of these conditions, several *in-the-middle* teachers reiterated worries about being unable to meet the glaring needs of certain children due to family financial and personal crises. Although their societal decline responses were not totally distinctive from the deficit-oriented responses of affluent mothers and *already there* teachers, teachers at working-class schools were attuned to the economic conditions that affected the families in their schools rather than to innate deficits in children and families.

Factory jobs in Hillsdale had dried up considerably in recent years and teachers at low-income schools talked about the recession felt by the working class and continuing lack of job opportunity for the long-term unemployed parents. In contrast to the school-related phenomena (standards and accountability movement) they observed and resented but might have done something about if they had more confidence and acted collectively, these trends were even more beyond their control. Yet the blending together of negative conditions may account for *in-the-middle* teachers assuming they had no power to be agents for change. It is my experience as a teacher educator that teachers enter the profession with an idealism about the constructive impact they will have on the lives of students. It seems that teachers are bound to be disappointed and hard on themselves if they do not live up to their own expectations. *In-the-middle* teachers especially conveyed that they had a nagging feeling that their best work was never quite enough to make a real difference in students' lives.

An issue that must be considered is whether—and how—demands on teachers are different in working-class than in affluent professional-class schools. Conditions at the former had been substantially worse in terms of class size, access to materials and resources, and physical conditions. National studies document that these unequal school conditions are not unique to Hillsdale (e.g., Kozol, 1991; Lipman, 1997; Orfield, 2000). Low-income urban schools have been described as chaotic, and such negative factors as dilapidated buildings, inexperienced teachers, large teacher turnover, and serious underfunding and limited resources are rampant (Bowes, 2001; Lien, 2001; Orfield, 2000). Yet, as a result of activism on the part of Hillsdale citizens both rich and poor who were persistent in bringing equity issues to the attention of the board of trustees and administrators, as well as the responsiveness of some brave superintendents who were attuned to equity issues, differences currently are not extreme in Hillsdale.

In the past, physical conditions were decidedly worse at low-income schools. Because ineffective principals tended to be assigned to those schools, teachers asked to be transferred to high- or mixed-income schools. So, less competent teachers ended up at schools in working-class residential areas. This does not seem to be the case anymore because of restrictions on teacher transfers. Teaching faculty at all schools are experienced and stable. Granted, there is more student turnover in working-class schools because poor families move for financial and employment reasons. Low-income schools are often poorly situated and their grounds are not attractive, but most were remodeled or rebuilt, so there is less visible evidence of qualitative difference in schools. Further, based on my own observations in Hillsdale schools, I would challenge certain stereotypes of low-income students as less motivated to learn or more difficult to handle or that parents are not supportive of the school agenda. Interviews indicated that some teachers confirmed my impression that working-class children are often better behaved and more respectful of teachers than affluent students. So, problems with local teacher morale seem mostly to be due to two factors: (1) they are bothered by their negative image in the community and (2) recent reform initiatives intensify the perception that low-income schools are failing schools.

DRAINED OF ENERGY BY THE DEMANDS OF TEACHING

Teachers spend a sustained amount of time teaching large groups of children in isolation from other adults. As parents are quick to admit after school vacations, simply caring for a few children is not easy; being with between 18 and 35 children in one setting for 7 hours a day, 5 days a week, can be exhausting for even the best managers and most energetic people. Calm, laid-back teachers still may find the perpetual noise and movement of the many small or large bodies in close quarters a strain. Containing students and maintaining classroom harmony is not enough. Accountable for student progress, teachers are to ensure cognitive, social, and emotional growth in their charges. Alice claimed:

> A teacher is like a parent, a social worker, a psychologist—you'd like to make them feel better when they don't feel good. My worst feeling is that I don't meet the needs of all my students because I'm one compared to 27, 28, 29. That's the real weakness—there are just so many children and I can't meet all their needs in a day—but I would like to. I really work hard, but you know you can only squeeze so much juice out of an orange. Some teachers are shutting their eyes to severe emotional and personality problems. We're not doing enough to help children.

Similarly, Audrey felt her peers "allowed kids to get credit for just sitting there," adding that "they are too tired to make a better effort." With 23 years of experience at Hillview, Bernice complained about the "lack of dedicated teachers, ill-prepared teachers. Starting salaries are low; salaries are especially low for the, you know, for me, the one supporting family member." Some mentioned the moral support of their colleagues in dealing with the stresses of teaching. Others said teaching kept them so busy that they only had time for hurried breaks in the teachers' room. Others not only avoided that room but claimed to have so little contact that they did not know what their colleagues thought about matters that certainly were of mutual interest and concern. Some who claimed that stress and burnout were common problems put themselves in that category.

In-the-middle teachers conveyed a deep caring for their students and a dedication to teaching, but many came across as bitter that they could never be entirely satisfied with their work or could never feel that their working day was done. As parents and spouses, they had home and family obligations. A compelling explanation for *in-the-middle* teachers' passivity in the public political domain is they were so exhausted by classroom demands that they had little energy left to organize to fight the unreasonable pressures that made their jobs hard and unrewarding or to advocate for an equitable education for children in their own predominantly working-class schools.

Regarding concerns about education, *already there* teachers mentioned curricular problems: "Educational bureaucracy is difficult to move. I am frustrated by things I am not allowed to teach like sex education and AIDS awareness" and "we have no systematic curriculum development because of a reluctance for central administration to insist on grade-specific curriculum content—they leave too much up to teachers so that there are major gaps in knowledge and some kids are sick of getting the same units (dinosaurs, pollution) year after year." Their replies centered around their sense of societal decline or that the complexity of modern life had repercussions: "how to respond to increasing demands placed on teachers because of modern problems—family and community breakdown" and "trying to reach kids who have too much stuff going on in their lives." A teacher was upset that "I have kids, second graders, who watch at least one video every night and many are violent or sexually explicit."

SETTLING FOR LACK OF CONTROL OVER JOB CONDITIONS

In discussing their concerns about education, many *in-the-middle* teachers used some form of the expression "power coming down on them from above." Dismayed about board of school trustee decisions, they rarely blamed Hillsdale administrators, who they felt understood local conditions and were on their side. Most complaints centered around state legislators, Department of Education officials, and, more often, vaguely identified groups outside the district who made arbitrary, illogical, degrading, and punitive demands and wielded considerable control over their teaching conditions. They launched into naming: "lack of monetary commitment to education," "teacher stress due to the reduced status of the teaching profession," "teachers taking blame for failure and not getting credit for success—this evaluation hurts," "American competition with the rest of the world and the pressure that puts on educators," "having to respond to increasing demands on teachers by politicians," "not knowing how to deal with the nature of modern problems that force schools to do more and more," "ambiguity about the mission of schools," "little attention to the affect of students or teachers (teaching can be lonely)," "we are made to put kids in boxes," "constantly changing state plans," "making us teach to the test," "difficulty determining what's worth teaching, whether to teach directly to tests or not," "lack of control of the educational agenda by teachers because of requests by administrators and pressures by state departments." Thus, they fretted about fluctuating reform initiatives or requirements that did not seem reasonable yet imposed responsibilities that took time away from what was educationally more important or left them working long hours outside of the school day. Some discussed the personal toll such initiatives took on them, stating that they felt exhausted, unsuccessful, and unappreciated as teachers. For example, Bernice said:

> Then there's the whole struggle—seems to be a power struggle between teachers and legislators, or whatever, over who's going to control things. Today we're hearing a lot about at-risk students, and so a lot of money in materials and training is supposed to be going into at-risk students. Of course, we've always had at-risk students at Hillview—though they've never been called that before—that is a popular saying that is being bantered about right now. I have always taught at low-income schools in Hillsdale and I have never seen any of that special funding. I wish we had the materials they have at Kinder or Beauford or Eastside. Public education makes a lot of swings: first this, and then we'll go to something else. It is too bad that it has to be swayed by those sorts of things. Teachers are put under a lot of pressure for doing those things, instead of praised for just doing a good job. Teachers need to spend time seeing their own weaknesses instead of waiting for public opinion to sway things.

Like other teachers, Bernice was prone to turn her frustration into criticism of other teachers: "It just gripes me to be around teachers who don't make the effort and complain about not getting enough money. That irritates me—it's a personal thing." She also was vociferous about "poor attitudes toward work, learning, and effort—there's a discipline problem that goes along with that attitude" among students and their parents. Political views about class inequities and problematic official mandates were diminished by a more salient dissatisfaction with colleagues and students.

School personnel told how they had collaborated to write standards or design assessments to comply with state accountability initiatives. Some resentfully rolled their eyes when telling about the extra efforts they had put in, especially when they feared these were temporary fads that would quickly disappear only to be replaced by other innovations they would have to address. There were different levels of discontent about the mandatory high school graduation exam that was required for students to earn the diploma. None claimed to support these tests, yet *already there* teachers mainly brought them up to illustrate how their schools compared favorably to other schools. Some personnel at low-income schools tentatively said the tests might have a positive impact if schools actually got the extra resources they were promised. Those critical of colleagues felt the test might make them work harder. Interviews were conducted at a time the test was being field tested (to set cut-off levels) but before its preventing failing students from receiving the diploma had gone into effect. High school teachers and administrators worried that the high-stakes graduation exit exam would increase dropout rates of low-achieving students and further demoralize teachers who taught in low tracks. They projected that they would increasingly have to teach to the test. Teachers at low-income schools grumbled about the tests; outspoken ones were disgusted and outraged, yet again communicated an obligation to comply with anything that "came down on them from the wisdom of the legislators or the Department of Education."

State standards and accountability pressures were described as bothersome and disruptive. Maureen, a Southside teacher, was frustrated by the new rhetoric of a state promise to spend more money to help failing schools improve their standardized test scores when they had not followed through on such promises in the past:

> In our school, one big issue for teachers is making the kids competent for competency testing. We are supposed to get funded for the programs that the states want implemented at certain low-achieving schools. Our kids at Southside usually do about second worst in the district—that is expected because of the income level of families—but we are still supposed to compete with other schools for high scores and are penalized if we don't do as well. It makes no sense whatsoever. I am concerned about where the state is going—that is the most frustrating thing about teaching for me. Every year we have a different plan. I wish they'd make a long-range plan and then work toward that so that we can get in gear and implement it—so that we know where we're going and can work to get there. I wish that we would actually get the funds that they keep promising.

Maureen says "wish" and fails to mention expressing her frustration either outside the interview space or working in a collective way to influence policy or practice. During debriefing, Maureen remarked that she "appreciated the interview because I was able to vent my spleen!"

THE ABSENCE OF ACTIVISM

One indication of teacher passivity was that interviewees were not specific about which individuals or governing bodies were responsible for the impositions about which they were bitter. They felt the oppression of externally imposed measures by distant adversaries but could not name them. None had written letters to the state superintendent or legislators. Some suffered in isolation; others cited teachers' room "bitch sessions." There apparently had been no formal meetings to discuss how to deal with the universally despised trends. They had not fought back by making collective commitments to educate policy makers about school conditions and there were no signs of any system-wide action to oppose gateway test legislation or, for that matter, any other state-mandated initiatives. The teachers' union had not made this a topic of their infrequent district-wide meetings. Indeed, the state teachers' association endorsed the adoption of the graduation exit exam, although many teachers were puzzled about why they did so. Some teachers described subtle opposition and noncompliance (passive aggression), but most were unenthusiastic conformists to the parade of changes they had witnessed during the past decade.

Bernice provides an example of an outspoken teacher who still stopped short of really challenging the system. Bernice had grown up in the industrial northern part of the state and was the only one of her siblings to get a college degree. Bernice claimed her working-class father had discouraged her from attending college.[3] She proudly announced that it was her choice to teach at Hillview—that she "would not want to teach with the stuck-up teachers at some schools." Bernice repeatedly referred to affluent students as spoiled and to parents and teachers as snobs or elitists. She framed her sentiments in openly political terms and did not apologize for speaking up about wealthy students' advantage in the district. Others expressed similar sentiments but usually asked that these remarks not be quoted. An enthusiastic supporter of the movement to include students with disabilities in general education, Bernice was the first at her school to volunteer to co-teach with special education teachers. She did not like ability grouping: "It's unnecessary. It just makes kids feel bad and makes twice as much work for teachers." Bernice flaunted her working-class identity and endorsement of unions. Bernice was Hillview's representative in the local teachers' union. Over the years, she often assumed district-wide leadership positions in that organization. Nevertheless, she did not talk about the union as a way to confront the external authorities that she felt made unreasonable demands of teachers and students.

The district's official teacher union is the National Education Association (NEA). Its role is to negotiate with administrators and the board of trustees to establish the school calendar, annual salaries, and fringe benefits. Because of the official collective bargaining role played by the NEA, a portion of the annual membership fee was automatically deducted from teachers' salaries. Many Hillsdale teachers did not pay the additional (voluntary) local, state, and national part of NEA dues, and through the years several had protested or filed lawsuits against having to pay any NEA fees. They lost on the grounds that all teachers benefitted from NEA activities, thus were responsible for paying the designated collective bargaining portion of the dues.

In the 1970s and 1980s, the American Federation of Teachers (AFT) tried to gain a foothold among teachers in the district. The AFT is the official collective bargaining body in many school districts in the more union-oriented northern part of the state. For some years, the AFT's membership was competitive with the NEA. Indeed, it was this AFT threat that eventually forced the NEA into acting more like a union (rather than just a professional organization) and to take on collective bargaining. During the

1980s, the AFT had a small but active and influential chapter for faculty on the university campus,[4] and there were attempts to have joint meetings and combined campus and school events. This collaboration was short-lived. By the 1990s, AFT membership had substantially declined in both settings.

Attendance at NEA meetings was said to be low except in times of crisis (delayed contract approval, threatened extension of the school day or school year), and the organization rarely had public sessions to discuss more general teaching issues. Few participants spontaneously mentioned the teachers' union. Those who did often were unhappy with it: "the NEA is too much money for nothing" and "teachers have a poor image due to the teacher organization." Teachers who complained about the incompetence of colleagues felt they were kept on due to the union's success in securing the impossibility of contract termination.

The lack of visible and viable opposition to what teachers felt were unreasonable external pressures and the absence of substantive collective stands were vivid signs of teacher passivity. Teachers excused their complacency by claiming nobody would listen to them or that they would be labeled troublemakers or, even worse, radicals—a self-image they eschewed. Besides claiming their actions would not produce results, they were apprehensive that activism, even collective activism, was risky. Their "don't rock the boat" attitude seemed to arise from their fear of job-related repercussions. What is troubling about these experienced teachers' fear of activism or even any public airing of opinions is that there would seem to be few risks involved for speaking about what was on their minds. Experienced teachers were purposefully selected for this study because they were tenured and would have few constraints about giving candid responses. The union exerted strong pressures against contract termination. Parents, teachers, and administrators all said "the system" could not get rid of incompetent teachers. Perhaps most bothersome was that in spite of their passionate indignation about the disparities that affected their schools, *in-the-middle* teachers seemed resigned— they had not done advocacy work in their students' behalf.

In a recent teacher education course, I mentioned that teachers complained about certain policies and practices but were not collectively trying to combat them. I said that in my opinion, if teachers organized around common issues, they could change things that they did not like. My 31 seniors quickly and excitedly enumerated the negative consequences that would result from such "political" activity. There was consensus that teachers might "lose their jobs." When I mentioned union safety nets, security in group actions, and a democratic right to free speech, they reiterated that "the system" would retaliate by conjuring up something teachers had done wrong that would warrant dismissal or they would be ostracized for being outspoken. I was surprised at the strength of their conviction that it was essential to conform to requests in order to keep their jobs.

EXPECTED MIDDLE-CLASS DEMEANOR AND SENSIBILITY

Fourteen first-generation college-educated personnel came from rural areas, which are known to be socially conservative and Republican. *In-the-middle* teachers, but even more *upward-striving* teachers, were conscious of incorporating a respectable middle-class identity, although, in the case of the former, not an affluent one. Their worry about the image of teachers and public opinion about their profession was visible in their criticism of others' actions and appearance and particularly in their rejection of union activities. *In-the-middle* teachers talked about social class directly and indirectly in their interviews. All noted class distinctions in student enrollment patterns of various elementary schools in Hillsdale; however, they tended to speak with empathy and sympathy about poverty and not social class.[5]

APOLOGIZING FOR NOTICING OR TALKING ABOUT CLASS DISPARITIES

Already there teachers did not hesitate to speak of educational and intellectual inferiority of poor children. They spoke of their own social class superiority with confidence—what might be judged to be an arrogant certainty about the truth and righteousness of their position and perspective. They touted prejudices in a way that conveyed their assurance that the interviewer felt the same way. In contrast, and what was perhaps most disconcerting about the interviews, was a consistent pattern of *in-the-middle* teachers prefacing or concluding descriptions of social class disparities with requests for the interviewer not to disclose their "radical" or "liberal" views to others. Esther, a high school teacher, elaborated on her concerns about class bias but then requested these not be made public:

> A strength of education generally is putting together the different groups in society, but that is a scary thing. In the past, all different kinds of [social] classes, age ranges, kinds of occupations mixed together. Society is much more rigid today. I see it as just frightening. You can map out Hillsdale—income and occupation—very, very much! One of the strengths of this country has been trying to keep this rigid caste system from developing. There is starting to be an alarming amount of class division—it's coming, it really is. There is not as much acceptance as there used to be in the past. We are creating a segmented society now. You have to be where everybody is like you. Kids get cliquey, nasty. Teachers treat kids from lower classes differently. Kids segregate by class. It's amazing how kids find their own level. I have the feeling that most teachers tend to go along with this social stratification that we are seeing in our society, in our town, and are quite comfortable with it. I think that my opinions about the problems are in the minority.

In debriefing, like other openly political teachers, Esther asked that these "liberal" views not be communicated to others. Similarly, after calling Kinder a "snob school," Audrey turned to the interviewer and said: "Don't put that in there! See that's where I don't want to be quoted." Corey, whose anger about teacher bias was quoted earlier, ended her interview with:

> I guess I am just kind of concerned that I don't want anybody in the school system to see it or know the things that I said. I don't want to be alienated any more than I am from certain teachers in the system. I really like what I am doing and I wouldn't be doing it if I didn't like it and I feel like it is an important thing to do.[6] And I do think that teachers do their best, and despite some of the negative things I've said about other schools within the system and maybe teachers, I'm just hoping that they're doing, you know, they're doing what they think is best and what is right. So, you know, who is to say what is right or wrong? It's a personal thing.

In spite of the hype about how demands for political sensitivity (correctness) silence right-wing people (see Wilson, 1995), in this study it was the left-wing teachers who were quick to apologize for their opinions while those who openly endorsed class advantage showed little hesitation or shame. Teachers' sense of a need to remain "apolitical"[7] is problematic in terms of the potential transformative role they could play in local school politics. Of equal concern is their lack of confidence in the validity of their own opinions. In personal interviews, most appeared to speak their minds openly and with conviction but did not want to take their voices to the bully pulpit and rally others to support their well-articulated private concerns.

WHY INSIGHTFUL TEACHERS ARE SILENT ABOUT SOCIAL CLASS INEQUITIES

I conclude this chapter by asserting that *in-the-middle* teachers (1) and their offspring do not personally benefit from an uneven distribution of school advantage; (2) are aware that affluent people negotiate for advantage for their offspring and others of their class; (3) acknowledge that teachers and administrators typically give in to influential parents' demands and anticipate their requests by creating favorable circumstances for affluent children without their parents having to make direct demands; (4) are deeply concerned with the inequities they observe in schools; (5) typically are silent about what they know; (6) feel inferior to, intimidated by, and powerless in combating the actions of more powerful Hillsdale residents; (7) are politically passive regarding local and state politics; and thus (8) are disempowered in terms of contributing to transformative reform.

I make the case for these assertions by referring to this subset of school personnel as being "in the middle of class relations," which means they do not think of themselves as being of the same status as more affluent and highly educated members of the middle class yet also do not position themselves as poor or oppressed. Hovering in the middle means that they have somewhat conflicted and ambivalent feelings toward low-income people in town but still do not generally condone stratified school structures and class-biased practices. They are bothered by wealthier people's actions to obtain and maintain advantage in schools, but, being subordinately positioned, they do not have the confidence to stand up as vocal advocates for equitable, democratic schooling. They do not voice their concerns and convictions publicly nor do they act on them. Therefore, they might be said to be inert in exercising authentic agency. Hence, being *in-the-middle,* or rather being lower than the demanding and controlling higher-income constituencies in Hillsdale, including the *already there* and *upward-striving* teachers and affluent parents, is a circumstance that mitigates against this fairly insightful group speaking up for what they believe and being advocates for themselves or lower-income constituencies.

THE NATIONAL PERSPECTIVE

This pattern of divisions of middle-class people, in which teachers rank low in the status hierarchy of professionals, may be somewhat unique to towns dominated by large or multiple universities. Universities attract a faculty from across the country and academics tend to be at least second-generation college (Dews & Law, 1995; Ryan & Sackrey, 1996); thus, there not only is a discrepancy between them and low-income parents but also between the more highly educated sectors of the middle class (doctors, lawyers, professors, business people) and teachers who are first-generation college. School personnel in urban districts would also be from more distinctive socioeconomic backgrounds than local residents. So, the social dynamics in Hillsdale caused by differences in educational backgrounds and current salaries may be a common phenomenon across the United States. There is a difference between the social class level of most citizens who run for school board and *in-the-middle* teachers. Hence, the pattern of teachers being *in the middle* (between higher and lower classes) and subsequently powerless in school decision making is likely to hold true nationally.

THE FINE LINE BETWEEN CRITICISM/PESSIMISM
AND ANALYSIS/CONSCIOUSNESS RAISING

When the case is made that a group has no power and influence, it is essential to add the caveat that all humans have the potential to exercise agency; that anyone at any place in a social hierarchy can choose to act to change the circumstances they abhor. On the other hand, it is also important to recognize the reality that humans are continuously socialized to engage in certain patterns of thinking and to enact and reenact certain role-related scripts based on characteristics of their habitus (Bourdieu, 1984). Overcoming the effects of long-term socialization is highly unlikely. Nevertheless, if democratic transformations are to occur in schools and society, it is necessary for people to become conscious of the realities of their lives and be inspired to change them in accordance with their ideals. For the purpose of raising consciousness, I have provided evidence to support claims about the passivity of *in-the-middle* teachers.

There is considerable evidence about the gendered nature of educational professions and the motives that undergird career choices from studies of teachers. Although my intention is not to demean or degrade the current teacher population, I think any class analysis of schooling would be remiss if it did not examine this part of the puzzle in an attempt to explain divided classes in schools. My mother spent her entire career as an enthusiastic elementary school teacher who volunteered in schools for more than a decade after her retirement. She made friends with low-income parents and tended to prefer teaching poorer students because she felt she could do the most for them, although her school was small enough to have comprehensive classes. She was a first-generation college student who went to a 2-year normal school to get her certification. Only after many years of teaching did she go back in the evenings and summers in order to get a bachelor's degree and move up the pay scale.

My eldest son was a dedicated secondary math teacher who taught by choice in a large urban school district that has been named as being among the more chaotic and least effective districts in the country. Although he was a competent and popular teacher who loved teaching, he was constantly bothered by such conditions at his school as the draconian and humiliating security measures, as well as the mandates that teachers had to use a teach-to-the-test curriculum that flew in the face of what he learned in his professional preparation and his own ideas about effective pedagogy and curriculum.[8] He was also alarmed by the difficult life circumstances of many of his students and by the high burnout rate among colleagues, whether they left or stayed in the profession. Partly to escape what he felt would be the eventuality of his own demoralization and partly to have more power to influence the field, he, too, chose to become a teacher educator.

I have spent my career as a special education teacher and a teacher educator. In our family's three generations of teaching, a burning concern has been class equity. My mother included students with disabilities in her heterogeneous classrooms decades before the term *inclusion* was ever mentioned. My son insisted on having recent immigrants integrated into his advanced math courses and spent his summers becoming proficient in Spanish to accomplish the goal of teaching them well. As I speak autobiographically, however, I must acknowledge that my family's outspokenness about equity comes from a sense of entitlement and empowerment that accompanies our class status. For a variety of historically specific and socially contextualized reasons, we were alert to inequity and pained about the fact that others of our status were content to ignore class privilege and intentionally turn a blind eye to inequities. As noted in my report of findings, teachers of working-class origins and with continuing working-class ties were aware of class discrepancies, grumbled about them, but were not active in transformative reform. Their fear of being seen as radical or losing job security meant they did not go public with their views. Their silence may also have been due to a habit of keeping "political" opinions to themselves. Whatever the cause, they did not confront affluent school constituents who control local policy and practice.

Through the years, as my first book about Hillsdale—*The Politics of Social Class in Secondary Schools: Views of Affluent and Impoverished Youth* (1993)—got local media coverage, these same teachers and administrators, along with other class-sensitive individuals in the district, would whisper to me that they were pleased that I spoke up about disparities. University colleagues made similar statements. Yet, while I was in the midst of disputes and struggles to dismantle inequities with powerful Hillsdale constituencies, few were present at board meetings nor did they write supportive letters to the newspaper editor. Why is it that astute sentiments about the benefits that those in power continuously receive are spoken only behind closed doors? Why do those with radical persuasions feel alone in beliefs about inequities and only speak their mind to strangers (see Eliasoph, 1998)? Why is it that insightful and caring individuals do not rally to confront unfairness in institutions? What feelings of entitlement and disenfranchisement cause Hillsdale residents, and Americans generally, to tolerate social class bias in our beloved country?

7

Succumbing to Demands:
Administrators under Pressure

I n Hillsdale, an elected board of school trustees hires the superintendent. These trustees are almost always affluent professionals.[1] The average tenure of appointed superintendents nationally is 2.5 years (Glass, Bjork, & Bruner, 2000), although these authors admit this figure depends on who measures it and how it is measured. In Hillsdale, one superintendent lasted almost two decades; another's 3-year contract was terminated in his second year. An interim superintendent had a 2-year contract renewed for a third year when a successor was not found, and an acting superintendent was appointed another year for the same reason. Summaries of interviews with the latter two as well as two assistant superintendents are included in this chapter. First, I provide an overview of school politics based on inspected documents (e.g., newspaper articles, editorials, letters to the editor; school records; school board minutes), a dissertation about central administration when Edwards was in office (Hutson, 1978), interviews with school personnel, and copies of my own communication with the school trustees and administrators. This admittedly sketchy history provides the background for the time just proceeding the formal data collection for this book.

ACHIEVING PROFESSIONAL LONGEVITY:
PLEASING POWERFUL CONSTITUENCIES

Donald Edwards[2] was superintendent of Hillsdale from 1966 to 1984. If Edwards's longevity is representative, there is a pattern to the administration of superintendents who are able to remain in office: they are quiet managers who figure out who important Hillsdale constituencies are and learn how to please them. They not only listen to influential people and consistently respect their requests but go further to anticipate their wishes and institute their known agendas so that they do not even have to ask for advantaged circumstances. Edwards was such an administrator. The pattern for short administrative careers involves trying to enact equitable school reform. Pete Rockenweil fit this second description—his term lasted from 1987 to 1989. Rockenweil's short tenure revealed that when their hegemony is threatened, the educated upper middle class scurry to put together a slate of similar-minded individuals to run for school board, spend time and money to advertise their slate, and warn neighbors, friends, and colleagues that some ill-informed educator is not meeting the needs of bright children by attempting to do away with the exclusive and advantaged conditions to which they are accustomed. Because Edwards left the state in 1984 and Rockenweil in 1989, neither were interviewed for this study.

THE LEGACY OF CLASS DISCRIMINATION: HILLSDALE IN THE EIGHTIES

High-income people trusted Superintendent Don Edwards and they had reason to—he managed the system so as to make sure their children had privileges and advantages (Hutson, 1978). Because of the asymmetric attention to school constituencies, various overt and covert[3] inequitable practices were solidly entrenched during Edwards's time in the superintendency. One way the district met the needs of the children of the affluent, educated class was to ensure they were always grouped exclusively together whether through the establishment of class-pure school catchment zones or separated tracks and ability groups. Affluent people use the rhetoric of the value of neighborhood schools to preserve their domains, yet a perusal of each elementary school's enrollment area reveals that boundary lines were configured not to have children in the closest school but rather to separate high- and low-income children. When affluent suburbs arose adjacent to low-income schools, in spite of openings in such schools, these pockets of affluent children typically were bused to schools in high-income neighborhoods. When boundaries could not be gerrymandered, liberal school transfer policies allowed knowledgeable (high-income) parents to choose schools for their children. Of course, they inevitably chose schools according to class composition. One reason given by Edwards and his fellow administrators for maintaining social class segregation was that to collect federal Chapter One funds designated for high-density low-income enrollments they had to keep a high percentage of low-income children in certain schools. After the federal policies guiding funding distribution for Chapter One changed, Edwards continued to use this rationale.

Another way that Edwards catered to affluent school constituencies was to make sure that they had new, modern schools with spacious and well-equipped classrooms, gyms, libraries, and playgrounds. Schools in low-income neighborhoods were shabby, run-down, and their grounds were not aesthetically landscaped. Some playgrounds were adjacent to, or mingled with, teachers' parking areas, and playground equipment was old and rusty. Low-income schools lacked adequate lunchrooms, auditoriums, teachers' lounges, and special subject classrooms. Art and music teachers moved from class to class with their supplies on pushcarts. Libraries had fewer books and older books (often hand-me-downs from affluent schools). Perishable supplies were distributed on the basis of fees collected from families within each school; hence, schools in low-income neighborhoods had substantially fewer funds to purchase materials, and their schools lacked advanced media equipment and often were staffed by part-time librarians.[4] It might be expected that the pupil-to-teacher ratios in low-income schools would be deliberately kept lower based on recognition of children's needs. The opposite was true. Affluent schools consistently had smaller class size—an advantage that might be attributed to affluent parents' vigilance and demands.

Site-based management had not yet become popular; nevertheless, Edwards maintained a hands-off policy regarding ability grouping in elementary schools and tracking at secondary schools. Probably Edwards did not set a policy because he did not want to take responsibility for inequities in schools' extensively tracked system. Without the backup of central administration, on a school by school basis, principals were unable to withstand the pressure to comply with powerful parents' demands for far-reaching tracking arrangements and exclusive high-track placement for their children, which happened whether or not they met placement criteria. If important parents were not satisfied, principals knew their tenure would be jeopardized.

In the early 1980s, I interviewed principals or counselors (depending on who was responsible) about how ability group or track placements were made. Rural schools and low-income elementary schools did almost no tracking and minimal within-class ability grouping. Affluent elementary schools' arrangements were based on standardized test scores and teacher recommendation. Secondary schools rather automatically placed students from the low-income elementary feeder schools or those with subsidized housing or other class-identifiable addresses in low tracks. As a counselor responsible for track assignments asserted: "Why should *they* be in college prep tracks? *They're* not going to college!" At a middle school with approximately 70% high-income enrollment, the counselor reported that they first sorted sixth graders into three groups according to standardized test scores. Because they only wanted two groups so as not to put all the "really low troublemakers together," they "randomly" assigned the middle cluster of students to either the high or low track. When asked what was meant by random, she glibly explained that they considered feeder school, parental occupation, and address in making decisions; that is, they sorted by social class. When she noticed my astonished expression, she defensively clarified that if they put high-income students in the low groups, the parents would be outraged and

demand a change. To avoid such ugly confrontations, they did not put affluent children in low-track classes unless they were "really, really low."

Toward the end of Edwards's administration, I distributed an unpublished paper, *What a Model Community Sweeps Under the Rug: Class Discrimination in the Schools,* to school board members, central administrators,
and the local press. This report contained the results of my tracking study
as well as other biased practices I had observed during my decade of visiting
schools regularly for field experience and student teaching supervision. I had
requested a public discussion of the paper at a board meeting, but Edwards
would not put it on the agenda. Four of the seven board members called to
thank me for bringing equity issues to their attention and inform me of their
concern about violations. Given the representation on the board at that
time, I believe their main worry was possible legal ramifications for themselves. I knew, and assume they soon learned from the school attorney, that
unlike racial or gender bias, which to some extent has been successfully
addressed by litigation, social class is not a minority category; hence, poor
people cannot legally be subject to discrimination.

In a private conversation in which Edwards was responding to my
report about social class bias, he excused himself from blame on the grounds
that he was "responding to the wishes of a highly educated class in town—
that he had no choice." He advised that if I were "so interested in equity,"
I should "talk to my peers at the university"—something I eventually did
and report in this book. Still, I told him that as an administrator, he was
accountable for school equity. In somewhat more subtle terms, I accused
him of choosing the easy but unprincipled path of giving in to powerful
patrons and ignoring class-based injustices.[5] During his administration,
social class bias in Hillsdale schools was substantial and visible to anyone
who wanted to see it; nevertheless, nothing was done about it during
Edwards's time in office. In my interviews with low-income parents, I
learned that they were acutely aware of disparities and upset about them
(Brantlinger, 1985a). As Delpit (1995) also pointed out, subordinates are
often aware of biases that dominant people presumably fail to notice. In
spite of their anger about discrimination, local poor people admitted they
did not speak up, perhaps because the same inequities exist in all aspects of
their lives and they knew from experience that bias would not be redressed.

REPERCUSSIONS OF SCHOOL CLOSINGS: THE BEGINNING OF THE END
FOR EDWARDS

After a baby boom from the 1950s to the 1970s, by the early 1980s, Hillsdale
school enrollment had decreased substantially. Yet, presumably not realizing
that growth had declined, Edwards and the board authorized building a large
high school on the northern outskirts of town and two large elementary

schools that were to draw from several rural areas on the north and south sides of Hillsdale.[6] After construction was underway, the district's anticipated growth did not occur, so large new schools as well as older city and rural schools where the school-age populations had declined had empty space for additional enrollment.[7] At the same time, a recession set in and the school district was financially overextended.

Giving the rationale that financial savings would accrue from school consolidation as well as that rural and poor children would benefit from the stimulation of their higher-achieving counterparts in modern, well-equipped schools,[8] Edwards recommended that the small, older schools in the district be closed. The board backed his decision. Despite neighborhood protest, they already had closed two downtown schools. One was sold to the hospital for storage and staff training, the other to the university for an art studio annex. Edwards was proud that these closings earned a small profit and involved "interagency cooperation." It is particularly interesting that they got away with shutting down schools based on ideologies of the benefits of economy of scale while building neighborhood schools in new suburbs.[9] In 1968, which was the third year of Edwards's administration, the district changed from a city to a consolidated county district. Hillsdale was in the center of the county and outsized surrounding rural villages. Without asking county constituencies, Edwards and the board presumed they knew what was best for rural people—that they would want their children to go to suburban or consolidated schools—or at least that they would not protest too loudly. Patron input should have been garnered; rural parents vehemently protested and for a short time successfully resisted the centralization initiative.

At a time of dire economic straits, the agenda of school closings could not be diverted for long. Superintendent Edwards's remedy was to propose shutting down more elementary schools and three of the five middle schools. Parents of children whose beloved schools were on the chopping block vied for the board's attention, each group pleading with them to recognize the importance of keeping their particular school open. Parent Teacher Organizations throughout the county held endless meetings to come up with strategies to save their schools. For several months, school board meetings were raucous affairs as the board reluctantly listened to parent input. Instead of meeting at the usual room at the Central Administration Building, board meetings were held at the high school auditoriums to accommodate concerned patrons. These large venues were packed with standing-room-only crowds. In the end, 5 of the 18 district elementary schools and 3 of the 5 middle schools were closed. Four elementary schools were rural and mainly low-income. One was the last downtown school with a fairly heterogeneous but mainly high-income enrollment—my own neighborhood school.

A TIME TO RECUPERATE—AND GET EVEN

The county was torn apart by consolidation, school closings, and redistricting. Citizens were angry about the miscalculations that had resulted in unneeded new school construction and, ultimately, the spate of school closings. Certain parties began to investigate Edwards's actions and within a short time there was enough incriminating evidence against him that the board was forced to meet behind closed doors to consider what to do about this personnel issue. Although the public was not informed of the exact charges against Edwards, leaks to the press alluded to mismanagement of funds, irregular use of the bidding system for awarding builder and bus driver contracts, and illegal insider dealings connected with negotiations for building sites and materials. Evidence was sufficient to force Edwards's resignation. He might have gotten away with these actions if he had not alienated county residents enough so that they pressured elected officials to take action against him and his loyal sidekicks.

After the upheaval of school closings and recurring financial woes of the district under Edwards, the board of trustees was determined to find someone who might be able to cool the myriad of stirred-up tempers and return the district to financial solvency. Dr. Vernon Dieken, who had been superintendent of schools for over two decades in a town similar to Hillsdale,[10] was identified by Department of Education officials as a popular leader. He was among the few superintendents in the state who had kept his district in the black during the recession. Due to retire in a year, Dieken was not in the job market. However, because he and his wife planned to move to Hillsdale after his retirement, he agreed to be interviewed and with considerable coaxing was convinced to accept a 2-year contract as Hillsdale superintendent. He eventually consented to stay on a third year after a failed search for his replacement. At the time of the school closings, six board members were professors or spouses of professors. They were not born or raised in the Hillsdale area. This existing board expected to find a superintendent who would uphold the status quo of Edwards's superintendency. Although they thought they found such a person when they recruited Dr. Dieken, to their eventual consternation, Dieken was not unconditionally on their side nor could he be micromanaged.

Dieken started his career as a high school teacher and had been a high school principal for 8 years before becoming a superintendent. He was a calm, dignified-looking man with a head of wavy white hair and an easy smile. He listened more than he talked in most social exchanges. He was polite but firm and articulate when he disagreed with others. Comparatively open about his positions in debates, he got along famously with newspaper reporters and routinely got good press coverage. Edwards had been a guarded person who had not been very accessible to the press. Whereas his predecessor often had been captured in newspaper pictures at intense and unflattering moments, Dieken smiled out from newspaper pages or was pictured shaking hands with others or listening in group settings. Good press certainly helped him gain community trust during his time in office.

In characterizing Dieken's leadership, it seems reasonable to conclude that he had three major commitments. One was a strong sense of the importance of education to all members of the community, which therefore meant he supported school equity and soon set out to reduce disparities between schools. Second, he respected school personnel and treated them as professionals with ideas of their own, encouraging building-level initiatives and autonomy. He had excellent relations with the teachers' union. Third, when he came to Hillsdale, Dieken knew he had been hired to solve financial problems, so he did not demand a high salary himself, which probably accounted for why teachers did not press harder for wage increases. Except for remodeling older schools and improving their physical resources, he discouraged expenditures and budgeting for suburban schools decreased after his arrival. Within 3 years, Hillsdale no longer had a financial crisis. Dieken saw himself more as a manager than a leader with personal visions, so he allowed others to propose and commit themselves to building-level reform. Although respected by most Hillsdale residents for his openness, honesty, integrity, and frugality, Dieken was despised by powerful school patrons. He did not approve of heavy achievement-oriented stratification, so during his administration the number of advanced course sections in secondary schools was reduced. Teachers were happy with these changes, but Dieken alienated affluent parents by not giving in to their requests for tightly framed, hierarchically stratified schooling.

UNDERCURRENTS OF DISCONTENT IN THE DISENFRANCHISED

Low-income people who lived in older downtown areas of Hillsdale had long been bothered that their neighborhoods had lesser schools with outdated, hand-me-down texts and inadequate resources. They were bitter that their children were always sorted into the lowest levels of ability groups and tracks in secondary schools and were not part of the mainstream school culture (Brantlinger, 1985a, b, c). After consolidation, rural residents joined the ranks of the discontented. Closings of country schools started with high schools, then junior highs, and culminated with elementary school closings. They occurred between the time when parents and grandparents had attended country schools where they were known and important and the time their children and grandchildren had to compete for high tracks and popular extracurricular activity spots without much hope for winning in the large, distant consolidated schools. Upset that their schools, which had served as community centers, were closed, they were becoming increasingly frustrated by their children's complaints of being looked down upon by teachers and peers in consolidated schools.

A SUCCESSFUL AND SURPRISING TAKEOVER

Having weathered the stressful times and extreme hostility that accompanied school closings during Edwards's administration, the school board incumbents chose not to run for reelection. With the exception of middle schools and the older downtown school, schools in high-income neighborhoods had not been affected by the rash of closings. Indeed, as their schools gained enrollment from transferred students, suburban dwellers felt secure that they would stay open in the future. Affluent professionals who typically came forward as candidates for school board were not motivated to enter the race. Having won out in the school-closing fracas, they had few issues, so were relatively unconcerned about the upcoming election.

In contrast, rural citizens were outraged by the loss of schools. The closings brought out the latent town/gown tensions in an extreme form. Several rural candidates threw their hats in to run in the school board election and a slate of four conducted an energetic campaign. Because candidates from various parts of the county supported each other and had church affiliates who were rallied to come to the polls, to the surprise of everyone— even themselves—rural candidates won the election.[11] Their success was partly because high-income candidates and their usual supporters were complacent. Until the final moments, they failed to actively campaign or take much interest in the election. For the first time, five[12] board members were townees—long-term local residents who were not connected with the university. They were small-time farmers, businessmen (e.g., bait shop owner), and blue-collar workers.

These new school board trustees were not just angry at Edwards; they were aware of, and resented, affluent people's control of schools. Long-term Hillsdale residents rightly perceived that university-affiliated people had not been raised in Hillsdale or even in the state. They were aware that these outsiders looked down on local folks—put-downs were evident in descriptors (e.g., "hillbilly," "redneck," "ignorant," "hick," "bible-thumping") used for the candidates who emerged from the countryside to run for the board. An anomaly in Hillsdale, this working-class board was motivated to hear complaints from teachers and parents at low-income schools as they set out to redress obvious inequities in local schools. Rid of Edwards and pleased with Dieken's leadership, they searched for a superintendent who would champion their children's education. They found Pete Rockenweil, who espoused the themes of equity and educational excellence for *all*.[13]

Rockenweil had been superintendent for several years in a school system in a western state that was geographically widespread but small population-wise.

The district had a state university that drew from a within-state population and thus a small and indigenous educated class who had not exerted much pressure for educational distinctions for their children.[14] Based on sterling reference letters, it appeared that Rockenweil's constituents were happy with his administration. He had been a popular principal who followed a superintendent whose educational philosophy was similar to his own. Thus, in implementing his ideas about democratic schooling, he had not encountered opposition from parents, teachers, or other administrators. In contrast, these same reform initiatives would substantially change Hillsdale schools. Hired on the basis of his reform ideals, the board gave Rockenweil full support and free reign to implement them in the Hillsdale district.

A NEW BEGINNING: A ROCKY PATH

After two decades with one superintendent and 3 years with a stopover administrator, a new superintendent was front-page news. Wary of the board of trustees, the newspaper staff was not inclined to approve of anyone they selected. Two holdover board members who were somewhat loyal to Edwards leaked negative reports from private board proceedings to the press. The first attack leveled at Rockenweil was cronyism. Apparently, fairly late in contract negotiations and after his hiring was announced, Rockenweil insisted that he could not work toward his visions without the support of like-minded associates. He threatened to back out of his contract if the board did not comply with his request to hire three colleagues (assistant superintendent of secondary education, two principals) who had worked with him in the west. The next headline targeted Rockenweil's salary—a substantial leap from his predecessor—and the salaries of his companions, which were larger than the local norm. To make matters worse, there had been a miscommunication about when their jobs (salaries) were to start. They expected to be paid for summer months that the board had not figured on. These contentious negotiations were given the most negative slant possible for the bumbling board and greedy newcomers.

In 1987, Rockenweil's team arrived with a plan for total transformation of the curriculum and pedagogy of Hillsdale schools. Generally favoring the progressive, equitable educational ideas of heterogeneous grouping, constructivist curriculum, and inclusive access to instruction, they endorsed such popular reform ideas as interdisciplinary and collaborative instruction within block schedules for secondary students and nongraded, multiage family-oriented elementary classes. During the summer, year-round personnel were apprized of plans to be enacted as well as the time lines for the initial phases of the transition.[15] Principals, many of whom had been in their positions for two or three decades, initially were impressed with the new team's articulation of plans, energy, enthusiasm, and commitment to ideals.

Those at high-income or mixed schools were pleased to have a central administrator to back them if they refused to give in to pressures from influential parents. Principals at low-income schools were delighted that material and human resource redistribution started by Dieken were also part of Rockenweil's plan. Regardless of how they felt about specific reforms, principals knew Rockenweil had the school board's endorsement.

The reform initiative involved extensive teacher in-service. The assistant superintendents and principals set up training sessions for the teacher preparation days prior to the fall semester and were to follow up by observing teachers on a biweekly basis and "scripting" suggestions about changes they should make.[16] As the summer drew to a close, principals became increasingly worried about the reaction of teachers to this intrusion on their classroom privacy as well as to the expectation that they radically modify their teaching styles. Indeed, when they received the schedule for fall orientation, teachers were alarmed to discover what was in store for them. The first 2 days of the school year were usually designated for senior faculty to meet new teachers, go out to lunch with colleagues, and prepare their classrooms for students' arrival. This year they were confronted with 2 days of orientation to the reform, then had to sign up for administrator observations.

Because of the many years of declining enrollment, the Hillsdale teachers were very experienced. When there was a retirement or resignation, the district policy was to hire their own graduates; hence, new teachers were offspring or friends of practicing teachers and were socialized by them. Teachers were used to having autonomy in their classrooms and principals were content not to waste time evaluating experienced teachers. Teachers interpreted the emphasis on teacher in-service to mean that they were being blamed for the system's problems and were annoyed that they were portrayed as inadequate by a stranger to the district. Reform came to a standstill; however, Rockenweil did insist that the prescribed scripting designed for faculty development be continued. Administrators had few chances to observe because teachers called in sick on the days they were to be visited.

School personnel's responses to the potentially transformative, democratic initiatives were diverse and often conflicted. Sentiments expressed by teachers and administrators in interviews made it clear that *already there* teachers disapproved of the rural board members, Rockenweil, and his reforms. The first-generation teachers, in contrast, would have approved if the new administrators had employed different tactics in introducing them.[17] Instead of working with staff and allowing them time to understand and adjust to his ideas, Rockenweil made top-down pronouncements and demands; the democratic collaboration[18] he proselytized for teacher interactions with students and each other was not part of his own game plan in relating to faculty. By alienating *in-the-middle* teachers, Rockenweil failed to gain the support of the personnel who might have agreed with his reform ideas and reform agenda. Instead, there was district-wide resistance not only to his plans but to his administration. Teachers and parents at mixed- and lower-income schools did not take a visible stand on the particulars of Rockenweil's reform agenda but stood passively by as their more assertive counterparts at affluent schools objected.

TAKING BACK THE REINS: AFFLUENT PROFESSIONALS ON THE OFFENSIVE

Edwards moved in circles with upper-income school patrons and endeared himself to them by making sure their children got the best the system had to offer—little attention was paid to the fact that advantage for some meant a second-class education for others. After Edwards was forced to resign, the success of rural folks in the school board election was a surprise to affluent people. University-affiliated people were suspicious of the school board and thus were not inclined to approve of its superintendent selection. During the summer, the first round of reform efforts were aimed at the teacher and classroom levels, so what was coming down the pike might not have been apparent to parents. Yet word spread quickly in high-income neighborhoods where schools had survived the recent spate of school closings and where there often were close relations between teachers and parents.

When details of Rockenweil's reform plans began to creep into the newspaper, panic quickly spread. Once this educated class was aware of the nature of Rockenweil's reform initiatives, a flurry of what might be categorized as hysterical or paranoid letters appeared in the paper. Eastsiders turned out at board meetings in droves. When confronted by these outspoken citizens, rural board members became defensive and hostile. Rockenweil tried to convince those who attended meetings as well as the local press about the reasonableness of his ideas; however, when his explanations made it clear that rumors about dismantling tracking were true, his audience became more irate and activist. Confronted with the prospect of losing honors and gifted and talented programs, Eastsiders united in expressing opposition. Groups organized to circulate petitions to halt the proposed changes. Newspaper coverage of the turmoil surrounding the would-be reform was, as usual, tactful in portraying the influential Eastsiders but antagonistic toward the trustees and administration.

What congenial personality Rockenweil might have had under calmer circumstances was not apparent when he was besieged by the groundswell of belligerent criticism—he was tense and aloof in public appearances and looked stern in media pictures in which he was inevitably encircled by his three colleagues—strangers who looked equally grim and unappealing. Rockenweil did not ingratiate himself to powerful university-affiliated patrons, perhaps because he misjudged their educational perspectives and/or underestimated their power to thwart his plans. Yet, unlike *in-the-middle* faculty, regardless of how Rockenweil approached these parents, they would not have endorsed reforms designed to take away their children's privileged education. When he tried to increase school equity and curricular access, those who benefitted from segregation and advantage—affluent parents, students, and teachers—promptly rose in protest.

Rockenweil and his team were advocates of progressive and democratic school reform. Because such ideals are associated with the educated classes and a liberal standpoint, it would seem that the majority of university-affiliated patrons would approve and less educated rural people would be against this reform. For reasons explained in chapters 3 and 4 however, east-side parents were content with the status quo of pedantically taught subject matter and segregation of social classes. Because he was cognizant of Hillsdale's heavily stratified pupil grouping structure, it seems that Rockenweil might have tried to seek out constituencies who potentially would have supported him. It is unclear where the supposed supporters of progressive and democratic education were during this fractious time. Perhaps the ferociousness of the east-side bloc's reaction made them wary of getting involved. Maybe it was that Rockenweil was a stranger who had forged ahead independently without gaining the trust of seemingly like-minded individuals. It may have been that the left-wing factions of the community, whose children often had attended the downtown schools that were closed, were battle-worn from their unsuccessful fight to prevent school closings or they were divided at having to make hard choices about which schools their children would attend after the closings. I think the most likely answer is that people who are radical in their scholarly work or about environmental and international peace issues are not as socially minded about their own children's education.

In response to the threat of progressive democratic reform, east-side vigilantes rallied a coalition powerful enough to take back control of school politics. Without mentioning their own agenda to increase and solidify advanced tracking, and couching their campaign slogans in the rhetoric of "excellence in education," a slate of parents of gifted and talented students ran a well-orchestrated, heavily financed, and much-publicized campaign for the next school board election. Commissioning expensive newspaper advertisements ensured kind treatment by the press. The slate, which included a doctor, lawyer, and two professors' wives, was elected by a landslide. Rural incumbents lost their seats.[19] Power swung back to its usual brokers, Rockenweil's contract was terminated, and his entourage was dismissed from their administrative positions.

Most people do not talk about Rockenweil. When they do, it is about greed, cronyism, and disrespect for teachers. As one who has long observed and critiqued the deeply embedded social class disparities in Hillsdale, I believe that Rockenweil's administration was ultimately brought down because he tried to dismantle the class-based hierarchies in district schools. This aspect of his being fired is not talked about. Rockenweil's team had the audacity to talk openly about the taboo subject of social class. They refused to be subdued by hegemonic discourse that touted the "unrealistic nature of ideals" in a town with such class-divergent and educationally disparate populations as exist in Hillsdale. Antielitist straight talk and action were not to be tolerated by the powerful, affluent, well-educated people.

RECUPERATING FROM DEMOCRATIC REFORM

Rockenweil was replaced by a retiring special education director who agreed to be acting superintendent for a year, then by an outsider to the district from 1989 to 1994. In 1994, after another failed search, Bill Calhoun, a former high school principal who at the time was personnel director and thus an insider to Hillsdale Schools, agreed to serve as interim superintendent. He was not a candidate for the permanent position because he did not have a doctorate. Like Dieken, Calhoun was born, raised, and educated within the state, started his career as a high school social studies teacher, then high school principal. He was popular with school personnel. Also like Dieken, but in contrast to Edwards, Calhoun was known for being accessible, open to new ideas, and concerned about equity. Rockenweil had not been able to put a dent in the class-biased system that prevailed in Hillsdale, whereas Dieken and Calhoun accomplished some of Rockenweil's proposed reforms because they had widespread support from teachers, positive press coverage, and, perhaps most importantly, were discreet in discussing changes. Another essential factor was that because they did not expect a long tenure or feel obliged to please the east-side power elite to retain their jobs, they acted on principle.

CLASS POLITICS IN THE 1990s

A positive consequence of the early 1980s school closings was that instead of five middle schools segregated by social class (two predominantly high-income, one low-income, one rural, one mixed), Hillsdale's two remaining middle schools were located on the north and south sides of town like the two high schools, so they cut across east–west social class residential patterns and had class-heterogeneous enrollments. In the early 1990s, the school-age population increased. Certain parents complained that middle schools were too large, so a decision was made to build a new middle school. Without public input in deciding on the location, a leak to the press indicated that it was to be built on the southeast side of town adjacent to a city park. It was not surprising that the site was in the center of an area with new affluent suburbs. My immediate reaction was that this would become the elite middle school and the existing two schools, especially the south-side school, would be seen as second rate as had been the pattern with the five class-distinctive middle schools in the 1990s.

A group of west-side members of the Bluffton Elementary Parent–Teacher Organization had the same concern. One had read my book, *The Politics of Social Class in Secondary School,* and he contacted me and asked me to go with the group to the board to protest the lack of community input in the decision on location and to persuade the board to consider a more neutral site. In the meantime, we investigated other locations in the county and came up with possibilities that would not alter the heterogeneity of current middle school enrollments. Because the newspaper editor was married to a teacher at a west-side school and the educational reporter's children attended west-side schools, our position was given positive press coverage in editorials, feature articles, and our own letters to the editor. Board meetings were broadcast over community access television and were widely viewed. At the end of some tumultuous confrontations between supporters of the proposed site and our opposition, the board voted to support the proposed east-side location. At the same time, they promised our group that they would ensure a mixed enrollment including children from two low-income schools and that they were constituting a redistricting committee to address our concerns about class segregation in the elementary schools.

The appointed 25-member redistricting committee with district-wide representation met for about a year. They were divided into subcommittees, and the five-member committee who were to consider diversity issues read *The Politics of Social Class* and met with me on two occasions. At these subgroup meetings, one member, a psychology professor, was openly hostile not only toward my position that schools should have a social class balance but toward me. A colleague of hers told me that she was obsessed about the possible negative repercussions of redistricting on her own young children and "extremely angry and insulted" at my portrayal of high-income parents as wanting exclusive circumstances for their children. The three working-class mothers on the committee all called me privately with their concern that she was dominating their subgroup report. The fifth member, a neighbor and acquaintance who had been appointed to the committee because she was active in the League of Women Voters, could only convey her concern that I was so openly radical. In the meantime, I sent the board ideas about ways they could achieve a greater degree of social class balance in schools without having to put more children on buses.

The redistricting committee's recommendation essentially left the existing catchment zones intact. I was not surprised. When I learned of the composition of the committee and noted that the chair was someone I have thought of as the penultimate of middle-class respectability, I was not optimistic about the outcome. Three board members, however, had been persuaded by my arguments about the benefits of social class desegregation. The night before they were to vote on the committee's recommendation, one called and asked if she and two others could come to my house to discuss my alternate plan. We brainstormed about how to convince one other member to vote against the committee recommendation. In the end, we were unsuccessful. Two of the members who voted against the plan as well as one who voted for it were interviewed by Michelle Henderson, a graduate student in education, and their views are included in chapter 8. The new middle school still includes the students from Southside Elementary and a rural school, so there is some social class mix. Nevertheless, as wealthy suburbs expand on the southeast—especially because parents who want their children to attend the new middle school buy houses in the area expressly for that purpose—and as school board members who promised not to let it become an exclusive school are replaced by other affluent parents who do not know the history of their commitment, it is inevitable that the two outlying lower-income schools eventually will be redistricted based on the neighborhood school ideology.

THE PERSPECTIVES OF CENTRAL ADMINISTRATORS

Edwards and Rockenweil left immediately after their respective terminations, so they were not interviewed. Two superintendents (Dieken, Calhoun) and Rockenweil's assistant superintendents (Hale, Husby) were interviewed and their perspectives are summarized in this section.

BRINGING ORDER TO CHAOS

In telling his own story, Dr. Vernon Dieken said that he felt fortunate to have been reared in a small rural community. Although his own high school had "limited equipment and limited options—typical of high schools in the forties—it had quality, dedicated teachers." Perhaps more important to Vernon was his sense that it had a "mission and a purpose" that students and others in the community understood. Students had been happy to be there because they "enjoyed the classroom, books, materials, and activities and tended to be optimistic about their futures." Dieken recalled that he had been "a well-organized hard worker with good work habits who challenged myself and was challenged by my teachers and parents."

When asked to evaluate current education, Dieken focused on a theme that he returned to many times: how schools should respond to public demands for accountability. Bothered that "education is the dumping grounds for politicians" and "people attach their fears for the future to a sense that educators are delinquent and irresponsible," he worried that "schools are to accomplish everything—too much—and that expectations are so beyond the ability of teachers that they feel overwhelmed." In contrast to his own education, Dieken felt the present curriculum was "too inclusive and not well ordered, so teachers are often unaware of what has been previously taught and skim the surface of ideas of too many subjects. It would be better if schools focused on a few things and taught them thoroughly." In spite of an obvious nostalgia for "a simpler school life of the past," he also claimed that "a weakness is that schools maintain outdated traditions such as the 9-month school year." Although Dieken had been a high school teacher for only 5 years before he began to climb the career ladder to become a very young principal, he clearly identified with teachers and often responded from their perspective. His sense of being part of a team, rather than outside it or above it, and his respect for teachers accounted for his popularity among school personnel. A strength of education was that "teachers are well prepared and committed to the responsibility of helping students learn." He felt that people should be proud that schools "are outstanding, well-equipped, and well-funded facilities."

Before reporting on the rest of the interview, it may be valuable to describe my own interactions with Dieken. Upon his arrival in Hillsdale, I sent him the 20-page report entitled *What a Model Community Sweeps Under the Rug: Class Discrimination in the Schools,* which I had given to Edwards and his board. This document detailed social class inequities that I felt needed to be addressed. Although he never got back to me to say whether he had read the report, Dieken corrected many of the problems during his administration that I identified, with the exception of a major redistricting to achieve a social class balance in elementary schools. Admittedly, the latter would have been an enormous and hotly contested undertaking. During the interview, I was unsure whether Dieken associated me with that report or whether he was aware that I had been part of the small group that persisted in bringing class disparities to the attention of Edwards and his board of school trustees, even threatening legal action if policies and practices resulting in inequities were not changed. Dieken's demeanor during our contact was so polite and formal that I hesitated to ask him if he was aware of my activism around class issues.

When I called to request the interview, he greeted me as if he knew me and promptly invited me to come to his home the next day. His wife brought us coffee and cookies and sat with us and chatted a while. He did not try to rush the interview and I was at his house for more than 2 hours. My admiration for Dieken grew as I heard my own opinions and sentiments reverberate through his replies. Those more cynical than myself might conclude that this savvy politician was posturing to please and appease me. At the time of the interview, however, Dieken had been retired for almost 4 years and had refused to run for a third term on the school board. At age 72, he and his wife had "ambitious travel dreams to pursue before it was too late." His animated references to class inequities convinced me that the empathy he attributed to "growing up in a small town where people were concerned about each other"[20] was genuine. Through newspaper reports, occasional attendance at board meetings,[21] and conversations with teachers and principals, I came to trust Dieken as someone who had the integrity to act on principle and the gumption to stand up to the elitism he condemned. I felt that he might have addressed class disparities on his own without the impetus of our group's information sharing and pressure for democratic reform. Nevertheless, external pressure would have helped Dieken convince the board of the need to reduce the inequities between high- and low-income schools.

In spite of his reputation for redressing a number of local wrongs related to social class, Dieken initially seemed compelled to be a tactful administrator who gave evasive responses during his interview to certain questions about the nature of social class relations in Hillsdale. For example, when asked to evaluate and discuss the quality of eight local schools (four with high-income and four with low-income enrollments), he responded that each was a "fine school." After making this same evaluation eight times regarding each school, he sat back, looked at me with a serious and somewhat regretful look on his face, and said:

> Look, I know how everybody else sees the quality of these [low-income] schools. I see this from a different perspective than others. Some are better schools than others in terms of adequacy of facility or the nature of the school community. The children in some schools have parents with more educational background, and the schools are typed because of these families. I tried to improve the facilities of some neighborhood schools so that they would be more equivalent to the rest in the community. But you can't change the impression made by school composition. For example, we improved Southside[22] so that it has among the best facilities in town, but, because of the quality of the school enrollment, it still has the reputation of being a weaker school—the concept about that school as a lesser school holds. People don't want their children to go there.

Although he observed that there was a negative stigma attached to schools in low-income areas, Dieken admitted to being "strongly committed to accepting the concept of neighborhood schools." Again, he did not mention the fact that over the years before he came to Hillsdale the district had been gerrymandered so that school enrollments were mostly class homogeneous. By looking at a map of school catchment zones, it would be evident to anyone that *de jure* as well as *de facto* segregation had been at work. Although a calm, smiley, soft-spoken man, Dieken looked troubled and his tone increased in volume and intensity as he forcefully asserted: "Putting kids on buses is a waste of time and money!" When asked about school equivalency, he elaborated:

> People just tend to live where they can afford to live.[23] When they can afford to live in better neighborhoods, they do. I am a proponent of the neighborhood school and believe that the concept has not created any kind of problem. I do know that television has raised aspirations of people in general. The Coleman reports did more disservice than service. We failed to keep older schools up-to-date. Low-income neighborhoods have older schools. They are left out of the process of getting new equipment and these schools soon become have-not schools. As an administrator, I was aware of this and made a conscious effort to serve the low-income establishment.[24] Now the facilities in high- and low-income areas are not wide-rangingly different. Probably, the poorest facilities are still the low-income ones, like Westside and Hillview. In terms of equipment, we have made a conscientious effort to provide equipment (computers, video cameras) with a high degree of standardization so that all schools get the same. They all have media centers and teachers have equal access to these centers. Whether they use them equally, I don't know. It is true that some of the low-income schools are the smallest schools, so don't have full-time librarians, nurses, and support staff like the larger schools. But we have not intentionally short-changed low-income schools. We have quit that part-time administrator business.

When asked whether school personnel distinctions resulted from involuntary transfers of inadequate teachers to low-income schools, Dieken was uncomfortable as he vaguely claimed:

> Teachers are assigned according to vacancies. In using the involuntary transfer method, I didn't note that teachers requested the better schools. I think they usually choose according to residential neighborhood—they choose schools close to where they live.[25] We have good teacher stability in Hillsdale.

Dieken puzzled about how low-income people might feel about equity issues and admitted his contacts with low-income members of the community were limited: "I do not have a good sense of how low-income people feel. I tried to get involved with Boys Club and Girls Club and other social agencies, but I still got a superficial view." His impression of cross-class contact among secondary students was: "By and large, children accept each other. I imagine there is some conflict and an occasional fight based on a game or incident of the moment rather than family background." In explaining social class differences in achievement outcomes, Dieken stated:

> Clearly the aspirations of high-income students are much greater than those of low-income students. I'm sure some low-income parents, such as single parents, have high aspirations. As a total class, aspirations of low-income parents and students are lower—and Hillsdale is not atypical in this regard. Still, low-income parents are glad for their children to graduate from high school. They see this as a major accomplishment. But university-related people have much higher aspirations and that makes a difference in the education they receive. I equate parental interest with attendance at conferences and only a small percentage don't come.

Dieken felt that special education was progress for some students but had misgivings about the increased rate of the mildly handicapped classification:

> Over a 20-year period we have responded to families feeling the need to have their seriously handicapped children educated. And this is fine. Previously they were "hiding." Instead of going to schools which were operated by families through fund-raising, the severe and profound were taught in special schools, which was better, but it soon became mandatory for public school teachers to be trained and for programs to be in schools that met the needs of the whole spectrum. That is fine. But, personally, the learning disabilities classification bothers me. I think that group is nebulously defined. There is a tendency to put some in learning disabilities classrooms and others—of a different race— in classes for mentally handicapped. The rapid increase in classified children resulted from vague definitions. We redefined some mentally handicapped children as learning disabled to keep them in their home schools. Principals felt that it didn't seem reasonable to send them elsewhere—that it defeated the needs of children. Besides, it was much easier to get parents to agree to their children being LD. Mental retardation is a stigma on the family—the parents see the label as reflecting on themselves.

When asked if the students in special education classes were primarily from low-income backgrounds, Dieken hesitated:

> I don't know. I really don't think so. But, maybe, maybe so. To the best of my knowledge, special education was not designed as a discriminatory practice, but it did result in discrimination. During my administration, I got kids sent back to their home schools and I made sure that special education classrooms had access to central space.

When asked if the education of poor children was equivalent to that received by affluent children, Dieken pondered:

It is hard to know if education of the poor is adequate—*equivalent* is a nebulous word. Educational opportunities for children from poor families are virtually the same as for those from high-income families. Then we have to ask if applying an equal standard of opportunity for meeting the needs of some children who have not demonstrated the same achievement is adequate. High-risk programs follow compensatory education guidelines regulated by the federal government. Based on my experience, I can't conceive of what we could have done differently to get different results.

In terms of his opinions about ability grouping and tracking, Dieken said:

Personally, I support the concept of heterogenous grouping. I think there are benefits of grouping children from different levels together. But children regroup themselves for social reasons. And we have to meet the demands of gifted children.[26]

At the end of the interview, after I had praised Dieken for his accomplishments in terms of achieving material equality at various schools, he spent at least a half hour at the door speaking off the record and more from his heart. Perhaps because my tape recorder was not running, he spoke earnestly about his regret about the class discrimination he now acknowledged was widespread in Hillsdale.[27] He confessed to feeling "a little uneasy about not having taken a stronger stand on tracking," then said: "Active parents put immense pressure on central administrators to increase the number of advanced courses offered at the junior high and high school levels" and "principals tend to have their hands tied, so give in to the demands of the active and influential people who make requests." Dieken said concern about continuing to combat these "personalized agendas of powerful people" was the reason he ran for school board after he retired. He was open about his alarm at the slate of candidates running for school board who "had an agenda and a prejudice and did not have the needs of the whole community in their hearts." Four parents (a doctor, a lawyer, and two professors' wives) of gifted and talented children were campaigning vigorously for reelection at the time and they were not admirers of Dieken. As is addressed in chapter 8, people probably run because of a personal agenda, although their rhetoric conceals personal ambitions for their children.

INTERIM SUPERINTENDENT BUT NOT THEIR GUY

Bill Calhoun became acting superintendent in 1994 after having served a few years in central administration as personnel director. Rumor had it that Calhoun wanted the permanent job but also that the board had insisted on hiring someone with a doctorate to prevent him from getting it. As principal, Calhoun had not been as enthusiastic about honors and gifted and talented programs as some parents (including those currently on the board) would have liked. Besides, Calhoun came from a rural within-the-state background and it showed. He had been All But Dissertation for a decade and was frustrated that the school administration doctoral program was "confused about its mission" and was "modeled after a Ph.D. in history, when it should resemble law or medical school—less academic and more practitioner oriented." His successor, George Schiller, was hired the next year and Cahoun went back to teaching for a while before he was hired as superintendent of a rural district not far from Hillsdale.

Like Dieken, Calhoun grew up in a "small cohesive community where everyone knew each other" and he described his own schooling as positive. He got along well socially and was the salutatorian of his class. Calhoun had good feelings about his undergraduate education at a small, private liberal arts college in the state. His instructors had doctorates, which Calhoun felt had a positive impact on the quality of his education. Calhoun was glad that he had majored in liberal arts (history) as an undergraduate because he felt that it broadened his knowledge and shaped his value system. When he came to the university the next year, he was ready for a larger institution. He finished a master's of education degree and landed a job as a high school social studies teacher in Hillsdale. Within the decade, he acquired an administrator's license and had become vice principal, then principal of one of the two Hillsdale high schools, a position he held for several years before he became personnel director for the district.

Calhoun echoed Dieken's concern that too much was expected of schools, so students and teachers faced many pressures:

> I worry about the ambiguity surrounding the mission of schools. We have a problem deciding and agreeing on the purpose of schools. We aren't sure what we are responsible for. After Sputnik, schools were given clear signals to pursue academic goals. Since that time we have been handed many social responsibilities. For example, to accommodate parents' working schedules we offer extended care programs from 6 A.M. to 6 P.M. The list of our responsibilities is endless. Teachers wrestle with what to teach. What content to choose is a persistent problem. Some societies may be less change oriented than ours. For us, curriculum questions are difficult to answer. The national goals always focus on cognitive areas. Yet, I feel, we give too little attention to the affective. Although discipline has not been a big problem in this county, drugs have been a problem. In this regard, parents are sometimes more involved in drugs than the kids and they are sometimes indulgent with their kids.

Like Dieken, Calhoun was perceived as identifying closely with teachers even though he had been an administrator for many years. When he was a principal, he ate in the teachers' room and teachers obviously were comfortable with him. He was particularly close to the special education teachers and most days sat with them and a few general education teachers who joined them. His concern about education was that "teaching can be lonely. We have tried a variety of programs, including the mentor program, to try to counteract the loneliness and isolation of teachers."

Calhoun described the ideal student as one "who has been taught what they need to know so they can teach themselves the rest. They have to know how to find information and how to process it—how to weigh alternatives. If they learn to do that, then they can so something with their education." However, Calhoun noted: "Too often we encourage passive students. As Dewey said, kids should be doing. It helps them understand; it may even help them keep memory." When asked about the purpose of education, Calhoun asserted:

> We say the purpose of education is one thing and then don't do it. We say, for example, that education is to transmit heritage—and then we don't do that. We say we want kids to think. But what about? We aren't sure what is good or bad. We have a hard time having our schools focus on major issues. We know what the issues are, yet we won't let teachers talk about them.

When I praised Calhoun for his effectiveness as a principal, he replied that although he received positive evaluations from others, he was not always satisfied with his own performance:

> Schools are too big. A school is too big if the principal doesn't know everyone. In my own experience [as a student] in high school, all the teachers knew everyone. Large schools don't transmit values well. Improving attendance is an unbelievably large challenge.

In comparing his four children's education to his own, Calhoun remarked:

> Better now. At least technologically better—better in science. Better in offering a broader range of services. Yet we still have egg crates.[28] Teachers are better in that they know more about the art and science of teaching, but I'm not sure they are as committed as my teachers. That may be true of society generally. Opportunities are better. Still, kids need to be in a less competitive environment. More attention to affect is needed. Schools are better academically, but not affectively. My affective experiences in school were better than my kids. I would trade the cognitive for the affective. My cognitive experience wasn't that bad. Attention to kids' hurting and sense of self-worth are critical.

He noted that his wife, a teacher, "spent the first month of school creating family in her class."

Calhoun had mixed feelings about special education. In recalling that his own schools had no special education classes yet had "handled slow learners quite well. Everyone just came along. Everybody was included." One of Calhoun's sons had been identified as learning disabled, and Calhoun clearly generalized many of his ideas about special education from his experiences with his son. As he said: "We all knew Mike was slow, but everybody included him. We have to make sure we don't segregate the slow kids." As a high school principal, Calhoun had been an early advocate for inclusion and began an initiative that resulted in the school's being a model for other schools planning to implement inclusion.

Calhoun did not bring up social class, race, or gender issues and used "diversity" in narrow reference to children with disabilities. In spite of making the global judgment that schools "dealt with diversity fairly well," when the topic of social class distinctions in local schools was initiated, he hesitantly but seriously made the observation that there was not much mixing of people from different social classes. He noted there was almost none at the elementary school level because of the location of neighborhood schools in wealthy and poor parts of town but claimed that there was more "mixing" at the middle and secondary levels. Calhoun went on to comment that there was very little mixing in community organizations. As he pondered the topic, he noted that "even scouts are organized by neighborhoods." At first he mentioned that churches might contain the most diversity, then changed his mind after thinking about it and remarked that churches were also divided into social class-homogeneous congregations.

It seemed that Calhoun was responding to questions about social class as if it were the first time he had thought about them. He may not have noticed the extent of class separation—an explanation hard to believe given that he had worked in a place where class difference and segregation are obvious. It is more likely that he saw social class segregation as a natural part of everyday life. Calhoun did note that "tension" was more apparent in school—a place where diverse children were brought together—than in the community where the families lived segregated residential and social lives. He recalled that as personnel director for the school system, he considered the academic credentials of teachers (the courses that they had and how well they did), but also, "because the student population is very diverse," he felt the "teaching population needed to be diverse as well." In this case, by "diversity" he meant "race."[29] Calhoun said that as a white male he had not personally experienced discrimination yet did recall that as a graduate student he took a history class and the professor advised him to

drop it, saying that as an education degree candidate he would have difficulty in it. Calhoun got *A*s on his exams and papers but received a B in the
course because he was not a departmental major. That was his only recol-
lection of having experienced discrimination.

In stating his preferences about local schools, he claimed none were
unacceptable, but Westside, Downing, Hillview, Southside (low-income
schools), and Eastside Elementary were "more acceptable." Calhoun noted
Eastside had "potential to be a yuppie school," but it was not due to the
international students' children who attended it. The rationale for his choice
was they were heterogeneous, whereas Beauford, Kinder, and Richards
"lacked heterogeneity" and he would "rather not educate my children in an
elitist environment." In spite of these declarations, his four children had
attended Richards and Beauford and his wife taught at Beauford. Perhaps
Calhoun answered in the way he did because he had known me and my
interest in social class for about 20 years at the time of the interview.

REMAINING LOYAL AFTER THE MENTOR IS GONE

Derek Hale had accompanied Rockenweil from the western school district
to be assistant superintendent for secondary education in Hillsdale. This
role encompassed responsibility for the professional development of secondary principals and teachers as well as coordinating junior high and high
school programs. Hale's contract as a central administrator was rescinded
when Rockenweil was fired, but he stayed on as an acting high school principal.[30] Shortly after the interview, Hale left Hillsdale to join Rockenweil,
who had taken an administrative job in another state. Hale consistently used
"we," which sometimes seemed to refer to people in general but usually to
himself and Rockenweil.

Like Dieken and Calhoun, Hale was the first in his family to go to college. He confessed: "Initially, teaching was just a job. I wanted to be a
teacher so I could coach. I didn't understand the relationship between
teaching and coaching. My experience of student teaching changed this."
Hale credits his student teaching supervisor with "pointing out the connections and shaping me into an effective, motivated teacher." A picture of
that man was displayed on a shelf in his office. Hale also praised his first
department chair for his "commitment to lifelong learning and growth,"
concluding: "Both shared a view that every student could learn." The third
role model identified by Hale was Pete Rockenweil, first his principal, then
superintendent in the western state. Hale eagerly claimed that Rockenweil
"experienced great success as a superintendent in the West; he's someone
who makes a difference."

Regarding the strong points of current education, Hale stated: "We give access to education to everyone. It's powerful to be part of that." Then said:

> Many, many people in the school system—though not all—have a deep commitment to education. A weakness is that there is a chasm between what we know and our ability to change important behaviors and what we actually do. In education we too often focus on beans, buses, and budgets.

In spite of their poor track record in gaining teacher consensus—or perhaps because of failed attempts—in retrospect, Hale maintained: "The secret to professional development is not telling someone how to do it but joining arms together to solve problems." He asserted: "My mission is to move teaching and teachers out of isolation." Although he never mentioned his dismissal from central administration, Hale did admit: "Change has slowed down here." When asked about his most negative professional experience, Hale quickly responded: "Encountering teachers who I have been unable to help—who I had to fire. I feel it's my fault."

The importance of student success and positive affect surfaced continuously as Hale talked. His ideal student was "someone who has a vision about himself that is positive—that feels good about himself as a human being." Of great concern was "too many children/people do not have confidence and this is reflected through the generations." He reiterated: "Each child has the right to perceive himself as a successful learner!" When asked to picture a child in the school system, he said: "I think of that kid positively. The student is thinking and feeling 'I belong in school. People here care about me and know me as a human being.' " In addressing the current issues facing public schools, Hale fervently expounded:

> My idea is that we now have the ability to help anyone learn about anything—95% of people can learn 95% of anything. I really believe that learning becomes a question of resources and how resources are distributed. The question for us now is are we willing to make that commitment and change our behavior in schools. We have to decide what is worth learning. What do children have the right to expect? One of those things that children have the right to expect is a successful learning experience. We should not fail kids. We should not tell them that they are not able learners. We have to create a mindset in all students that they can learn. This is not a tradition in most schools in this country. Locally, up until now we have had the opposite. We've had a ladder that people fall off of at different points—we've had a sorting out of students. This is the key issue that concerns us. We have ideas, but public education is very bureaucratic and difficult to move. Those who are unwilling to grow—who like to be secure and stable—need to examine the situation. Since change is seen as demanding inordinate resources, we have consequently

sought to increase the role of business and industry to contract with us to provide particular services. That approach may result in money making and cost effectiveness, but in the end we need to examine the situation and ask who are our clients and how well are we serving them. When we refer to at-risk kids, we are not just talking about certain kids. At-risk kids can be any kids.

Hale then told a story of a "good student" who one day just disappeared and noted that this kid who was a high achiever from a middle-class home "should also be considered to be 'at risk.'"

Hale was more than willing to discuss his concerns about Hillsdale schooling. Although he claimed that as a newcomer he had "limited exposure and information," Hale noted: "There seems to be little class contact in this town in elementary schools, and as soon as they get to the high schools, they are class segregated in tracks." Then, in an animated way, Hale conjectured:

> Everyone wants to teach the stars because it's really fun. There are not enough supermotivated kids for all who want them. As administrators we should consider where we are putting our new, rookie teachers and where superstar teachers should be used. In a community where 50% of the kids are high ability and the other 50% are poor, these are conditions that support the creation of tracks. This has clearly created a caste system. We have a rigid tracking system in which gifted and talented are at the top, then honors, then another high level, and then the basic track. Students at that level are dramatically different. They don't expect to learn. They're given *Weekly Readers* (in some cases) to read with a few little activities. Hillsdale has more tracking than most towns. Because English core and math core are that way, social studies follows and then all other classes in the schedule follow. We get all homogeneously grouped classrooms. Art classes and the basic choirs get unsuccessful learners; the [prestigious] swing choir is filled with superstars.[31]

This form of enthusiastic speech—and its implications for the district—was exactly what caused his former boss Rockenweil trouble in the district.

In addition to his concerns about tracking, Hale expressed dismay at the national and local growth in children classified as disabled:

> If kids don't fit in, they test them. Once we put a label on them, then teachers think "they are yours, not mine." The way we fund special education rewards schools for finding more disabled kids. We weren't remediating, they were gone forever. As a principal I wouldn't allow that to happen. We need special educators to help regular teachers be successful with learning problems to help teachers generate solutions for learning problems. Even if a kid is dyslexic, we can help him wrestle with the same concepts as other kids. Itinerant programs can help. We've got to take labels away. They are destructive.

Hale was a strong advocate for heterogeneous grouping, which was "more reflective of the basic values of our society. There are no disadvantages to mixed groupings, but there are challenges. People like to be around folks who look the same and behave the same." It was difficult not to feel that I was in one of his school personnel in-services when he then gave the following example of an approach he had implemented as a principal:

> When I was back west, we had Wolf Packs, a kind of homeroom concept, which met every day for 20 minutes with the specific objective of becoming a team that would go through school together. My job as principal was to shake hands with kids who were graduating prepared for the future they wanted. Everybody else (teachers) set on this goal too for their 15 to 20 students. We did something similar to this here prior to the state-required testing. We broke up the staff and had teachers meet several times a week with small groups of heterogeneously grouped kids to tell them what the test was about. You know what was remarkable during the week that we tested, teachers said: "We've never seen our kids so well behaved." Those kids (the ones in low tracks) are always with poor role models. In this setting, we had spread them out. They were with kids they had never been with, who they perhaps admired. Their behavior was *so* different. Now Johnnie, the outlaw, may be sitting next to Susie, the cheerleader, and now he's not an outlaw. Faculty commented on how nice it was to see those different kinds of kids together, taking breaks together, going out to buy a pop together. Social class becomes hidden because it is our blind side—we don't want to see it.
>
> I observed classrooms at South. In one class, kids are presenting themselves as successful figures in class. In another class, they're just reading the *Weekly Reader*—only they're not really reading it. Many are making vulgar signs on it. I know that it's in expectations. It's the way we treat kids that we haven't noticed. We have lower expectations for kids from poor homes who don't have braces on their teeth, who don't smell very good. We plan to do an analysis of the state test data on the basis of sex and SES. When we did this in the west, the teachers realized the nature and breadth of the problem.

Hale discussed attitudes "in the west" nostalgically, but in the interview he never gave direct accounts of the failure to implement similar reforms in Hillsdale.

Hale had six school-age children from two marriages. The youngest three, two of whom were preschoolers, lived with him. Although Hale felt that he had been "better taught" than his own children, "they had access to a greater variety of learning experiences." Because Hale had bought an older home on the west side of the city, his son went to Hillview, a school attended predominantly by low-income children, although because of redistricting after a new elementary school was built and some gentrification of west-side neighborhoods, Hillview had a somewhat more heterogeneous enrollment than previously. As Hale said: "At a Christmas concert at Hillview you see both social class extremes. There is the parent with the finest camera equipment and the parent who does not have a coat even though it's cold out." Hale was generally satisfied with his son's education, claiming that he was learning about people in a way he would not have at a high-income school. Although Hale claimed "Hillview is fine," he said:

> My druthers would be Westside. Westside has a super principal.[32] It has a loving, accepting, and caring environment. Teachers are just that way. The principal has brought these teachers together with a commitment to young people. Everybody feels they belong; students have real dignity.

Hale maintained that all Hillsdale schools were acceptable except Kinder and Beauford, and he eliminated those on the grounds that:

> They have artificial environments where most kids are more similar to each other and not as diverse as at other schools. The skewed population can easily permit average students to be seen as poor. Because the pressure is high, adjustment problems are more likely to be high. I'm not sure that I want my kids to have all that pressure. Some students can get a good education anywhere in town; others can accidentally get a good education. But kids with low skills at Beauford would really be at risk. I think we need to take a serious look at this kind of environment.

Compared to Dieken and Calhoun, Hale was more enthusiastic and fluent in articulating a democratic theoretical educational perspective. Yet he conveyed an assurance that verged on arrogance of the correctness of his own views. He never alluded to teachers' ideas. He also spoke disparagingly of low-income families, for example, he expressed the common belief: "Many families don't see much value in learning. That 'got to get that diploma' is not an attitude they represent." So, in many ways, Dieken and Calhoun's more respectful and humble views positioned them more squarely in the equity camp. After Rockenweil's contract was terminated and he left town, many mixed- and low-income elementary schools independently and aggressively moved to nongraded family arrangements and the inclusion of students classified as disabled in general education classrooms. Few attribute this to a legacy of Rockenweil's brief and conflicted administration, yet I believe that his ideas did stimulate principals and teachers to think critically about their ability grouping, tracking, and segregated special education practices. Nevertheless, secondary schools have reverted back to hierarchical grouping, particularly under the pressures from a board of school trustees who ran because of their interest in increasing gifted and talented programs and advanced placement and honors sections.

A LESSON IN SURVIVAL

Assistant superintendent for elementary education, Dr. Scot Husby,[33] supervised elementary teachers and principals, monitored the elementary-level curriculum, and oversaw a week-long outdoor education program for fifth graders. He had also assumed responsibility for understanding and interpreting state initiatives and regulations for the school corporation. He began in this position under Superintendent Edwards and retained it through the administrations of Dieken, Rockenweil, and Calhoun. Husby got along with his bosses of various ideological persuasions and with disparate administrative agendas seemingly equally well. His tenacity in the changing system was certainly due to the fact that he was knowledgeable about education and worked hard but perhaps more to his ability to change his educational philosophies to match whoever was on the board or in the superintendent's office and, more generally, his attempts to convince everyone with whom he interacted that he was on their side. This interview was conducted shortly after Rockenweil left and it might be noted that ideas expressed by Husby about the issues facing education closely resembled not only those of Hale and Rockenweil but my own ideas about schooling, which he knew well. I wonder what he would have said to current board members who favored "putting kids in boxes." At any rate, Husby stated:

> We have a problem with putting kids in boxes—this is a national problem. This problem turns us into a selecting and sorting kind of school instead of a teaching and learning school. We have convinced ourselves that if someone is different, someone else should take care of them—therefore special classes. It is important to create environments that build success. Every kid should succeed in more of a heterogeneous group. That's a real challenge! I am more and more convinced that we can group that way, but we need to develop our teachers so they can do it. We need to develop an attitude that says you are here, and regardless of your differences, I'm going to teach you.

Concerned about the "meaning of professionalism," Husby was disgusted at the work ethic of teachers who demanded pay for tutoring children after hours or attending workshops.

Husby's two children were in college. Comparing his education to that of his children, he felt that theirs had been superior because their teachers were more skilled but not necessarily more committed in terms of caring. He said his own children, who had attended Kinder, "probably had been exposed to a smaller range of kids." Husby said: "The fact that their father was a school administrator and not a janitor narrowed the range." Husby had grown up poor—his father was a janitor and his mother was "depressed and suicidal" most of his life. In addition to embarrassment and worry about his family life, Husby had been the smallest kid in the class and had not felt very accepted socially. When he grew in high school, he was a happier, more motivated student. Husby had gone to a private church school and was grateful that no one had made an issue of how poor he had been. He planned to major in science in college but had not had enough background in high school, so he struggled and never caught up enough to go on. In education he had professors who believed in him and encouraged his success; he fondly remembered the one who suggested that he get a doctorate. Husby had been an elementary teacher in Hillsdale for a few years. He believed that because he developed a meaningful math sequence for the school, his leadership ability was recognized and he was offered an administrative position.

Husby felt that the purpose of education was to "facilitate, allow, assist, and help students become learners so that learning could continue without teachers" and stated that "in modern times, students needed to know how to access and process information." His ideal student was "intrinsically motived and his home frame of reference was that education is valuable." This student would also "trust that people who work with them want them to learn." In picturing a student, he first recalled a student of his, Sara, who was "not real bright but bright enough." Another student, Dennis, came to Husby's mind. Dennis could not read and Husby was concerned that he "never got to him. I didn't help him." Husby felt a strength of public education was that "it serves all children and is more successful with them than most other nations, and the large percentage of graduates from our schools is a strength." A weakness was that educators have tried to convince parents that they (educators) could fix all problems. Husby believed that "the public does support public education, but we don't tell our story to the public. Only 27% of households have kids in schools; the rest have no access to information about schools."

Husby's discretion surfaced when he was asked to rate the quality of local schools. He first said "any would be okay," then, although his own children had attended the elementary and middle schools with the highest percentage of high-income, professional parents, Husby offered:

> My druthers are Westside and Hillview because of the quality of the staff.
> I wouldn't want my children in Southside because expectations are not high
> enough. My daughter went to Kinder and Northside Middle School. She pre-
> ferred Northside because of the wider mix of kids. At Kinder there were a
> bunch of snobs. Northside, Westside, and Bluffton have a high level of
> professionalism.

When asked about variation in the social class composition of Hillsdale schools, Husby evasively noted: "All schools are mixed to some extent, some skewed down, but Kinder isn't. I believe kids tend to interact with one another, especially in the elementary grades when they don't sense the difference. My son had friends at both ends." When asked if students could get a good education at any school in town, he hesitantly said "yes and no" but would not continue. When prompted about resource distribution, he responded: "I guess low-income schools have sort of less resources than high-income." He also brought up that the book-rental procedure used to discriminate but proudly volunteered that it no longer does.[34] When asked about relations with teachers, Husby first said that their expectations are biased but quickly claimed: "Teachers teach to the average kid in class and kids who could do better are not challenged." At this point, Husby rather defensively elaborated on his belief in the importance of aspirations and efforts, and the validity of meritocratic schooling:

> Probably the biggest differences we have in the schools are the expectations of the parents: the Ph.D.s' expectations on the one hand and parents who feel their kids need only stay until they are 16 on the other. Like with Dennis— that's all that mattered to him. He quit when he was 16 and that was just fine with his parents. Another poor student, Jennie, was able to overcome her background. It was just a wonder to see Jennie break a mold. There is opportunity for kids who come from that environment. I know, I did that. I knew another student, Jan, who was a member of the church youth group that I led. He was overprotected and overcontrolled. He was an excellent student, an academic all-star. He named me as the person who had most made him grow. In this town, more kids can get "over the hump" because the college is here.

When asked about social class-related achievement patterns, Husby claimed: "As much as I hate to admit it, the conventional pattern for high- and low-income kids' achievement holds here in Hillsdale. Higher-income kids get higher grades." Husby admitted the class correspondence with special education, adding: "In some categories, like learning disabilities, there are fewer low-income kids." In spite of repeatedly emphasizing his own low origins and what sounded like rhetorical opposition to "putting children in boxes," Husby told many tales about poor children "making it" and consistently slipped into blaming-the-victim explanations for children's school failure. Moreover, he narrated reasons why stratified grouping arrangements were justified.

All four central administrators who were interviewed were first-generation college. I categorized Dieken, Calhoun, and Hale as *in the middle* because of how they conveyed their own class origins and identification, their sentiments about schooling, but also what I observed of their actions as administrators. In terms of current family circumstances, Calhoun had connections with *already there* school personnel through his wife's job at Beauford and his children's education at high-income schools. Still, he was accepting of the lesser achievement of two of his four children, was quite critical of influential parents, and was known for standing up to some while he was a principal. Husby's chameleon-like quality of reflecting the sentiments and endorsing the practices of whoever was in charge and his discourses about the fairness of meritocratic schooling put him in the *upward-striving* cluster of school personnel. Like *upward-striving* teachers Karl and Marsha, Husby did complain about personal rejection of himself as well as such treatment of his children by peers when they attended Kinder, an exclusively high-income family school.

What seemed most apparent to me in talking with Husby and Calhoun was their seeming lack of awareness of class relations in Hillsdale and how they treated their glimmers of awareness of school inequities as something beyond their control. In contrast, Dieken articulated a specific agenda for reducing disparities and was disappointed that disparities remained after his administration as well as annoyed at the attitudes and actions of parents who negotiated for their children's advantage. Hale's verbalization of his and Rockenweil's progressive vision for schools was deliberate and constant, but his failures in working democratically with others and in understanding how change might be implemented made him appear somewhat quixotic and out of touch with reality.

Four elementary and secondary principals were also interviewed. Because of their building-level loyalties and perspectives, their narratives are integrated into chapters 5 and 6 with those of teachers. However, taking the liberty to consider them with administrators here, it is important to note that the two *already there* principals revealed an astute awareness of social class politics in Hillsdale and were willing to discuss between-school disparities. In that respect, these two were quite different from *already there* teachers and affluent mothers. Perhaps having to deal with affluent parent demands had made them cognizant of the entitlement felt by elites. The most salient feature of the narratives of the *upward-striving* and the *in-the-middle* principal was their sense of being forced to comply with the board, central administrators, or parents ("the system"), so they could not achieve valued outcomes for their own schools. In recognizing their lowly place in the social dynamics of Hillsdale, they felt that their hands were tied in terms of reducing disparities. In this sense, to some extent, all administrators took on *in-the-middle* status.

8

School Board Perceptions of Policy and Power

MICHELLE HENDERSON

In the town of "Hillsdale," the idea of diversity is well known and is generally considered to be well accepted. There is a city-sponsored committee created for the purpose of encouraging tolerance for diversity and preventing hate crimes. Many local residents pride themselves on their politically liberal viewpoints and consider the town to be one of the most open-minded and liberal in the state. For those people, Hillsdale is seen as a haven of progressive ideas encircled by a sea of conservatism in the surrounding rural counties. And it is true that in many ways Hillsdale is a relatively progressive and liberal community. However, this study was inspired by the idea that acceptance for progressive ideas often stops short when considering diversity in the schools of Hillsdale.

The idea of racial and ethnic diversity is well understood by members of the Hillsdale community, and the idea of accepting those who do not belong to the dominant culture of European descent is publicly portrayed in a positive manner. There are international festivals and frequent musical and artistic events that highlight non-American and non-Western cultures. On a community level, there is certainly a public message that is positive toward accommodating those with disabilities. But somehow, when it comes to tolerating or particularly appreciating or embracing the idea of diversity in the schools, these messages become more ambiguous. These observations about the cultural climate in Hillsdale are based on the researcher's experience of living in Hillsdale for 9 years, having two children attend school in Hillsdale, and observing student teachers in many of the schools serving the Hillsdale community.

The university community is notorious among conservative county residents for the liberal ideas of the faculty and students. For these residents, the university influence is also seen as unjustly powerful and brings an unwelcome liberalism to local politics. Just as there are class and economic divisions between town citizens who hold positions of power at the university and those who work in other sectors, there are class and economic divisions in the town, which are mostly evident in the east-side/west-side layout of Hillsdale. The university is on the east side of town, and the neighborhoods and schools that serve the university have tended to attract and maintain a higher-income population. The west side of town, especially the near west side, has traditionally been lower income. This was the area where the African American neighborhoods and schools were located at the turn of the 20th century, and although there is now more racial and economic diversity, the west side is still considered "less desirable" by realtors.

Brantlinger and colleagues have (1993, 1995) written on the attitudes of lower- and upper-income students toward secondary school and about the views of upper-income mothers toward schooling in Hillsdale (1996, 1998). The purpose of this study has been to look at the school board as a group of elected officials who have certain types of power in terms of how they make decisions and implement policy. This study was undertaken with the hope of gaining an understanding of school board members' perceptions of education in Hillsdale, their values and goals regarding education, and their views of diversity, especially in terms of how they see the social class of children as influencing their education in local schools and in terms of the need for separated academic levels within the schools.

GOALS OF EDUCATION: CONSERVATIVE AND PROGRESSIVE VIEWS

This study is framed by concepts surrounding the nature of conservative and progressive views toward education. The specific focus on education is considered to be different than general political ideology because it does not always correlate with educational ideology. The chapter specifically orients around the democratic concern of how best to support diversity in education. People have general neutral associations with the terms *conservative* and *progressive* regarding education, but it is important for me to specifically define what is meant when using these terms in the context of this study. Individuals with a "conservative" educational perspective have positive attitudes toward "teacher-directed," "traditional," or "didactic" education. Individuals with a "progressive" educational perspective have a positive regard for "student-centered" or "constructivist" educational ideology. Although these alternative terms vary in their subjective connotations according to specific usage by different authors, Brantlinger and Majd-Jabbari's (1998) definitions of the progressive and conservative views are used in this study.

According to Brantlinger: "Conservatives favor a technical or classical curriculum in which knowledge is predefined and separated into linearly sequenced steps with fairly rigid boundaries between subjects as well as between ranked levels of achievement" (p. 431). Progressives, on the other hand, "believe that students, when in a stimulating environment, naturally construct knowledge and acquire competencies and skills as they are needed or wanted from meaningful phenomena in their surroundings" (p. 432). Brantlinger focuses on differences in educational philosophy in chapters 3 and 4. One essential characteristic of progressive educational philosophy for Brantlinger is that advocates believe in the social inclusion of a broad range of gender, race, and achievement levels for students.

The goals of education look very different from conservative and progressive perspectives, and the goals of education shape the pedagogy, curriculum, and applications of education. Conservatives tend to look at the classics and traditional academic disciplines for inspiration (Beane, 1990, p. 92). According to Kohn (1997), who is a widely acclaimed critic of conservative ideology: "Children are—pick your favorite metaphor—so many passive receptacles to be filled, lumps of clay to be molded, pets to be trained, or computers to be programmed" (p. 434). The overriding goal of conservative models, according to Beane (1990), is to produce citizens who will maintain and protect the status quo while ignoring issues such as pluralism, complexity, and context.

The conservative view of what curriculum should include is sometimes based on a "classical humanist" or "liberal arts" foundation that draws almost exclusively from Western civilization—university curricula provide a prime example of this curricular paradigm. According to Beane (1990): "This approach to curriculum . . . represents a world known to and experienced primarily by white male intellectuals for whom the classical tradition is a lived experience, and its perpetuation a condition of stable existence in university departments in which most of them work" (p. 94). Conservative educators at all grade levels believe that there is a body of knowledge that is crucial for all members of society to know in order to keep society from falling into chaos (Beane, 1990). In critiquing this dominant culture curriculum perspective—this insistence on one right perspective that favors and perpetuates—the dominant culture is seen by critical theorists as being problematic. Noddings (1992) also claims this restriction does not take into account the fact that Americans now live in a pluralistic and global society. To clarify my own curricular perspectives, I believe that students need to be both implicitly and explicitly taught to look at the world from multiple perspectives, because multiple postitions and perspectives exist in the real world of everyday life. Thus, an understanding of diversity is key to understanding multiple perspectives and living fairly in a complex and multifaceted world.

The goal of education from a progressive perspective is to address the idea of creating a more just and enlightened society. Progressive educational goals are often traced back to Dewey. Dewey (1909) saw education as the key to influencing young minds in such a way that students could change their own lives, and thus society, for the better. This sentiment is echoed today by progressives such as Noddings (1995), who writes: "In direct opposition to the current emphasis on academic standards, a national curriculum, and national assessment, I have argued that our main educational aim should be to encourage the growth of competent, caring, loving, and lovable people" (p. 366).

The goal of education for progressives is to promote positive social change based on a student-centered pedagogy that will result in an appreciation for democracy, dignity, and diversity for all individuals in the educational system (Beane, 1990). This goal results in a positive environment in the classroom as teachers guide students in working together in accomplishing both group and individual goals rather than attempting to force all students into a standardized vision of what a successful education should be and what educators should strive for.

It is my opinion that an appreciation of diversity—as opposed to tolerance or acceptance—is the key to realizing a sense of cooperation and community in classrooms. Appreciation of diversity in schools must also go beyond the surface issue of race—a true appreciation of diversity includes different levels of socioeconomic status and different levels of academic achievement. The conceptual framework of the researcher is progressive rather than conservative, and has been strongly influenced by Dewey's (1909) ideas in *Moral Principles in Education:*

> Interest in community welfare, an interest that is intellectual and practical, as well as emotional—an interest, that is to say, in perceiving whatever makes for social order and progress, and in carrying these principles to execution— is the moral habit to which all the special school habits must be related if they are to be animated by the breath of life. (p. 17)

In focusing on community welfare, Dewey urged educators to adopt a curriculum that would cultivate an awareness of social ties. Dewey wrote that children can only learn to be successful in society if they are given the chance for the same experiences in the classroom that they will find in society. With this idea in mind, it is the researcher's belief that it is crucial for students to be enriched by a diversity of experiences while in the classroom. This includes working with students of all different ethnicities, social class levels, and ability levels.

Bowles and Gintis (1976) have written about the pervasiveness of hierarchical relationships in schools and the use of those hierarchies to teach students to conform to the current social order, thus perpetuating inequity in the classroom and in society. Kozol (1991) has strongly criticized the inequity of the American educational system, including the hypocrisy often involved in addressing the injustices that are currently inherent in schools: "What they mean, what they prescribe, is something that resembles equity but never reaches it: something close enough to equity to silence criticism by approximating justice, but far enough from equity to guarantee the benefits enjoyed by privilege" (p. 175). Brantlinger (1985a, b, c, 1987, 1993) has been critical of the inequity of Hillsdale, where my study also takes place.

The conceptual framework of the researcher is also based on critical theory and has been strongly influenced by the writings of Noddings. Noddings (1992) writes critically about the current status quo in which competition and privilege determine much of the school curriculum and agenda, leaving behind those who are different and powerless. In *The Challenge to Care in Schools,* Noddings writes in favor of a "curriculum of caring" which would replace the current ideology of authoritarian control in education with one "in favor of shared living and responsibility" (p. 62). This study was undertaken with the goal of understanding the educational ideology of some past and present school board members, as well as the way their perceptions of social class and inclusion reflect their level of acceptance for diversity in the schools and within the classrooms of each school. It has been the goal of this researcher to look at the impact of both educational conservatives and educational progressives on the school board in the community of Hillsdale.

METHODS

This research was implemented in an effort to gain a better understanding of the perceptions that members of the Hillsdale Board of School Trustees have about their role in policy making, both in terms of the personal power they have had in influencing and making decisions within the group and the power the group has had in negotiating with others in the administration and community Four main ideas were explored:

1. How do school board members negotiate decisions between themselves in controversial situations?
2. How do school board members interact with members of the administration and members of the community in controversial situations?
3. How do school board members perceive social class issues in Hillsdale?
4. How do school board members perceive diversity (especially diversity in terms of academic ability) within the schools?

In previous chapters, Brantlinger discusses the contradictions between stated liberal and progressive educational ideals of middle-class mothers and the contradictions that arose when it came to accepting class or academic diversity in their children's schools and classrooms. This study was undertaken to explore elected officials' awareness of social class and diversity issues and whether they would support the need for economic and academic diversity—an educationally progressive stance—in the community they are serving.

In a conversation that Brantlinger had with a current school board member, names of six current and past members of the board of school trustees were listed as likely resources of information about the board and its relations with school administrators. These were identified based on their varied perspectives on diversity in local education and length of residence in Hillsdale. The recommended past and present local school board members were contacted to request an interview for this study. Special efforts were made to interview school board members whose term of office included a controversial period in which a new redistricting plan was developed and implemented. In addition to school board member interviews, a middle-class member of a west-side neighborhood who had been a long-term observer of board activities was interviewed in order to gain a perspective on educational and social class issues on the west side of Hillsdale. A document analysis was also conducted and included minutes from school board meetings as well as newspaper articles written at that time. The researcher attended one school board meeting to get a better understanding of the way the meetings are structured and the interpersonal interactions during the meetings.

Potential participants were contacted by phone. For those who agreed to take part in the study, a time and place to meet for an hour-long interview was set up. Six board members were contacted and four agreed to participate in the study. Two past male school board members never replied to a message requesting their participation left on their answering machines. All four participants are of European American descent and all are female. Participants are all mothers, and all have between one and four children who are of middle school age or older. All participants had full- or part-time professional jobs at the time of the interviews. The interviews began with general questions about their motivation for running for school board and their general thoughts about the schools attended by the participants and their children. Questions then became more focused on the nature of school board activities, including relationships between school board members and with administration and members of the community. Participants were asked specific questions about their perceptions of the role of the school board and about controversial policy decisions, specifically about redistricting and the issues of tracking and inclusion. Interviews were audiotaped and transcribed. Pseudonyms have been used to protect the confidentiality of all participants.

RESULTS

All school board members openly discussed social class issues. All were aware of the town demographics and the role that family income plays in determining where children live and thus where they are most likely to attend school. All participants discussed social class in a politically liberal manner. Based on these comments about social class, they might be expected to have progressive educational views and voting records. Differences in what was discussed and the way it was discussed arose around the topics of redistricting and inclusion. When it came to issues of interactions between board members, all were guarded in identifying any other board member by name when discussing past decisions, and all were extremely diplomatic when discussing other members of the school board who they currently serve with or have served with in the past. As Ann put it: "I don't think there was any board member I ever served with that I would say negative things about now. We might have disagreed on some things, or lots of things, but there's no board member that I served with that I don't have nice things to say about." Despite being protective of the confidentiality of the way decisions are made on the school board, all participants seemed to be open and honest about their own beliefs and goals for education in the community of Hillsdale.

The results of this study have been analyzed in terms of three major areas: (1) the relationships between school board members in terms of how decisions were made, (2) the relationships between school board members and parents in the community, and (3) the attitudes of these school board members toward diversity in the schools in terms of social class, inclusion, and tracking.

SCHOOL BOARD RELATIONSHIPS: BALANCING POWERFUL IDEAS

There was agreement among the four members of the school board who were interviewed that there were a variety of personality types on the school board, and personality affected who was more influential when it came to voting on controversial issues. Mary talked about consensus building as a group:

> I think we do try to come to a consensus, but depending upon the group, see . . . the board is a constantly changing entity. That makes a difference. You have some people come to the board who don't have experience with consensus building and it takes a while to learn that they're not going to get their way every time, that people are going to disagree. And that even happens with people who've been on the board for a while. Everybody may not agree with something they want to do.

Debra felt that the goals of school board members affected the way they made decisions:

> The problem with school boards, I've found, is that you either have change artists, you have people who really want to focus on children and what's best for them and use the research at hand and base their decisions on that. And there are other members who are more interested in making sure the superintendent manages the school district without getting in their way. And there's a real dichotomy, and it's been really interesting, and I was glad that the board (at least for my first 8 years) was more of a progressive board, willing to wade in on difficult decisions and most of the time that was very effective.

Ann felt board members could be divided into leaders and followers, as well as those who were less informed and those who were more informed:

> In any group that exists, whether it's the school board or any other group, there are leaders and there are followers. That's been my experience. So, I think that's true for every school board and every organization . . . and there are also people who are more informed and less informed. And there are people who are hard workers, and there are people who are lazy. And the people who are more informed and work harder are hopefully the ones who have the influence, and often that turns out to be the case.

All four school board members mentioned that different people had different issues that really mattered to them, and those were the issues in which they were very unlikely to change their minds or their votes, regardless of how strongly they were urged to do so by others on the board. As Mary put it:

> There have been times when one of us has brought an issue to the board and kept it there by the sheer strength of our personalities. Sometimes that's gotten the board into kind of a little mess. You don't go out and lightly run for an election. It's a lot of hard work. So people who do it tend to be relatively sure of themselves and relatively convinced that they are right. And so, you get a strong-willed group of people, and sometimes some of the stuff that comes up, you know, if it doesn't matter to other board members, they'll go along mainly because of the strength of the argument and will support the board member. If it matters, there are times when I've . . . we've . . . had real acrimonious discussions.

Debra discussed the ways that she worked to create more informed board members in the hopes of changing the redistricting vote:

> But Fairview became a real lightning rod . . . I worked for 2 months to get one board member, and I was focusing on Ann, 'cause I'd always worked with

her and because she was of pretty much the same political philosophy that I was . . . hoping that I could get her to change [her vote]. I brought in all the political leaders in the community that she most respected who agreed with my perspective. I mean, I did a great job, but I couldn't get her to change her mind. I think it was pure torture for her, because she knew what I was doing, it was so very clear . . .

WHO DECIDES TO RUN AND WHY

The system of selecting board members appears to have some influence on the way that members are more likely to vote once they have been elected. Three of the four board members mentioned being asked to run or fill a vacant spot by current board members at the time of the elections. During elections, those who are asked to run by the current board members have the benefit of running together on a slate with the public acknowledgment that they are recommended by the school board. This method of recruitment gives any existing school board the advantage of selecting members who will be more likely to be in agreement with them. Mary explained it like this:

> Quite frankly, when school board elections come up, school boards actively look for people in that community, and we have meetings to invite people to see how it works and everything so that they're not going into it blind, and we actively look for people who have already shown an interest in education and look like they would be good candidates for the school board.

In addition to having the power to increase the likelihood of gaining members who are in agreement with the agenda of current members, there seems to be an unspoken but powerful influence when it comes to voting after those candidates have been elected into office. Kris spoke of feeling a sense of obligation to vote a certain way, knowing she had been selected because of having similar views as other members of the board:

> That was a very difficult position to be in because when some of the issues came forward, the people who voted for me felt that I somehow should be on board with their positions, that they picked me because I agreed with them. But then there were times in the remaining 4 years that I didn't agree with them and every once in a while I heard a little bit of that kind of discussion.

CHOOSING A LEADER WITH A SIMILAR EDUCATIONAL AGENDA

The school board also has the power to select and keep a superintendent who shares their values—or fire a superintendent with whom they are not in agreement. Two of the board members interviewed were involved in the process of hiring a new superintendent after not renewing a controversial superintendent's contract. They both spoke of the importance of being able to work with the superintendent. Ann recalled:

> We hired a new superintendent about a year or two after I got on the board. The superintendent, um, left, and we hired a new superintendent. And so, I think it's not surprising that you always have a better relationship with somebody that you hire. We hired him because he shared our goals.

Mary also spoke of the problems with the superintendent before she was elected and her feelings about hiring a new superintendent with whom the board felt they could work:

> One of the things I'd talked about a lot in my election and that I wanted to see happen was that we get a superintendent we could live with and work with and that there wouldn't be any changes. We'd had too many changes. And I wanted a board superintendent relationship that was good. We'd had such an antagonistic relationship between the board and at least one of our previous superintendents, and I wanted us all working towards the same goals instead of fighting with each other, because when the board and the superintendent fight, things do not get done.

The superintendent is presumably motivated to work well with the school board since his or her job is at stake. This would tend to perpetuate the status quo in terms of the agenda of the school board, thus affecting the continuation of systemic inequity, whether that outcome is intentional or not. This is illustrated by the power dynamics that Kris experienced during the redistricting controversy:

> The issue that caused the biggest conflict for me was the redistricting plan. I had a strong opinion about that, and I communicated it to the superintendent and to the individual members of the board. And as it came down to it . . . either no one wanted to come forward with this, it was too politically sensitive to come forward with it, or they just didn't agree. And I did not support the redistricting plan. And some other really stronger members of the board did. Um, the superintendent told me that he supported my position, but, you know, he's in a tough political position, and you know, he doesn't vote anyway, and so the redistricting plan passed.

SCHOOL BOARD ACCOMPLISHMENTS: USING POWERFUL NEGOTIATIONS

When working with the community, the school board was able to negotiate power in order to achieve their goals. These goals, as stated, generally tended to be more (though not all) educationally progressive in nature. The school board accomplishments that were mentioned by the four participants included building a new middle school, starting an alternative school, building new schools, starting extended-day/full-day kindergarten programs, eliminating corporal punishment, aligning curriculum so that it was similar in all schools, and doing renovations where needed.

One way in which these school board accomplishments were achieved was through the use of "work session" meetings held between the monthly public meetings. These work sessions are open to the public, but attendance tends to be much lower than at the monthly school board meetings. Controversial decisions were often discussed during the work sessions, and votes were discussed and sometimes changed ahead of the public meeting. This gave members a chance to work together to change a crucial vote. Mary spoke frankly of the importance of these work sessions:

> Almost everything on that agenda we've had in our hands for a while. Some of it we've been discussing for a year or two, and we do work sessions, and this stuff gets talked about, talked to death. The superintendent is very good about bringing us the things he thinks we're going to have to deal with, you know, a little early, so we get some study time on it, so that we get a chance to talk about it, and get our ducks in a row.

She also expressed annoyance toward board members who break the unspoken rules of the work session process:

> I can tell you one thing that's been a little frustrating to me is to go to a work session, where it's designed that we talk through all this so that we don't have a board wrangle at our meetings—they can make meetings longer, and they make it so that you get involved in that [issue] and then don't pay attention to other issues . . . or things of that nature, and then have a board member put it back on the table at a meeting and have to go through it all over again. I really am unhappy with that. . . . I think it's "I didn't get my way here, so I'm going to try again." Usually I'm finding it doesn't make any difference. People come out of work sessions usually with their minds set one way or the other.

Work sessions are conducted in a more private environment than the monthly board meetings. So, much is determined before issues are brought to the more public forum of the monthly school board meeting with requests for public input.

WHO SPEAKS IN HILLSDALE AND WHO GETS HEARD

When working with members of the community, all four members spoke of the louder voice of the upper-income parents among their constituents. In some cases, there was a sense of indignation on the part of the board member for what he or she perceived as unreasonable and unfair demands made by these parents. Kris recalled the upper-income parents complaining about changing schools as part of a redistricting plan:

> You know one of the things that was part of the plan that passed was that High Park would go to Northview. And those High Park parents, I mean, they were not happy with that. They saw that as moving away from South-view, which was in their view a higher-end school, a white school, and at that time before Southview was renovated, the handicapped were all at Northview. We don't have a racial issue in Hillsdale, but the few minorities that we do have probably were more at Northview. So they did not want their kids to go there.

Debra also recalled the controversy around that portion of the plan and the attitudes of the high-income High Park parents: "The other part that was contentious was High Park going to Northview, where we've got a high-income group of people being transferred, and they were extremely, unlike the Hillview crowd, they were extremely vocal, drove us crazy." Mary recalled the heated public debates around this topic as well:

> We had adults who treated students despicably in those meetings. If I'd of had the power I'd have spanked some of those adults! We had way too many people with their own self-interest in front of us—not an interest in the whole community. I mean, nothing like redistricting brings out the people who are totally self-interested and not interested in what is good for the whole community or what's good for students as a whole. And unfortunately, it's usually the ones who can afford to make up the difference who are standing up there screaming bloody murder.

There was also general agreement that the voices of the lower-income parents were not heard often. Ann and Kris cited the problems of logistics—lack of transportation to attend meetings and phones to make calls—which they felt kept lower-income parents from making the same kinds of demands as upper-income parents. According to Ann: "I would get calls from people who were pretty low-income, but in terms of frequency, high-income people tended to be more vocal. Just as they tend to be more litigious, file lawsuits more, or appeals more, because they're more skilled at it."

SCHOOL BOARD CONTROVERSIES: SEEKING POWERFUL SOLUTIONS

The school board members who were interviewed were very articulate and impassioned when discussing their feelings about the way they felt schools should be run. All four spoke of their desire to work for the good of all students as a major factor in their decision to become members of the school board. When speaking of their work in general, especially when discussing their reasons to run for school board and their ideals for schooling, all school board members used progressive terminology ("for the good of all the students," "it's not fair to students," "importance of diversity"). Their views of what was best for students differed, however, in terms of representing conservative or progressive educational ideology. Controversial issues brought out the more conservative educational views in several cases.

REDISTRICTING: DIVERSITY WITHIN SCHOOLS

The most conservative school board perceptions of how schools should be affected by redistricting were not represented in these interviews. The board members who voted to support the conservative redistricting plan that passed and was implemented were happy to discuss the effects of social class in Hillsdale in general but did not address their own part in perpetuating the inequity through their votes on redistricting. Mary showed a great depth of understanding of the effects of social class on local schools in discussing Kinder, an upper-income school:

> In Hillsdale, I think that you can see the difference in the students from different types of neighborhoods. Not that a student from a neighborhood from a lower socioeconomic [class] can't do well, and I think he gets a good education here, but you can see the differences. You take Kinder school, which is made up of a neighborhood where the socioeconomic status is high, your at-risk rate is low . . . and there's a standard in those neighborhoods that's kept. And it's not only a standard of finance, but it's a standard of behavior and expectation that comes in those neighborhoods. That's why that school does so well. To be in those neighborhoods, your parents have got to be educated.

Mary went on to discuss Hillview, where the lowest-income students were placed in the redistricting plan:

> And then you compare that with Hillview, where some of our very poorest students go, and you look at the family . . . I mean, like two-thirds of that school moves every year. And they don't move out of town. They move to another school. And frequently they're moving because their parents can't pay the rent. The parents can't pay the rent because they don't have an education, they can't get a decent job . . . too many people in that school only have one parent in the home, that parent is stressed out, the parent can't participate in the school, show an active interest, they frequently might be working long hours. Those kids aren't getting the attention they need, so socioeconomic plays a great deal.

One board member (who was not part of this study) was frank about his conservative beliefs when interviewed for the local paper at the time of the redistricting controversy:

> Instead of moving kids around to balance socioeconomic levels, XXX said, why not send resources into schools that need extra help? "It bothers me a little that we're hung up on this socioeconomic thing," he said. "What is equitable to the child? What we need to do is look at what's the need for services." He advocates putting resources where they are most needed. "Give the critical care to those schools that need it and the first aid to those that don't," XXX said. (*H-T,* 10/12/96)

Kris confirmed this view, stating that those who were against mixing the socioeconomic levels in the schools justified their decision by stating that it would be better to put all the poor students together and focus the additional resources all in one place. One of the people, who was a very prominent person on the board, said "I think it's a better idea to put all of the needy kids in one place, then we can address their needs—more social workers, another assistant principal . . . and they did that at Hillview, but I don't know what the result was." Another justification for keeping the poor children grouped together was to keep the upper-income parents happy so that they would keep their children in the public schools of Hillsdale. As Kris explained:

> Another argument was that if we don't give special . . . stuff . . . to the high end, then there's going to be a big movement to create a private school for their kids and it's going to be like other major cities in the U.S. where the high-end kids aren't even in the school system. . . . But that was the other thing, that we've got to keep the high-end kids, the gifted and talented kids— they loved to talk about the gifted and talented kids—we've got to keep them in the school system. And so that means we can't make them go to school with poor kids, we can't make them serve as role models for poor kids.

All school board members recalled that the controversy over redistricting was framed as being for or against "neighborhood schools." Debra expressed surprise that members of the board weren't familiar with the historic connotations of segregation that the term brought up for her. Those who were against a socioeconomic mix in the schools felt that students should attend the school closest to them. The fact that poor neighborhoods tend to surround poor schools was apparently ignored or overlooked. But not all members were willing to do so. Debra couldn't understand why others wouldn't listen to the speakers she brought in to advise the school board:

You know, they were really looking at this with tunnel vision. It was really bizarre to me. They weren't listening to the city council rep from that area; they weren't listening to the mayoral candidate. I got a lot of people there who I know they voted for (laughs) and who we all respect, who live in that neighborhood and who have worked in that neighborhood, or whatever.

And Kris felt that other solutions could have been examined:

I guess I just wanted to be proud of what we were coming up with, going back to redistricting. We didn't come up with anything that looked very different than you know, we're gonna draw little circles, and it lacked . . . it seemed to me that we weren't being very creative . . . if people had been willing to adopt the basic philosophy that this would be a helpful thing.

The term "busing" was used to provide negative connotations during the redistricting controversy—not only did upper income families not want their children to ride a bus a long way to a school but even families in the low-income neighborhoods protested against the idea. But Debra countered that argument:

I was trying to get them to focus on the fact that suddenly Hillview, up until that time, it was 45% at-risk students, which was bad enough. Now we're moving this huge new subdivision into the school that would make it, they said, 65%, but we knew it would be much higher . . . because more of that subdivision was being moved in . . . so it was a real concern to me. And I did a lot of research on it, and the idea of the neighborhood school idea, you know, none of these kids around Hillview actually walk to school . . . but at any rate, most of them are bused to the school, so that was an idiotic argument.

Mary expressed a continuing concern about busing—but in this case she is concerned about lower-income students being bused so that upper-income students can stay at the schools they prefer:

I'm really concerned when they start busing west-side students extreme distances to avoid busing east-side students little distances. And this is class speaking. Because the west side is less populated does not necessarily mean that they need to be treated like they are less than the other students. And quite frankly, those people chose to live on the east side, and if the population is larger over there, that doesn't mean that because they chose this house and it was in Southview [district] that it's going to remain in Southview.

Members of the school board who voted against the redistricting plan that was adopted spoke emphatically against the segregation of upper- and lower-income students. They felt that students from both socioeconomic levels lose out when there is no mix in the schools. Kris quoted one board member as saying that "high-end kids are not in school to be role models for other kids," and she went on to say:

> I didn't agree with that statement. Because I think that what we're trying to do in public education is prevent long-term poverty. . . . But if you segregate kids like that in schools and that's all they see, these poor kids who come from poor environments like they do, and they don't see that education is . . . parents don't push education as a core value in the home. They aren't going to see anything other than what they see in their little neighborhood. And I thought that a mix of kids would have been a better thing.

Despite efforts to convince other members of the board that not only individual students but the entire community would benefit from more diversified schools, the votes of Kris and Debra were overpowered by a final vote of four to three in favor of the conservative redistricting plan that would continue to keep the low-income students together in a small number of schools.

INCLUSION AND TRACKING: DIVERSITY WITHIN CLASSROOMS

Having progressive views about diversifying the schools by social class did not mean that school board members had progressive views about diversifying schools when it came to levels of academic ability in the classroom. Kris, who was passionately opposed to the segregation of rich and poor at many of Hillsdale's schools, was equally passionate about the importance of keeping expectations high in the classroom, which for her meant being against inclusion policies:

> It [tracking] did not exist, and there was a big emphasis at the time at Northview High of the integration of the handicapped, or . . . whatever the current terminology was at that time, I can't remember . . . which I thought was overboard. I mean, I'm not someone who thinks we ought to segregate the handicapped and put them in the basement with special ed, I don't mean that, but there was no college track.

Ann concurred with this viewpoint, stating that MCCSC has gone "way too far" in terms of inclusion, and that in terms of tracking, "this school corporation hasn't had tracking for years. They didn't have tracking when I came on the board and they don't now. I don't remember when they last had tracking. But they have things that have other names that some people think are tracking or seem similar." Ann's proposed solution to the problems of inclusion and tracking would be to allow students to choose from a three-level system. As she explained it:

> The plan that I've always liked the best, and I'd call it differentiated curriculum . . . the idea of it was that there would be at least three levels, and one would be more like for an advanced student, and one would be for a non-advanced student, and one would be more for a student that needs help, but my idea of how this should be run . . . and this is how it differs from tracking: Tracking is where the school system says you will be in this track. With this differentiated curriculum, the school offers various levels, and you tell us where you want to be. . . . Now, if you are an extremely bright student, maybe you want to be in that class. If you're not so bright but you're a real hard worker, you might also like to be in that class. If you're really bright and you're really lazy, maybe you do not want to be in that class. So we won't tell you which class to be in, but all these choices will be available to everyone.

Mary, on the other hand, voiced a relatively progressive view on inclusion:

> I would say that on the whole it's good for special education students and good for the other students in that they do have to see and deal with those students. I am not going to say that at times they don't create distractions and take up large portions of the teacher's time, because I think they do. I'm a supporter of the idea.

Mary went on to discuss the problems of funding inclusion so that all students would be able to benefit fully in an inclusion program:

> I like the idea better when it's adequately funded. And I think that's where we fall down and it's simply because we can't afford it. But those classrooms need to be smaller and they need to have more aides and more help from people trained to deal with the multitude of problems. We're not talking about the same problem with every one of our disabled students. Those problems are a whole gambit of things. There's no way you can expect every classroom teacher to be trained in every one of those problems. I think they affect learning, particularly with the children who are more easily distracted. But I don't know how you solve that problem. Because I don't think those kids should be shut up.

Debra mentioned the importance of research that supports the idea of inclusion:

> There is a local research project which found that all the kids in an inclusion classroom, special ed, and non–special ed, benefitted greatly and statistically

significantly . . . from the inclusion program. And my own conclusion from this summary of their research [is that] having two teachers in the classroom obviously is beneficial.

Because inclusion is state mandated and is not under the control of the school board, there were no controversial votes or policy-making issues that would cause members to vote in ways that supported or refuted their spoken views on inclusion. Perhaps for this reason, the conservative or progressive ideologies are not taken at face value.

The school board members who were interviewed for this study discussed an interesting mix of conservative and progressive ideas. Rather than school board members being conservative or progressive in all aspects of their educational thinking, each member expressed different areas in which they were conservative or progressive. The complexity of working as a policy-making group was evident.

For these school board members, certain types of power are easily obtained, such as having the time to debate and decide topics in work sessions where members of the general public are rarely present, the ability to have a strong voice in who will be elected as members of the group, and the ability to hire and fire administrators. However, other types of power are not possible, such as keeping the same group of members together over a long period of time when they are working well as a team, being reelected, determining the amount of money available to the district, and determining curriculum and standards for the district.

School board members did not discuss their own level of power and their ability to maintain or change the status quo in these interviews. They were more likely to be critical of upper-income parents for making unreasonable demands in terms of redistricting and of lower-income students for not being motivated and hardworking in terms of tracking issues. In this respect, school board members tended to be unlikely to support the progressive goal of diversity, especially in terms of supporting academic diversity (inclusion) in all schools and in all classrooms in the district.

9

Conclusion: Choosing a Democratic, Communitarian Ethic for Schools and Society

It is widely acknowledged that social class-related hierarchies prevail in American education. Although few professionals deny that school circumstances and outcomes correspond to social class status, it seems they presume this results from adults of their class striving hard to succeed in occupations and settle in good neighborhoods, parents of their class caring about schooling and providing intellectually stimulating home environments, and children of their class being smart and having high aspirations and good work ethics. Thus, they are inclined to attribute stratified school structures and outcomes to the essentially superior traits of higher social classes and the natural result of fair competition in meritocratic schools and job markets. Furthermore, they insist that for life to become more equitable, the poor must become more like themselves.

Scholars react in a range of ways to social class distinctions. Most convey a resignation to hierarchies and are not deeply introspective about their own role in producing them (Brantlinger, 1997, 1999a). They focus on failing students, offering continuously newer technical remedies to fix kids and reduce failure. As Sleeter (2000) puts it: "Researchers from dominant groups have a long history of producing knowledge about oppressed groups that legitimates their subordination" (p. 10). Few turn the scholarly gaze upward to understand the dynamics of class relations and the stratification that continuously intensifies. Yet concern is expressed about school and societal disparities and considerable effort is put into hypothesizing about its causes. Numerous interventions have been designed purportedly to make things more equal. Nevertheless, stratified school structures are remarkably resilient in resisting reform efforts (Bowles & Gintis, 1976; Oakes & Franke, 1999;

Oakes, Quartz, Ryan, & Lipton, 2000; Tyack & Tobin, 1994). Scholars who address the failure of school reform sometimes name such reasons as the absence of flexibility in teachers or the lack of effective leadership for realizing or sustaining change (Fullan, 1993; Sarason, 1990). These hypotheses are based on the tacit assumption that people who have the most control really want schools to be fair and equal.

In contrast, Colker (1992) contends that stratified institutions are durable *precisely because* they serve dominant group interests (p. xi). Similarly, Roth (1992) argues that school hierarchy and disparate outcomes are the *products of desires* and *actions* of powerful people. Thus, Ball (1994) insists that to transform social hierarchies, it is necessary to understand groups that have the power to control them. Similarly, Mirel (1994) writes that such fundamental political aspects as "who controls schools, whose security is threatened by reform, and who attempts to protect and expand their turf" are as important to reform as "exciting ideas, strong financial backing, and committed reformers" (p. 515). Few bring up the likelihood of intentionality behind class stratification; hierarchy creation and justification phenomena are neither directly confronted nor scrutinized by scholars, politicians, the press, or school personnel.

Instead of accepting the validity of common deficit attributions for class distinctions, the studies included in this book were designed to provide evidence related to the hypothesis that both social inequities and school hierarchies result from the personal intention and design of the dominant class. The educated middle class, who are primarily in control of schooling whether consciously or not, consistently arrange school structures to benefit children of their class. So, rather than attributing school outcome disparities to problems in low-income constituencies and seeking ways to change that class, I turned my scholarly gaze upward and inward at educated middle-class people's desires for school distinctions for their children and at their descriptions of working toward that end. I was particularly interested in how supposedly liberal, progressive people explain and rationalize their children's school advantages.

Liberal and right-wing thinking and agendas are believed to be different and in conflict; however, Popkewitz (1991) claims both have similar assumptions and implications. The studies summarized in this book support Popkewitz's claim and lead me to conclude that the affluent professionals speak a liberal rhetoric, but their actions reflect conservative neoliberal ideology. Whether professionals are conscious of their advantage or aware of the self-interested nature of their actions is not clear (Danforth, 1996). Bersoff (1999) concludes that "unethical behavior" does not result from a moral judgment hiatus but from corruption driven by a desire for personal gain. Certainly, the Enron and WorldCom scandals support their claim.

Rorty (1998) condemns "suburbanites, who know social mobility advanced their parents' fates," and still they see nothing wrong with "preventing the mobility of Others, belonging to a hereditary caste, and having a secession of the successful" (p. 86).

Some surmise that Americans' egalitarian commitment has receded over time (Fraser, 1989; Lasch, 1984, 1993, 1995), whereas Piven and Cloward (1979) believe it has never been possible to compel concessions from dominant groups (e.g., get them to give up advantage). This lack of generosity arises from there not being room at the top for everyone. Social standing is relational. Hierarchical societies have a top and a bottom. The only way to reduce class disparities is for those who currently have more to give up some of their status and advantage. If equity is desired, it is essential to question the motives of professionals who occupy top positions (Apfelbaum, 1999) and of parents who insist on advantages for their children (Eichstedt, 1998; Kohn, 1998).

The idea of class advantage is not new. Mills (1956, 1963) referred to a "power elite" who had vested interests in stratified and exclusive institutions. Counts documented upper-class control of school boards (1927), challenging educators to use schools to build a "new social order" that was not based on social hierarchies (1932, 1934). Rorty (1998) cites Dewey as offering an account of "institutionalized selfishness" and hoping to "mobilize political agents to work toward a 'truly democratic' America" (pp. 17, 25).

In the Preface, I alluded to my premise that people who act to the detriment of a broad social good and lack a sense of commonality with other humans—indeed, with other creatures or inanimate objects in nature—are the truly deficient. Further, I charge that human incentives are flawed when they center around having more status and resources than others. The mentality behind such material and prestige goals results in wars, interpersonal strife, self-defeating personal agendas, nonproductive competition, illogical hoarding of goods and monopoly of spaces, unstable financial conditions that undermine people's security, destruction and depletion of natural resources, and misuse and contamination of the environment, among other dire consequences for human and nonhuman survival on the planet. Acts that are based primarily on self-interest, regardless of the political ideologies espoused, are detrimental to the common good and ultimately to achieving democracy (Rorty, 1998).

LETTING GO OF THE COMFORTING (AND PERNICIOUS) NEOLIBERAL AND MERITOCRACY MYTHS

Through the roles of concerned parents, responsive school officials, and dedicated school board trustees, the college-educated class may believe that they design schools as meritocracies in which all children have opportunity to realize their potential and get ahead. For meritocracies to be fair, however, there must be a comparable distribution of resources and some homogeneity in student status; school conditions must be equal, students should have access to quality learning, and the curriculum must be pertinent and culturally relevant for all. Meritocratic schooling requires a neutral, level playing field if those with natural intelligence and competence, a will to succeed, and a constructive work ethic are to do well. In spite of the sense that democratic education and social mobility are the American way, unequal school property tax–based funding combined with extensive residential class segregation means the possibility of equal school opportunity for low-income students is slim. The actual American educational system slants the field to give the best chances to those who are already advantaged; advantage and winning are just as circular as the long-acknowledged cycle of poverty and failure.[1] Both patterns exist across generations. It is well documented that equitable conditions, equal access, and fair treatment are not currently available, nor have they ever been in American schools. Given the prevailing school and university funding formulas and the highly stratified wage structures of adults in the United States, it is unlikely that equitable conditions will be reached in the near or distant future.

If schools really could be made equal, there is still the consideration that meritocracies are not the best form of schooling in a democracy. The dark side of any meritocracy—fair or unfair—is that its benefits are partial and particular. Competition is integral to meritocracies. As Watt (1994) notes: "Americans are dominated by the egoistic conception of equality as equality of opportunity to compete for society's prizes" (p. 227).[2] Yet, even if by some miraculous sweep of a wand schools were to become fair to all social classes—it would have to be magic because we are not moving toward equity now in spite of the awareness of scholars and rhetoric of politicians[3]— meritocratic schooling still would not lead to a leveling of stratified social class structure, a reciprocal morality among citizens, or the democratic country of our ideals. I would go further to assert that truly equitable, integrated, and high-quality comprehensive schooling could never be accomplished in an unregulated capitalistic country where adult life circumstances are so discrepant. This book, however, was not intended to cut so wide a swath. My aim was to examine problems in current practice that would inspire readers to think about ways to make schools better for a broad range of children and create places with a lively intellectual climate in which students consider the issues and develop the competencies to sustain a democracy and decent life on the planet.[4]

The educated middle class is believed to be liberal, progressive, and, in contrast to conservatives, empathetic, generous, and attuned to the best interests of working-class and lower-income people. It is important to challenge these class-based assumptions. On a rhetorical level this class is pop-ulist and democratic, but on subconscious and unspoken levels we eschew both equitable distributions of resources and substantial inclusion of others into our exclusive communities (Zizek, 1989). Scholars, educators, and col-lege-educated parents are positioned to shape schools (Horvat et al., 2002; Lareau, 1989). Most of us, especially those of us on the left, think of our-selves as exceptions to the flaws we perceive in others and thus choose to exempt ourselves from our own class analyses (Bourdieu, 1996). But are we exceptions? Should we excuse ourselves from the scrutiny we apply to others? Do our personal life actions regarding social class and schooling match the philosophies espoused in our writings and teachings?

hooks (1990) writes: "It always astounds me when progressive people act as though it is somehow a naive moral position to believe that our lives must be a living example of our politics" (p. 48). Based on this study, my response to hooks would be that most members of the educated middle class in spite of pretense, are neither progressive nor deeply concerned about Others. But I would agree with her that scholars on the left certainly should walk the talk. When we do not, we become a class with deeply divided intel-lect, affect, and spirit.

IDENTIFYING MORAL DEFICIENCIES

The studies reported in this book indicate that unless the desires and inten-tionality behind advantage and the negotiations of the winners in stratified schools are examined and confronted, school reform that is (purportedly) aimed at increasing equity will never succeed. To give what I believe is a valid analogy, a well-accepted truism in all successful psychological or rela-tionship therapy is that *the real problem* must be identified and acknowl-edged, and there must be *a genuine desire for change* **before** treatment can be successful. As long as the lay public, policy makers, school managers, and educational scholars locate *the problem* in school losers and direct their efforts at changing them, a dent will not be put in the ubiquitous class-biased practices in school.

If equitable schooling really is a national aim—as it definitely should be in a democratic country—then the factors that prevent reaching that goal should be scrutinized. Ball (1994) suggests Foucault's advice be followed: "The real political task is to criticize the working of institutions which appear to be both neutral and independent, and to criticize them in such a manner that the political violence which has always exercised itself obscurely through them will be unmasked so that we can fight them" (p. 27). Said (1994) also believes that the challenge of intellectual life is to dissent against the *status quo* (p. xv). Scatamburlo (1998) calls for a ruthless criticism of everything existing—one that is not afraid of its own conclusions or of conflict with existing power relations. Given that privilege and deprivation are integral to school and society—that institutional structures and dominant culture are intertwined—transforming hierarchy is not an easy task. The common metaphor "money speaks" readily translates into "voices of wealthy white people are heard and influential." "Power corrupts" applies to those who support public policy that directs disproportionate resources to their own class. As Kincheloe (1999b) writes:

> Even conservative analysts have come to understand the negative psychological impact of market-driven capitalism with its commodification of desire and its destruction of community. The quest for economic opportunity drew farm children from their extended families to the isolation of the city and has been shattering communal ties ever since. Business relationships have undermined friendships for decades, and industrial/postindustrial workers have had to repress significant portions of their psychic energy in order to perform boring and miserable jobs, submit to authority, and live with low-status, subordinate positions. Even among the affluent, who are released from the emotional indignities of the lower socio-economic classes, an emotional/spiritual emptiness often undermines emotional health—a vacuum that consumption of sex, drugs, or rock n' roll can't fill. It has become a cliché by now to assert that psychological progress has not matched technological progress. (p. 5)

To heal from moral deficits and bring coherence to the realms of intellect, affect, and spirit, the problem of what hoarding status and material benefits mean for Others must be addressed.

ACTIVISM BASED ON A SOCIAL RECIPROCITY MORALITY

In contrast to what I think might best be called the ethics of greed and vanity, the ethics of social reciprocity, which is based on seeing others as being as valuable as self and in which one's actions toward others are consistent with the way one wants to be treated, has been embraced as a central concept by the world's major religions,[5] secular philosophies, and enlightened local and national democratic governments. Despite the tendency for social hierarchy creation, consciousness about the value of social reciprocity appears universal to varying degrees. (Brown, 1991). However, the ethical perspective of "do unto others" tends to be eroded by other human drives or purposes. It slips away into obscure shadows when certain people in a community focus almost exclusively on self-gain for various reasons. The personal aggrandizement motive that allows agents to buy into hierarchical ranking and resource distribution schemes is contrary to the aims of a social reciprocity or communitarian ethic that is essential to a strong democracy (Barber, 1984; Greene, 1993; Harvey, 1996; Rawls, 1971; Young, 2000). Humans are diverted by what might be characterized as a false consciousness[6] of the purposes of schooling—indeed, the purposes of life, or what I may go so far as to call the "false gods" of pride, greed, and commodity fetishism. Greene (1993) notes that Dewey envisioned schools as an inclusive "Great Community" that would prepare students for genuine democratic participation.

Transformative democratic and communitarian reform depends on consensus[7] and collective action; therefore, my goal in writing this book is to inspire readers to join a movement that opposes stratifying measures and works to lessen or eradicate hierarchical and excluding relations in school and society. Granted these ideas are utopian; however, in order not to drift toward undemocratic social conditions and so that our daily professional efforts allow progress toward prized goals, an ideal community must be imagined to guide our practice (Anderson, 1983) or praxis (Freire, 1989). "Do unto others" with its emphasis on social reciprocity is an appropriate motto for a democratic country in which equality and social responsibility are major goals (see Sober & Wilson, 1998).

Although he conceives of social justice as a heterogeneous set of concepts, Harvey endorses a "decentralized communitarianism which espouses egalitarianism, nonhierarchical forms of organization, and widespread local empowerment and participation in decision-making as the political norm" (p. 181) and favors anything that mitigates destructive, degrading, and debilitating racism (and classism). In terms of a constructive role for activists, Rorty (1998) observes that "initiatives come from people who have enough security, money, and power themselves, but nevertheless worry about the fate of people who have less" and gives such examples as "muckraking exposés by journalists, novelists, and scholars" (p. 53). Rorty claims there is already some consensus about what is meant by social justice: "decent wages and working conditions, and the end of racial prejudice" (p. 59). Bourdieu (1996) insists that reason and rational knowledge are the best weapons against domination. Although Harvey (1996) recalls the Frankfurt School's criticism of hegemonic instrumental rationality, he notes they sought an alternative rationality that had the power to give a deeper meaning to life through a rough solidarity around moral values.

CONFRONTING STATUS HIERARCHIES: IS IT A JOB FOR SCHOLARS?

Bourdieu (1998) claims that neoliberalism[8] succeeds in presenting itself as self-evident because nothing is put forward to oppose it. Professional class inaction regarding inequity is consistent with Freire's (1973) judgment that subordinates cannot rely on dominant groups to change conditions for them. Scholars are, in fact, integral to the world of educational hierarchies. When we ask Gramci's "who benefits" from educational stratification, we must admit that we do. Harvey (1996) feels that academics err in being individualistic, professionally fragmented, and involved in egotistically driven enterprises. Speaking of the field of sociology, Feagin (1999) claims: "Much mainstream research has drifted away from the urgent moral and practical concerns voiced by critical sociologists since the first decades of this [20th] century" (p. B4).

Evidence from my research indicates that professionals and scholars have a divided mind—one that allows a public or theoretical rejection of hierarchies but retains a personal desire for them. This split affinity, or hypocracy, is something that we live with but rarely talk about.[9] Indeed, the status connected with high educational attainment is seductive in drawing even critical scholars into competition for advancement and recognition. This trend for intellectuals may be of modern origin, particularly coinciding with expanding education and extensive credentialing of professions. Foucault (1980) observes that "universal intellectuals have been replaced by specific intellectuals who have credentials to use technical expertise and work within a discipline" (p. 7). Martin (1998) notes Gramsci's observation that intellectuals from working-class backgrounds cease to serve the interests of their original class and play a conservative role by supporting the status quo of institutional and political life.

Inequity is by definition the conflict of relational (Whitty, 2000) and social positions. So, advocating for Others destabilizes the power and status of the mainstream and threatens academic stature. Wells (2000) observes that in the present (rightist) political and economic climate, people who question neoliberalism are promptly dismissed. Leftists who go against the conservative grain in higher education are vulnerable to censure and rejection (Whitty, 2000; Wilson, 1995). Fine (1992) claims that although politics "saturates all research, those of us who 'come clean' [identify as being on the left] run the risk of being portrayed as distinctly biased" (p. 230). Yet, as Zizek (1994) maintains, everything is ideological and political, so it is best to locate ourselves within this complex reality and be open about our politics and ethics.

Although nothing is neutral, I use "political" in an honorific way for theories that address the intentionality of actors' self-serving orientations and that connect to an agenda for transformative change. Within these parameters, it is possible to ask pertinent questions about the nature of social life. We must comply with Becker's (1963) request that scholars answer the fundamental question: Which side are you on? We should not just be for social justice theoretically but must work for change in our personal and professional lives and be willing to give up material advantage and social status so that egalitarian ideals might be realized. Thus, we are not exempt from our own critical insights (Bourdieu, 1998) and our prescriptions for others.

My breakdown of morality constructs an overly neat dichotomy of sup-porters of hierarchies (the bad) and opponents of hierarchies (the good). I am not alone. Rorty (1998) writes: "Understanding evil was basic to the Progressive Movement in American politics" (p. 34). Yet in naming evil it is important not to assert the same sense of moral superiority we condemn in others. It is necessary to point out that binaries represent a continuum in which there are few pure cases at either end. Most of us vacillate between various confounded, intertwined, and overlapping strands of hierarchical and reciprocal thinking and acting. Freedom from the false consciousness of hierarchical thinking that causes oppression is founded on awakening a consciousness (Freire, 1973) of the value of a reciprocal morality. Con-sciousness raising must further result in an informed agency that inspires people to be brave enough to be activists for social justice. There are excel-lent models of such activists (see Crocco, Munro, & Weiler, 1999; Freire, 1985; Horton, 1998; Walker, 1997).

In terms of defining roles for intellectuals—although I assign a think-ing and theorizing role broadly to all humans and not just erudite people with cultural capital and credentials—those of us who are paid to set trends in schools of education or lead in public schools should be held most accountable for deep, critical thinking about how to improve life circum-stances for all citizens. According to Martin (1998), Gramsci defines intel-lectuals as consciously reflective social analysts (who interrogate their own tacit sociocultural knowledge and class-embedded ideologies). For Gramsci, the test of intellectual production by organic intellectuals is the extent to which their thinking fuses with the life of the masses—an approach con-sistent with Freire's (1973) consciousness raising through literacy instruc-tion. Said (1994) claims real intellectuals are moved by metaphysical passions about disinterested principles of justice and truth, and they de-nounce corruption, defend the weak, and defy imperfect and oppressive authority (p. 6). So, too, for Mills (1963), intellectuals have impassioned social visions.

Although Harvey (1996) notes that it is dangerous in academia these days to confess to being meta about anything (p. 2), he believes that the grand metanarratives about social equity (e.g., Marx) and the Enlighten-ment ideals of equality and justice (see Latour, 1993) are relevant to today's society. Walkerdine (2000) notes that subject positions have been created for people, thus advocating that new spaces be created so that people can reinvent themselves [and Others] in more positive ways. In discussing gen-der relations, she recommends that as women's roles change, men must be prepared to cope with the loss of a particular kind of masculinity. In a sim-ilar vein, it is clear that if social class relations are to change, not only should materials and status be redistributed but new roles and identities must be developed for the traditional oppressors as well as the traditionally oppressed.

OPPOSITION TO DOMINATION: A ROLE FOR TRANSFORMATIVE INTELLECTUALS

Considering what might work in modern times, principles can be drawn from such intellectuals as Polanyi (1957), who claims that reciprocity—giving and receiving according to need, which has been the dominant mode of exchange in traditional societies—should be the principle for social relations in complex industrial economies. Rawls (1971) recommends a distributive justice in which the neediest in society are the first to get scarce resources. Kittay (1999), the mother of a severely disabled child, examines the dependency work of women and writes that her aim is to "find a knife sharp enough to cut through the fiction of our independence" (p. xiii). Koggel (1998) suggests that instead of limiting thinking to what individuals need as independent, autonomous agents, a relationship approach to equality asks what moral persons embedded in relationships of interdependency need to flourish. Relationships should include all community members.

TRANSFORMATION OF SCHOOLS

Meier (1994) pressures educators to look at the purpose and nature of schools so that their means and ends align better. She insists that high-stakes measures are not the answer (Meier, 2000). It is imperative that educators not create debilitating roles for children by implementing differentiating educational policies and practices (Oakes, Quartz, Ryan, & Lipton, 2000), by providing subtractive education to the children of powerless families (Noddings, 2000), or by consenting to destructive measures advocated by a corporate elite whose main concern is personal profit and not children's interests (McNeil, 2000a). Middle-class parents must be convinced that they and their offspring will benefit if democracy is improved through valuing and including Other people's children. Administrators must "respect the moral bottom line" and not give in to illegitimate requests of self-centered school patrons (Kohn, 1998, p. 576). Teachers might follow the model of Pruyn (1999), who during his 9-year teaching career in a Los Angeles refugee neighborhood, took a Freirean approach to helping students become aware of and change their societal positions. The editors of *Rethinking Schools* (2000) set forth principles to guide reform initiatives that resonate with my beliefs, including schools must be responsible to communities, not the marketplace; actively multicultural and antiracist; promote social justice for all; be geared toward learning for life and for the needs of a democracy; receive adequate resources; collaborate with parents and other community members. These editors also insist that communities as well as schools be revitalized.

Due to routine noninvolvement of teachers in real decision making and the disruption of top-down reform pressures, Herr (2000) advocates creating change from within schools by having teachers name their own concerns. Saavedra (2000) recommends that teachers have more control and respect so that they will get over their fears and quit privileging the expert, external knowledge that is often aligned with corporate interests and demands. She appeals to them to quit allowing themselves to be pathologized and forced into unhealthy competitiveness with each other so that they become disempowered technicians—they should fight the oppressive control forced on them in the name of somebody else's idea of reform. Saavedra sees a need for solidarity and authentic partnerships among teachers, and suggests they join with teachers' movements. An example of teacher activism is 6 Florida teachers who traveled 6 hours to return their bonuses (for students' high test scores) to Governor Jeb Bush in order to focus attention on what they see as a misuse of the Florida comprehensive achievement test to rank schools (Fairtest, Winter 1999–2000b, p. 5). But a movement for equity and social justice on the part of teachers must be joined by others. If social activism is to be successful, it must be revitalized and broadened to have the critical mass necessary for an effective social movement (Marwell & Oliver, 1993; Tarrow, 1998). Such activism will require work and commitment as well as the bravery to not just leave the mainstream but reject it and confront it. Social movements are necessarily extrainstitutional; for change to be durable, activism and collective movements must disrupt rather than interrupt dominant practice (Katzenstein, 1998).

THE POSSIBILITY OF TRANSFORMATIVE MOVEMENTS

As conditions are in flux, improving dramatically for some and worsening drastically for others, democratic principles and ethical social relations are in jeopardy. Moral vacillation is the history that has become apparent to Hunt (2000). She surmises that only periodically do people come up with moral "truths" that they hold to be "universal" and "self-evident." This thinking occurs during revolutionary periods. The French Revolution spawned the Enlightenment. Americans' break from England resulted in the writing of the Constitution. In both cases there was a groundswell of populist thinking about basic human rights and the nature of civic relations. Idealistic thinking apparently happens only periodically when there is a reason to be hopeful, or when some major form of societal upheaval causes people to be anxious about social life. Perhaps at other times people get so caught up in the banal routines of daily life that they do not see the big picture or think past the mundane.

Reflecting on Hunt's theory, it seems that the rapid technological development as well as the fast-paced rate of economic and political globalization constitute a revolutionary period in which the social class polarization of wealth and power has caused many to react by becoming both idealistic and activist. Protests against the World Trade Organization in Seattle, the World Bank in Switzerland, and the Summit of the Americas in Quebec City represent a growing contingent of Americans who are willing to participate in public activism.[10] These movements are not directed at the power of the government per se but at its links with transglobal corporations.

Governments can be political entities and moral agents with transformative potential (Martin, 1998, p. 73). Indeed, regulations to curb the potential destruction of the free reign of capitalism are sorely needed at this time. Social institutions and the professionals who run them have the potential to enhance social justice and equity. Various philosophies about the role of government in relation to social institutions, citizens, and business enterprise wax and wane. With market deregulation, rampaging consumerism, fluctuating economic and monetary stability, global colonization by abusive industries, rapid ecological decline, and rightist control of institutions, many feel a sense of urgency about the disastrous dividing and impoverishing effects of global capitalism. "It transpires that there is not a region in the world where manifestations of anger and discontent with the capitalist system cannot be found" (Harvey, 1996, p. 430). Rather than being passive (Eliasoph, 1998), it is time that citizens take stock of trends and make deliberative democratic decisions about the future (Elster, 1998). Oettingen (1996) asks that people generate positive fantasies and mental images depicting future events; that optimism has beneficial effects on motivation, cognition, and affect. Schudson (1998) advocates the need to capture the national imagination with a large moral mission.

Notes

PREFACE

1. Hillsdale is a pseudonym as are all names for people and places in this book.
2. *Poor* and *low* refer to financial and achievement status.
3. A hodgepodge of disasters are forewarned: school failure, grade repetition, low test scores, dropping out of school, early unwed pregnancy, substance abuse, inadequate parenting, chronic unemployment and/or underemployment.
4. The Enron scandal broke as I was writing this book. The moral outrage and indignation about that intentional economic fiasco came from both the left and the right; however, it was implied that the practices connected with this situation were rare rather than common business tactics.
5. *Negotiates* implies deliberate actions: "confer with another so as to arrive at the settlement of some matter"; "deal with some matter or affair that requires ability for its successful handling"; "arrange for or bring about through conference, discussion, and compromise" (*Merriam Webster's Collegiate Dictionary,* 10th ed. (1993). Springfield, MA, p. 777).
6. I use *rationalize* rather than *justify* or *legitimate* because it refers to psychological functions. It is defined as "to invent plausible explanations for (acts, opinions, etc., that actually have other causes)" (*Webster Desk Dictionary of the English Language* (1983). Springfield, MA: Merriam-Webster). "To bring into accord with reason or cause something to seem reasonable"; "to attribute (one's actions) to rational motives"; "to provide plausible but untrue reasons for conduct"(*Merriam Webster's Collegiate Dictionary,* 10th ed. (1993), Springfield, MA, p. 969).
7. Low-income people mainly live on the west side and high-income people on the east side of Hillsdale.

CHAPTER 1

1. The differences in overall family assets make the gap even more discrepant than just comparing current salaries (Conley, 1999; Oliver & Shapiro, 1995).

2. Lee (2002) and Gee (2002) claim that the historical gap between the test scores of white and black students narrowed until the late 1970s but has widened since then. Gee claims neoliberal educators know why the trend reversed (equity was not emphasized) but choose to ignore it.

3. According to Mirel (1994), such fundamental political aspects of education as "who controls schools, whose security is threatened by reform, and who attempts to protect and expand their turf" are as important to reform as "exciting ideas, strong financial backing, and committed reformers" (p. 515).

4. For example, current myths about dominant group strengths are promoted by advocates for the standards and accountability movement as norms that are advantageous for all people.

5. When a capital O is used, it means that a process of marginalization is at work that involves stigmatizing classifications, segregation or banishment, and even bodily violence.

6. Brown also concludes that people recognize the benefits of a reciprocal morality.

7. Relatedly, women often attribute their lesser status to personal inadequacies rather than gender bias even when they know better (Acker & Feuerverger, 1996; Aisenberg & Harrington, 1988; Assiter, 1996; Bartky, 1990; Crocco, Munro, & Weiler, 1999; Fine, 1992; Hauser, 1997; Martin, 1994; Ortner, 1996; Walkerdine, 2000).

8. The pretense of scholarly knowledge as authorless, disinterested, and value-free is what Nagel (1986) calls the "view from nowhere." Apfelbaum (1999) would locate the sources of such knowledge in those at the powerful center of mainstream institutional life.

9. Consciousness is the part of mental life that is discursively accessible to one's own awareness (Wright, 1985, p. 245).

10. According to LiPuma (1993), Bourdieu sees the origins of symbolic power as lying within a necessary period of socialization or habitus in which the basic principles of an initial culturally arbitrary system of beliefs, values, norms, and practices are inculcated or internalized so that they perpetuate or reproduce the authority and dominance of a powerful group or class.

11. "Symbolic forms include a range of actions and utterances, images and texts, which are produced by subjects and recognized by them and others as meaningful constructs" (p. 59).

12. For example, *even in America,* criminals and people with disabilities were sterilized and incarcerated to prevent the "breeding" and danger to society (Brantlinger, 1995).

13. The front-page billing of *The Bell Curve* in *Time* and *Newsweek* initially appears critical, but a close reading reveals ambivalent views on class, race, reproduction, intelligence, poverty, and the nature of school achievement.

14. Deprivationists see immorality and family breakdown (personal inadequacies) as the cause of poverty, whereas McDermott and Varenne (1996) see caring behavior set against a breakdown of job opportunities (structural constraints).

15. Perhaps much of the multicultural education scholarship that focuses on diversity without acknowledging structural inequality falls within this genre.

16. Work by scientists who attempt to generate (objective) knowledge about Others and develop interventions to improve these Others' performance. Schnog (1997) and Bruner (1996) critique social scientists for naturalizing oppressive and dehumanized standards of adjustment.

17. Supposed, because the "woe" is never located in low working-class salaries or lack of jobs for the unemployed or underemployed but rather in our country's rivalry with other nations.

18. Credentials give authority to some and take it from Others (Bourdieu, 1996).
19. Control paradigms only emerge in inegalitarian conditions (Rosaldo, 1984).
20. Although the focus is on cultural assimilation, the increasing ratio of people of color is always announced as problematic. Then, too, poverty is to be eliminated regardless of the fact that the lifestyle of the poor puts less of a strain on the environment than that of the wealthy.
21. These arguments are not new. In *Stigma,* Goffman (1963) wrote of how professionals' classification leads some to have permanent out-group status. Mills (1943) observed how norms and values relate to distributions of power and professional ideologies create social pathologies.
22. Special education classification and marginalized service arrangements have parental permission carefully written into such laws as Individuals with Disabilities Education Act (IDEA) and its predecessor, Education of All Handicapped Children Act (EHCA).
23. Another instance of ideological storytelling to justify student rankings.
24. In contrast, high-income adolescents approved of these arrangements.
25. Globalization is "a set of processes by which the world is rapidly being integrated into one economic space via increased international trade, the internalization of production and financial markets, the internationalization of a commodity culture promoted by an increasingly networked global telecommunications system" (Gibson-Graham, 1996, p. 121).
26. This echoes Marx's theories about the relation between base and superstructure.
27. Bourdieu (1998) and others (e.g., Gee, 2002; Wells, 2000) define neoliberalism as the dominant discourse of political submission to economic rationality, undivided reign of the market, and withering away of state regulation of business or provisions for human welfare.
28. Although many countries have become independent from western colonization, Ahmad maintains that decolonization has mainly involved bringing a national bourgeoisie to leadership positions, typically not people who had been in the dangerous forefront of their country's anticolonial struggles (p. 18). Power changes hands in decolonized nations, but the class structure does not change nor does the class character of imperialist nations diminish.
29. The media does, however, stress the perils of declining markets and the importance of remaining a military superpower.
30. The public got temporary reprieve from the constant harangue about school failure when the press was distracted by the tragic events of September 11, 2001, and the war against Afghanistan.
31. Anyon reports that 50% of workers are just above the poverty line and 24% are under it. One fifth are part-time with no fringe benefits or job security. One in ten make over $65,000 annually.
32. For example, white working-class men hold blacks accountable for their own economic insecurity and conditions of job fragility (Weis & Fine, 1996).
33. "Brazilianization" refers to a phenomenon of the tax base—hence public-sector jobs for the educated middle class—to be squeezed out in countries with extremes of wealth and poverty.
34. Related to apathy is the high level of nonproductive contentiousness among the political parties during elections and in interactions afterward (Meyer & Tarrow, 1998).

CHAPTER 2

1. In about 1949, this national system stopped in my area. It was bought by the Ford company and deliberately shut down so that people would buy cars. Because my father worked in St. Paul, we were among the families forced to buy a car when our streetcar line closed.

2. I included an autobiographical sketch in my 1993 book but only wrote about the small-town atmosphere, substantial cross-class contacts, and fairly equitable nature of our school. My older sister remarked on her surprise that I had not mentioned how aware we were of the class differences between summer and winter people.

3. My middle-class perspective might not match that of my lower-income classmates, but my best friends were daughters of our garbage collector, a farmer, an auto mechanic, an office worker, and a dentist. At a recent school reunion, I was pleased that my memory of good relations across social classes was confirmed by others.

4. All of the students at my "Lake Wobegon"–like school were white.

5. Practicum sites included a youth shelter (temporary housing and schooling for runaways), a juvenile correction facility, an inpatient treatment center for elementary and secondary students with serious emotional disabilities, an adult literacy program, work-related programs for adults with severe cognitive disabilities, an alternative high school, and an independent school for K–8 students with dyslexia. I also placed students with social workers who worked with parents with mental retardation who had abused or neglected their children and with home programers who worked with infants and toddlers with disabilities and their families.

6. For an overview of some repercussions of this local activism, see Brantlinger, 1999a.

7. A problem with our decision was that our son was adopted and African American. Some neighbors who had been angered by my attempts at social class desegregation of schools let it be known that we might not have made the same decision if he had been a birth child. During his second year at Southside, when he was in a class of 39 for the second year and had a teacher who had been transferred from a high-income school because of multiple parental complaints, we exercised our right to choose and sent him to Richards Elementary. This was a trying time. What assuages my guilt about subjecting our son to bad school conditions is that good things happened: (1) the four high-income parents made such a fuss about poor school conditions that we inspired other Southside parents to become activists and successfully pressured the board and administration into replacing the old school, stopping the biased involuntary teacher transfer policy, and funding schools on a per capita rather than fees-collected basis; (2) our popular son made friends at Southside, and when he got to middle school, he brought students from diverse classes together in a constructive way; and (3) this now adult son is proud that his parents are principled and has no ill feelings about our sending him to a lesser school.

8. As an adjunct professor of special education, I was already studying sexuality and disability issues, so this research was not related to career goals at the time, although social class later became my strongest interest.

9. A residential census approach to participant identification.

10. Morrow and Torres claim that classic social class reproduction theory operated exclusively at the level of systemic analysis and thus reduced agents to passive, interpellated subjects. In contrast, purely hermeneutic and humanistic sociology focused on actions of individuals or groups at the expense of systemic analysis of institutions.

11. A third middle school has since been built close to new affluent suburbs.

12. Most mothers rank in this class because of their own professions and salaries; others (clerical worker, homemaker) achieve this status through the occupations of their spouses.

13. The effect of having a "foreigner" conduct interviews has been discussed by Chang (1992), Lamont (1992), and Varenne (1986); that is, while participants explain how things are in the United States to an outsider, they reveal much about themselves and their perspectives.

14. Initial interviewees identified people they perceived as sensitive to class issues and as politically liberal.

15. The U.S. Census Bureau (1990) identified roughly 95% of local residents to be European American and 4.02% to be African American.

16. Families whose children had attended secondary (social class comprehensive) schools were purposely selected.

17. Actually, school volunteers or those actively involved in school affairs had typically been mothers rather than fathers.

18. Another reason that men may have relegated participation to wives was that the contacting person was a woman. Participants were informed that couples could take part, yet only one father was present and he chose to be a silent observer.

19. My original intention was to interview more nonprofessional staff, but because time constraints prohibited this, the one interview with a secretary is not reported in this book.

CHAPTER 3

1. Win in school and win in rendering themselves morally superior.

2. Felski (2002) concludes that the "common belief that everyone in America is middle class makes no sense in a country that boasts some of the largest income disparities in the Western world" (p. 24).

3. Lynn adds "even" in telling of her husband's involvement. The powerful force of a professional man backing her up supports Atkinson's (1985) interpretation of women's in-between place in status production and power relations. Of course, a powerful father is likely to be symbolically present in school personnel's minds even when mothers do most of the negotiations regarding their children's school careers.

4. Ideologies construct knowledge for their subjects that allow them to utter ideological truths as if they were the "authentic authors" of these truths (Larrain, 1992, p. 97).

5. In spite of expecting the best resources for their children, mothers also held the illusion that the poor received more resources, which were a drain on those available to their families.

6. Seven taught in local schools or worked at social service agencies.

7. Bias was diminished by attributing it to personal (residing in some teachers) rather than institutional (structure of schools) factors. Critical views were present but were not overarching.

8. Middle-class mothers may not seem to be a powerful group, but in the educational context, especially when they act as spokesperson for a family headed by an influential male, they wield considerable power in determining school policy and practice not only for their own children but also by default for Other people's children.

9. Swartz (1993) calls "replacement codes" (where they belong, in their own neighborhoods") "hegemonic constructions" (p. 501).

10. This is where "false consciousness" is apparent in the middle class.

11. Hartsock (1987) states that male dominance is maintained by the sexual division of labor and that men achieve masculinity by distancing themselves from home. Fraser

(1989) claims that male dominance is intrinsic to—rather than accidental to—classical capitalism and that the institutional structure of this social formation is actualized by means of gendered roles.

12. Because fathers were not included in this study, I cannot make definitive claims about comparative gender roles in the reproduction of the vertical class system. Because the few fathers who did answer the telephone relegated participation in the study to their wives, it seems that mothers were perceived by couples as the ones who should take part in a study about schooling. Mothers talked of their heavy responsibility for their children's school possibilities and rarely mentioned their husband's role regarding children or school, except as a backup person when they were unsuccessful in having their requests met by school personnel.

CHAPTER 4

1. Sandra Harding (1998) maintains that much of the Western European knowledge base is really an accumulation of ideas from a variety of nations and cultures, but Westerners colonize this knowledge and claim it as their own. Hence, what we often think of as the superior Western culture and techniques really is an aggregate of artifacts from many world cultures.

2. Carnoy (2000) claims that one effect of globalization has been a focus on quality, and Shweder (1991) reasons that "hierarchy is a concomitant of excellence" (p. 35).

3. Achievement could include creative projects done for the self-satisfaction or social contribution of students (progressive conceptualization) or expectation to excel academically (compete for high scores) to ensure access to top-ranked settings (a conservative agenda).

4. Metcalf makes the case that the textbook companies oppose whole language because they want to sell their basal readers, phonics workbooks, and other commercially made supplies. Whole language, with its emphasis on trade books and expressive writing, put an immediate dent in the traditional material sales, but trade books and blank paper are also commercially produced, so it seems that the gains for corporations would be the same in the long run.

5. It is interesting here that mothers imply their children are not so self-motivated and school oriented as they described when they contrasted them with low-income children.

6. New programs or regulations were the result of the civil rights actions of African Americans, Chicanos, and Native Americans. It is unlikely that the injustices and inequities would have been visible or seen as problematic if it had not been for the litigation, social movements, and fervent demands of these groups. Although middle-class European Americans responded to the demands and threats, that does not mean they would have given up power and advantage if they had not been forced to do so. Also, most of the social initiatives did not affect middle-class white Americans. When they did, such as when desegregation plans involved two-way busing, parents vociferously protested (and delayed or prevented their implementation), sent their children to private schools, or moved to more distant suburbs that were not part of desegregation plans. When nondiscriminatory housing regulations actually were enforced, advantaged people chose with their pocketbooks and resettled in new exclusive neighborhoods.

7. Another way to look at the funding of social initiatives that are supposedly aimed at helping the poor or disadvantaged is that they usually mean an expansion of social services—an expansion that means additional professional jobs for college-educated members of the middle class. A simple proof of this assertion is that the poor have stayed poor—their ranks have expanded, their conditions have worsened, and their

isolation has increased while the social service sector has grown as have the credentials needed to be a professional.

8. It may not be valid to equate liberal with progressive, but in common usage they seem to be somewhat interchangeable or overlapping concepts.

CHAPTER 5

1. One of the characteristics of qualitative designs is that issues and data arise that were not originally anticipated but do turn out to be relevant upon close examination of results.

2. Thirty interviewed teachers and administrators seemed too many for all to be named, yet because I quote a few of them several times and they have somewhat distinctive perspectives, I use first-name pseudonyms so that readers can see the connections between some of their responses.

3. In a study of preservice teachers, Lexmond (2002) found they chose middle school students similar to themselves to write about in their "observation of a student" papers.

4. Betty did not specifically mention this, but Symbionese Liberation Front members Bill and Emily Harris had taught at Beauford for a couple of years prior to moving to California.

5. Harvey (2001) writes how people's spacial imaginaries are linked to national boundaries. His theory also can explain how Hillsdale residents from various parts of town view each other.

6. Due to criticism of bias in the teacher transfers, the district had put a restriction on interschool personnel transfers. These could occur only when the teacher/pupil ratio at a school made it necessary or when a teacher with a particular type of certification was needed at another school.

7. In my study (1985b), low-income parents confessed that they never went to school to complain about something unless they were extremely upset and they were less likely to achieve an outcome—they expected school personnel to ignore them—than to express their anger.

8. Karl sees a correlation between students and teacher class background at local schools.

9. Tracking involves dividing whole classes by achievement; ability grouping subdivides a class into achievement levels for small-group instruction in reading and mathematics. Tracking is usually done at the secondary level and ability grouping at the elementary school level.

10. Note that she ends by stating exclusion is in the best interest of the excluded students.

11. Children eligible for gifted and talented classes had the option of being bused to a school-wide program at Eastside. Beauford teachers believed that their advanced classes were roughly equivalent to the gifted and talented classes at Eastside, and bragged that because parents felt the same way, they often declined the invitation for their children to attend that program.

12. Beauford had "average" and "advanced" tracks, but teachers usually called them "high" or "top" and "low." Most students were in advanced tracks. My own observations and conversations with teachers indicate that low-income children were usually in average tracks.

13. Beauford is a predominantly high-income school; however, about 10–15% of its enrollment come from a lower-middle- and working-class neighborhood within its catchment area. The class correlations with track placement are obvious.

14. Three *already there* teachers used this exact phrase in reference to low-income students.
15. *Already there* teachers readily, and with no apology, dismissed low-income schools as inappropriate for their children, but *in-the-middle* teachers asked not to have their identity revealed when they rejected high-income schools on the grounds of their being elitis.

CHAPTER 6

1. Some of this information comes from newspaper coverage; however, as a member of Jobs with Justice and a Local Workers Rights Board, I have been involved with hearings, petitions, and protests related to local corporate activities and economic conditions in Hillsdale.
2. In the spring of 2002, a Marriott Hotel fired all local workers and contracted with a company that brought in a team of Czech maids and maintenance workers who were "guaranteed" a 48-hour work week at $2 an hour.
3. She conveyed that her father's opposition was due to working-class pride.
4. The campus AFT petitioned successfully for opening faculty records on the tenure and promotion process, having open access to salaries of all faculty and administrators, and initiating review boards that would hear cases of unfairness to faculty. It also encouraged the formation of the Graduate Student Organization and helped them secure improved benefits and better salaries.
5. Speaking about "poverty" frames a "charitable" perspective that does not challenge social hierarchies, whereas addressing "social class" implies an interrogation of hierarchies.
6. A year after the interviews, the caring and insightful Corey left the field of teaching to pursue a full-time career as an artist. She had no intentions of returning to teaching.
7. Supposed "neutrality" and "passivity" about inequalities certainly are very political acts.
8. In his first year of teaching, when the principal gave him a test-oriented curriculum to follow for 2 months until the tests, my son refused to use it. The principal explained several times that he was required to follow it and my son repeatedly refused to; the principal finally said: "Just don't tell me you are not using it." When my son's students tested considerably higher than other classes, the principal "rewarded" him by assigning him all advanced sections the next year.

CHAPTER 7

1. Such school board representation is not unique. Gross came to the same conclusion about national elected and appointed boards in 1976.
2. Because these central administrators were referred to by their last names by other participants, their last names will be used in this chapter. The author admits that it is problematic to use first name pseudonyms for mothers and teachers (mostly women) and last names for men.
3. Hillsdale residents would have been aware of social class discrepancies, although they were rarely mentioned at school board meetings nor did they receive attention in the local press.
4. Principals at some low-income schools had half-time administrative duties, so they were assigned as *the* librarian for the other half day. Because principals had so many administrative duties they rarely got to the library part of their job. Hence, libraries were mostly unavailable to children.
5. To penalize me for speaking up and instigating criticism from others about his practices, Edwards retaliated by drawing the line for which children could ride a bus to

school on the alley (no major thoroughfare or straight boundary) beside my house. Some neighbors also affected by this decision were angry at me but in the end heeded my advice. We lined our children up at the bus stop on the first day of school. The bus driver said nothing and from then on no one prevented our neighborhood children from riding the bus. I presume that Edwards knew he would not win a court battle over that issue and also learned he could not intimidate me.

6. Within 5 years, the north-side school was sold to a local manufacturer who used the building to house his eventually famous drum and bugle corps and his charter bus enterprise.

7. Several knowledgeable Hillsdale residents warned that the population expansion of the 1950s and 1960s was over and that projections for the future should not be based on past growth. The board and administration did not listen. Many speculate that because of real estate and construction business connections they chose not to hear this sage advice.

8. This rationale contradicted reasons he had given through the years that poor children had to be clustered in separate schools so that the district could receive Chapter One funding for compensatory programming, which depended on schools having a high ratio of poor children.

9. When some of us pointed out this contradiction, Edwards, who was talented at justifying his actions, informed us that new school construction came from a separate budget and so was not adding to the already apparent financial problems of the district.

10. This town was slightly larger, industrial, and its university neither as prestigious nor as large.

11. The four newly elected board members had been leaders in actions to preserve their rural schools and were not long-term politicians or activists with a reputation for informed leadership. Although cast by many as ignorant country bumpkins or prejudiced rednecks, these individuals were articulate and had sound ideas about democratic education for the community's schools.

12. The local chiropractor's term was not up.

13. "Meeting the needs of all" is used rhetorically by affluent parents to mean their children need high tracks and differentiated curriculum. Rockenweil used "all" to refer to lower-middle-class, working-class, and rural children—a usage that converged with the trustees' interests.

14. Northern and western states appear to have a better record for school equity than some districts in the central middle-western states.

15. Elementary students already had been assigned reading and math books at different levels and secondary students to tracks, so in spite of first insisting on immediate heterogeneous groups, Rockenweil was convinced by principals and the assistant superintendent of elementary education (retained from Edwards's administration) that this would be too difficult at such short notice.

16. In the 12 years since his departure, teachers and administrators still refer to Rockenweil as "Dr. Scripting" or facetiously refer to his 2-year administration as the "scripting time."

17. Sensitive *in-the-middle* teachers were especially hurt by the implied criticism of teachers.

18. Granted, this was somewhat before site-based management had gained momentum.

19. Knowing the likely composition of the new board and its agenda, Dieken agreed to run for school board and was elected. When I interviewed him, he was serving his

second term on the board. One reason it took so long to hire a replacement for Rockenweil was that board members had such disparate and conflicting perspectives that they could not agree on a candidate.

20. An upbringing and perspective that matched my own.

21. Mostly because of the personal stress of my local activism (see Brantlinger, 1999a), I rarely attended board meetings for a number of years after Superintendent Edward's departure.

22. During his administration, the dilapidated old building was torn down and a beautiful new building was constructed on the same spot. Additionally the grounds were landscaped and the playground was improved so that it could be the showcase school of Hillsdale.

23. Dieken was interviewed in his own rather small home in a modest older suburb, which is one of the reasons that he was categorized as *in the middle* (see chapter 5).

24. The improvements he addressed here had been identified as needed to redress discriminatory practices in my *Model Community* paper. Again, for reasons I cannot now explain, perhaps my own shyness or discomfort about "being radical," I did not ask Dieken if he knew me by reputation or by my writing. His responses led me to believe that he did.

25. Dieken came to the same conclusion about the correspondence between schools where school personnel work and their own social class affiliation, which I address in chapter 5.

26. As a board member, Dieken consistently opposed the creation of additional tracking.

27. In my experience with interviewing, I have found that the best "data" tend to come after the tape recorder is turned off, the pen and paper are put away, and I am standing at the door ready to depart, so I must quickly reconstruct responses when I get back to my office.

28. Which, upon questioning, he defined as sorting students into categories and tracks.

29. As a personnel director, Calhoun was known for actively recruiting and hiring African American teachers.

30. It is likely that Hale had been hired as acting principal because of the board's fear of legal ramifications from his dismissal as assistant superintendent. He knew he would not be reappointed to that or any other administrative position on a permanent basis.

31. And, he might have added, the children of the wealthiest people in town.

32. This principal had accompanied Rockenweil and Hale to Hillsdale.

33. Unlike Dieken, Calhoun, and Hale, all of whom I categorized as having *in-the-middle* status, I dub Husby as an *upward striver* not so much because of what he said in the interview but because of where he lived, where his children attended school, and what I knew to be his actual position based on observing his actions over a number of years.

34. Certainly he recalled that I mentioned a per capita fee distribution policy in my *Model Community* report and petitioned long and hard for that change. During Edwards's administration, Husby himself told me that a per capita rather than an "as fees are collected" basis for resource distribution would be illegal.

CHAPTER 9

1. The *cycle of poverty* is often mentioned, whereas the *cycle of advantage* is not.

2. Watt then recommends that schools be guided by an alternate, noncompetitive conviction that all people are equally and uniquely valuable, and have the same claim on the respect of their fellows and the benefits of the society.

3. School inequalities are announced but never eliminated—an interesting and disconcerting phenomenon that is highly relevant to the purpose and findings of this book.
4. Regarding education, emancipatory scholars who scrutinize tightly framed, discipline-
   based knowledge conclude that because much of it is unrelated to people's lives, its
   value is mainly as class-distinguishing cultural capital (Bourdieu, 1977, 1984; Freire,
   1989; Shor, 1999). Hence, critical educators must focus on the nature of curriculum
   as well as ranking systems.
5. "What is hateful to you, do not to your fellow man. That is the entire Law; all the rest
   is commentary" (Judaism). "Hurt not others in ways that you yourself would find
   hurtful" (Buddhism). "No one of you is a believer until he desires for his brother that
   which he desires for himself" (Islam). "Do unto others as you would have them do
   unto you" (Christianity). "Blessed is he who preferreth his brother before himself"
   (Baha'i Faith).
6. I use false consciousness perhaps in a rather idiosyncratic way to mean that if it is
   agreed collectively that democracies should be based on a social reciprocity morality,
   then individual purposes tied to self- rather than common interests are false because
   they are socially and ultimately self destructive.
7. Nader (1996) warns of the dangers of consensus; however, it seems important to
   interrupt the current solidarity around the benefits of the market and meritocracies
   and replace them with a consensus about more inclusive, equitable social goods.
8. Again, neoliberal ideology is faith in the rationality and goodness of the market
   accompanied by the sense that acting in one's own self-interest in competitive milieus
   will ensure economic security for self and a contribution to societal progress.
9. I cannot name one among my colleagues who at an abstract or theoretical level does
   not claim to oppose school stratification, yet they/we all want their/our children to be
   in high tracks.
10. These movements and demonstrations get very little serious mainstream press
   coverage.

References

Acker, Sandra (Ed.). (1989). *Teachers, gender, and careers.* Philadelphia, PA: Falmer.

Acker, Sandra, & Feuerverger, Grace (1996). Doing good and feeling bad: The work of women university teachers. *Cambridge Journal of Education, 26*(3), 401–422.

Ahmad, Aijaz (1992). *In theory: Classes, nations, literatures.* London: Verso.

Ahonen, Sirkka (2000). What happens to the common school in the market? *Journal of Curriculum Studies, 32*(4), 483–493.

Aisenberg, Nadya, & Harrington, Mona (1988). *Women of academe: Outsiders in the sacred grove.* Amherst, MA: University of Massachusetts Press.

Alexander, Patricia A., Schallert, Diane L., & Hare, Vivian C. (1991). Coming to terms: How researchers in learning and literacy talk about knowledge. *Review of Educational Research, 61*(3), 315–343.

Althusser, Louis (1971). Ideology and the ideological state apparatus. In *Lenin and philosophy.* New York: Monthly Review Press.

Althusser, Louis (1974/1976). *Essays in self-criticism.* (G. Lock, Trans.). London: New Left Books (original work published in 1974).

Ames, Carole, & Archer, Jennifer (1987). Mothers' beliefs about the role of ability and effort in school learning. *Journal of Educational Psychology, 79*(4), 409–414.

Anderson, Benjamin (1983). *Imagined communities.* London: Verso.

Anderson, Gary L. (2002, April 2). *Performing school reform in the age of the spectacle.* Presented at the Annual Meeting of the American Educational Research Association, New Orleans.

Anderson, Gary L., & Irvine, Patricia (1993). Informing critical literacy with ethnography. In Colin Lankshear & Peter L. McLaren (Eds.), *Critical Literacy: Politics, Praxis, and the Postmodern* (pp. 81–104). Albany: State University of New York Press.

Anderson, Gary, L., & Saavedra, Elizabeth (1995). "Insider" narratives of transformative learning: Implications for educational reform. *Anthropology and Education Quarterly, 26,* 228–235.

Anijar, Karen (1999). The rubber band club and other fables of the urban place. In Frederick Yeo & Barry Kanpol (Eds.), *From nihilism to possibility: Democratic transformation: Democratic transformations for the inner city* (pp. 37–70). Cresskill, NJ: Hampton Press.

Ansalone, George (2001). Schooling, tracking, and inequality. *Journal of Children & Poverty, 7*(1), 33–47.

Anyon, Jean (1980). Social class and the hidden curriculum of work. *Journal of Education, 162,* 67–92.

Anyon, Jean (1981) Elementary schooling and the distinction of social class. *Interchange, 12*(2/3), 118–132.

Anyon, Jean (1997). *Ghetto schooling: A political economy of urban educational reform.* New York: Teachers College Press.

Anyon, Jean (2000, April 25). *Political economy of an affluent suburban school district: Only some students get the best.* Paper presented at the American Educational Research Association Annual Meeting, New Orleans, Louisiana.

Apfelbaum, Erika (1999). Relations of domination and movements for liberation: An analysis of power between groups. *Feminism & Psychology, 9*(3), 267–272.

Apple, Michael W. (1992). Education, culture, and class power: Basil Bernstein and the neo-Marxist sociology of education. *Educational Theory, 42*(2), 127–145.

Apple, Michael W. (1993). *Official knowledge.* New York: Routledge.

Apple, Michael W. (1996). *Cultural politics and education.* New York: Teachers College Press.

Apple, Michael W. (2001). *Educating the right way: Markets, standards, God and inequality.* New York: Routledge-Falmer.

Apter, David E. (1964). Introduction. In David E. Apter (Ed.), *Ideology and discontent* (pp. 15–46). New York: Free Press of Glencoe.

Apter, Terri (1996). Expert witness: Who controls the psychologist's narrative? In Ruthellen Josselson (Ed.), *Ethics and process in the narrative study of lives* (pp. 22–44). Thousand Oaks, CA: Sage.

Arons, Stephen (1997). *Short route to chaos: Conscience, community, and re-constitution of American schooling.* Amherst: University of Massachusetts Press.

Artiles, Alfredo J., & Trent, Stanley (1994). Overrepresentation of minority students in special education: A continuing debate. *Journal of Special Education, 27,* 410–437.

Asante, Molefi K. (1991). The Afrocentric idea in education. *Journal of Negro Education, 62,* 170–180.

Assiter, Alison (1996). *Enlightened women: Modernist feminism in a postmodern age.* London and New York: Routledge.

Associated Press (2000, June 8). Cheating teachers increasingly common: Emphasis on top test scores fuels adult deception, critics say. *Bloomington Herald Times,* p. A4.

Atkinson, Paul (1985). *Language, structure and reproduction.* London: Methuen.

Auerbach, Elsa R. (1989). Toward a social-contextual approach to family literacy. *Harvard Educational Review, 59*(2), 165–181.

Bailey, Alison (2000). Locating traitorous identities: Toward a view of privilege-cognizant white character. In Uma Narayan & Sandra Harding (Eds.), *Decentering the center: Philosophy for a multicultural, postcolonial, and feminist world* (pp. 283–298). Bloomington, IN: Indiana University Press.

Bakhtin, Mikhail (1975/1981). *The dialogic imagination* (C. Emerson & M. Holquist, Trans.). Austin: University of Texas Press (original work published in 1975).

Bakhtin, Mikhail (1983). *Rabelais and his world.* Bloomington: Indiana University Press.

Bales, Kevin (1999). *Disposable people: New slavery in the global economy.* Berkeley: University of California Press.

Ball, Stephen J. (1993). Education markets, choice and social class. *British Journal of Sociology of Education, 14* 3–19.

Ball, Stephen (1994). *Education reform—a critical and post-structuralist approach.* Milton Keynes: Open University Press.

Ball, Stephen J. (1998). Educational studies, policy entrepreneurship and social theory. In Roger Slee, Gaby Weiner, & Sally Tomlinson (Eds.), *School effectiveness for whom? Challenges to the school effectiveness and school improvement movements* (pp. 70–83). London: Falmer.

Ball, Stephen, Kenny, Anthony, & Gardiner, D. (1990). Literacy, politics, and the teaching of English. In Ivor Goodson & Peter Medway (Eds.), *Bringing English to order* (pp. 47–86). London: Falmer.

Banks, James A. (1997). *Educating citizens in a multicultural society.* New York: Teachers College Press.

Bannerji, Himani (1995). *Thinking through: Essays on feminism, Marxism, and anti-racism.* Toronto: Women's Press.

Barber, Benjamin (1984). *Strong Democracy.* Berkeley: University of California Press.

Barber, Benjamin (1992). *An aristocracy of everyone: The politics of education and the future of America.* New York: Ballantine Books.

Baron, Dennis (2000, February 1). Will anyone accept the good news on literacy. *The Chronicle of Higher Education,* p. B10.

Barrett, Michele (1994). Ideology, politics, hegemony: From Gramsci to Laclau and Mouffe. In Slavoj Zizek (Ed.), *Mapping Ideology* (pp. 235–264). London & New York: Verso.

Bartky, Sandra (1990). *Femininity and domination.* New York: Routledge.

Barton, Len, & Oliver, Mike (1997). Special needs: Personal trouble or public issue? In Ben Cosin & Margaret Hales (Eds.), *Families, education and social differences* (pp. 89–101). London & New York: Routledge in Association with The Open University.

Baumeister, Roy F. (1996). Self-regulation and ego threat: Motivated cognition, self-deception, and destructive goal setting. In Peter M., Gollwitzer & John A. Bargh (Eds.), *The psychology of action: Linking cognition and motivation to behavior* (pp. 27–47). New York: The Guilford Press.

Beane, James A. (1990). *Affect in the curriculum: Toward democracy, dignity, and diversity.* New York: Teachers College Press.

Becker, Howard (1963). *Outsiders: Studies in the sociology of deviance.* New York: Free Press.

Belenky, Mary F., Clinchy, Blythe M., Goldberger, Nancy R., & Tarule, Jill M. (1986). *Women's ways of knowing: The development of self, voice, and mind.* Stockbridge, MA: Basic Books.

Bell, Derrick A. (1994). *Confronting authority: Reflections of an ardent protester.* Boston: Beacon Press.

Bellamy, Elizabeth J. (1998). "Intimate enemies": Psychoanalysis, Marxism, and postcolonial affect. In Robert Miklitsch (Special Issue Editor), *Psycho-Marxism: Marxism and psycho-analysis late in the twentieth century* (pp. 341–359). *South Atlantic Quarterly, 97*(2).

Berliner, David (2000, November 14). *What business ought to be concerned about in American Education.* Indiana University School of Education Distinguished Lecture Series.

Berliner, David C., & Biddle, Bruce J. (1995). *The manufactured crisis: Myths, fraud, and the attack on America's public schools.* Reading, MA: Addison-Wesley.

Bernstein, Basil (1971). On the classification and framing of educational knowledge. In Michael F. D. Young (Ed.), *Knowledge and control.* London: Collier-Macmillan.

Bernstein, Basil (1973). *Class codes and control. Vol 1: Theoretical studies towards a sociology of language.* London: Paladin.

Bersoff, Donald M. (1999). Explaining unethical behavior among people motivated to act prosocially. *Journal of Moral Education, 28*(4), 413–428.

Biklen, Sari K. (1995). *School work: Gender and the cultural construction of teaching.* New York: Teachers College Press.

Bingham, Richard D., Haubrich, Paul A., White, Sammis B., & Zipp, John F. (1990). Dual standards among teachers: This school is good enough for other kids but not my child. *Urban Education, 25*(3), 274–288.

Borsa, Joan (1990). Towards a politics of location. *Canadian Women Studies, 11*(1), 36–39.

Boudon, Raymond (1990/1994). *The art of self persuasion: The social explanation of false beliefs* (M. Slater, Trans.). Cambridge, UK: Polity Press (original work published in 1990).

Bourdieu, Pierre (1977). *Outline of a theory of practice.* Cambridge: Cambridge University Press.

Bourdieu, Pierre (1984). *Distinction: A social critique of the judgment of taste.* Cambridge, MA: Harvard University Press.

Bourdieu, Pierre (1996). *The state nobility: Elite schools in the field of power.* (L. C. Clough, Trans.). Stanford, CA: Stanford University Press.

Bourdieu, Pierre (1998). *Acts of resistance against the tyranny of the market.* New York: The New Press.

Boutwell, Clinton E. (1997). *Shell game: Corporate America's agenda for schools.* Bloomington, IN: Phi Delta Kappa.

Bowes, Catherine A. (2001). *Roads from a secret place: Beginning European American teachers' beliefs, pedagogies, and contexts of learning in a predominantly African American public middle school.* Unpublished doctoral dissertation, Indiana University.

Bowles, Samuel, & Gintis, Herbert (1976). *Schooling in capitalist America.* New York: Basic Books.

Bowles, Samuel, & Gintis, Herbert (1987). *Democracy and capitalism: Property, community, and the contradictions of modern social thought.* New York: Basic Books.

Bracey, Gerald W. (1997). *The truth about America's schools: The Bracey reports, 1991–1997.* Bloomington, IN: Phi Delta Kappa.

Brandau, Deborah Mayne, & Collins, James (1994). Texts, social relations, and work-based skepticism about schooling: An ethnographic analysis. *Anthropology & Education Quarterly, 25,* 118–136.

Brantlinger, Ellen (1984). *What a model community sweeps under the rug: Class discrimination in the schools.* Unpublished manuscript.

Brantlinger, Ellen A. (1985a). What low-income parents want from schools: A different view of aspirations. *Interchange, 16,* 14–28.

Brantlinger, Ellen A. (1985b). Low-income parents' perceptions of favoritism in the schools. *Urban Education, 20,* 82–102.

Brantlinger, Ellen A. (1985c). Low-income parents' opinions about the social class composition of schools. *American Journal of Education, 93,* 389–408.

Brantlinger, Ellen A. (1986a). Aspirations, expectations, and reality: Response to Olson and Weir. *Interchange, 17,* 85–87.

Brantlinger, Ellen A. (1986b). Making decisions about special education: Do low-income parents have the information they need? *Journal of Learning Disabilities, 20,* 95–101.

Brantlinger, Ellen A. (1993). *The politics of social class in secondary schools: Views of affluent and impoverished youth.* New York: Teachers College Press.

Brantlinger, Ellen (1995). Sterilization of people with mental disabilities: Issues, perspectives, and cases. Westport, CT: Auburn House.

Brantlinger, Ellen A. (1996). The influence of preservice teachers' beliefs about pupil achievement on attitudes toward inclusion. *Teacher Education and Special Education, 19*(1), 17–33.

Brantlinger, Ellen A. (1997). Using ideology: Cases of non-recognition of the politics of research and practice in special education. *Review of Educational Research, 67,* 425–460.

Brantlinger, Ellen A. (1999a). Inward gaze and activism as moral next steps in inquiry. *Anthropology & Education Quarterly, 30*(4), 413–429.

Brantlinger, Ellen A. (1999b). Class moves in the movies: What *Good Will Hunting* teaches about social life. *Journal of Curriculum Theorizing, 15*(1), 105–120.

Brantlinger, Ellen A., & Majd-Jabbari, Masoumeh (1998). The conflicted pedagogical and curricular perspectives of middle-class mothers. *Journal of Curriculum Studies, 30*(4), 431–460.

Brantlinger, Ellen, Majd-Jabbari, Masoumeh, & Guskin, Samuel L. (1996). Self-interest and liberal educational discourse: How ideology works for middle-class mothers. *American Educational Research Journal, 33*(3), 571–598.

Britzman, Deborah (1991). *Practice makes practice: A critical study of learning to teach.* Albany: State University of New York Press.

Britzman, Deborah P. (1992). Teachers under suspicion: Is it true that teachers aren't as good as they used to be? In Joe L. Kincheloe & Shirley R. Steinberg (Eds.), *Thirteen questions: Reframing education's conversation* (pp. 73–80). New York: Lang.

Britzman, Deborah P. (1997). The tangles of implication. *Qualitative Studies in Education, 10*(1), 31–37.

Brock, Colin (1999). Introduction. In Nafsika Alexiadou & Colin Brock (Eds.), *Education as a commodity* (pp. 7–8). Suffolk, England: John Catt Educational.

Brown, David K. (1995). *Degrees of control: A sociology of educational expansion and occupational credentialism.* New York: Teachers College Press.

Brown, Donald E. (1991). *Human universals.* Philadelphia: Temple University Press.

Bruner, James S. (1996). *The culture of education.* Cambridge, MA: Harvard University Press.

Bryk, Anthony S., Lee, Valerie E., & Holland, Peter B. (1993). *Catholic schools and the common good.* Cambridge, MA: Harvard University Press.

Bryson, Mary, & de Castell, Suzanne (1997). En/gendering equity: Paradoxical consequences of institutionalized equity policies. In Suzanne de Castell & Mary Bryson (Eds.), *Radical interventions: Identity, politics, and difference/s in educational praxis* (pp. 85–103). Albany: State University of New York Press.

Burbules, Nicholas C. (1992). Forms of ideology-critique: A pedagogical perspective. *International Journal of Qualitative Studies in Education, 5,* 7–17.

Burton, Ramona L. (1999). A study of disparities among school facilities in North Carolina: Effects of race and economic status. *Educational Policy, 13*(2), 280–295.

Caplan, Paula J. (1995). *They say you're crazy.* Reading, MA: Addison-Wesley.

Capshew, James H. (1999). *Psychologists on the march: Science, practice, and professional identity in America, 1929–1969.* Cambridge: Cambridge University Press.

Carlson, Dennis (1999). The rules of the game: Detracking and retracking the urban high school. In Frederick Yeo & Barry Kanpol (Eds.), *From nihilism to possibility: Democratic transformation: Democratic transformations for the inner city* (pp. 15–35). Cresskill, NJ: Hampton Press.

Carlson, Dennis (2002, April 4). *Small victories: Narratives of hope in a neo-conservative age.* Paper presented at the Annual Meeting of the American Educational Research Association, New Orleans.

Carlson, Dennis, & Apple Michael W. (1998). Introduction. In Dennis Carlson & Michael W. Apple (Eds.), *Power/knowledge/pedagogy: The meaning of democratic education in unsettling times* (pp. 1–38). Boulder, CO: Westview.

Carnoy, Martin. (2000). Globalization and educational reform. In Nelly P. Stromquist & Karen Monkman (Eds.), *Globalization and education: Integration and contestation across cultures* (pp. 43–61). Lanham, MD: Rowman & Littlefield.

Chang, Heewon (1992). *Adolescent life and ethos: An ethnography of a U.S. high school.* London & Washington, DC: Falmer.

Childs, James M. Jr. (2000). *Greed: Economics and ethics in conflict.* Minneapolis: Fortress.

Cicourel, Aaron V. (1993). Aspects of structural and processual theories of knowledge. In Craig Calhoun, Edward LiPuma, & Moishe Postone (Eds.), *Bourdieu: Critical perspectives* (pp. 89–115). Cambridge, UK: Polity Press.

Cole, Michael (1996). *Cultural psychology: A once and future discipline.* Cambridge, MA: Belknap Press.

Coleman, James (1988). Social capital, human capital, and schools. *Independent School, 48*(1), 9–16.

Coleman, James S., Campbell, E. Q., Hoson, C. J., McPartland, James, Mood, A. M., Weinfeld, F. D., & York, R. L. (1966). *Equality of educational opportunity.* Cambridge, MA: Harvard University Press.

Colker, Ruth (1992). Abortion and Dialogue: Pro-choice, pro-life, and American Law. Bloomington: Indiana University Press.

Collins, R. (1992). Women and the production of status cultures. In Michele Lamont & Marcel Fournier (Eds.), *Cultivating differences: Symbolic boundaries and the making of inequality* (pp. 213–231). Chicago: University of Chicago Press.

Conley, Dalton (1999). *Being black, living in the red: Race, wealth, and social policy in America.* Berkeley: University of California Press.

Connell, Robert W. (1987). *Gender and power: Society, the person and sexual politics.* Stanford, CA: Stanford University Press.

Connell, Robert W. (1993). *Schools and social justice.* Philadelphia: Temple University Press.

Connell, Robert (1998). Masculinities and globalization. *Men and Masculinities, 1*(1) 2–23.

Connor, Mary H., & Boskin, Joseph (2001). Overrepresentation of bilingual and poor children in special education classes: A continuing problem. *Journal of Children & Poverty, 7,* 23–32.

Cookson, Peter W. Jr. (1992). The ideology of consumership and the coming deregulation of the public school system. In Peter W. Cookson, Jr. (Ed.), *The choice controversy* (pp. 83–102). Newbury, CA: Corwin Press.

Corson, David J. (1992). Social justice and minority language policy. *Educational Theory, 42,* 181–200.

Cose, Ellis (1993). *The rage of a privileged class: Why are middle-class blacks angry? Why should America care?* New York: HarperPerennial.

Counts, George (1927). *The social composition of boards of education.* Chicago: University of Chicago Press.

Counts, George (1932). *Dare the school build a new social order?* (Reprint). Carbondale, IL: Southern Illinois University Press, 1978.

Counts, George (1934). *The social foundations of education.* New York: George Scribner's Sons.

Crocco, Margaret S., Munro, Petra, & Weiler, Kathleen (1999). *Pedagogies of resistance: Women educator activists, 1880–1960.* New York: Teachers College Press.

Dale, Roger (2000). Globalization and education: Demonstrating a "common world educational culture" or locating a "globally structured educational agenda"? *Educational Theory, 50*(4), 427–448.

Danforth, Scot (1996). Autobiography as critical pedagogy: Locating myself in class-based oppression. *Teaching Education, 9,* 3–14.

Daniels, Harvey (1995). Right wing attacks yet another reform: Is whole language doomed? *Rethinking Schools, 10*(2), 1, 5.

David, Miriam. E. (1993). *Parents, gender and education reform.* Cambridge, UK: Polity Press.

De Castell, Suzanne, & Bryson, Mary (1997). Introduction: Identity, authority, narrativity. In Suzanne de Castell & Mary Bryson (Eds.), *Radical interventions: Identity, politics, and difference/s in educational praxis* (pp. 1–11). Albany: State University of New York Press.

de la Luz Reyes, Maria (1997). Chicanas in academe: An endangered species. In Suzanne de Castell & Mary Bryson (Eds.), *Radical interventions: Identity, politics, and difference/s in educational praxis* (pp. 15–37). Albany: State University of New York Press.

Delamont, Sara (1989). *Knowledgeable women: Structuralism and the reproduction of elites.* London: Routledge.

Delpit, Lisa (1988). The silenced dialogue: Power and pedagogy in educating other people's children. *Harvard Educational Review, 58,* 280–298.

Delpit, Lisa (1995). *Other people's children: Cultural conflict in the classroom.* New York: The New Press.

Derrida, Jacques (1982). Sending: On representation. *Social Research, 49,* 294–326.

Dewey, John. (1909). *Moral principles in education.* Boston: Houghton Mifflin.

Dews, C. L. Barney, & Law, Carolyn Leste (Eds.). (1995). *This fine place so far from home: Voices of Academics from the working class.* Philadelphia: Temple University Press.

Deyhle, Donna, & Swisher, Karen (1997). Research in American Indian and Alaska Native education: From assimilation to self-determination. In Michael W. Apple (Ed.), *Review of Research in Education, 22* (pp. 113–194). Washington DC: American Educational Research Association.

Dibos, Alessandra (2002). Democracy as responsibility, meaning, and hope: Introductory reflections on a democratic project in education. *Journal of Thought, 37*(1), 54–65.

Dickstein, Morris (1996, April 4). Moral fiction. *NY Times Book Review,* p. 19.

DuBois, William E. B. (1965). *The souls of black folk.* New York: Avon.

Dunn, Lloyd M. (1968). Special education for the mildly retarded: Is much of it justifiable? *Exceptional Children, 35,* 5–22.

Dyson, Michael E. (1993). *Reflecting black: African-American cultural criticism.* Minneapolis: University of Minnesota Press.

Eagleton, Terry (1990). *The ideology of the aesthetic.* Oxford: Basil Blackwell.

Eagleton, Terry (1991). *Ideology: An introduction.* London: Verso.

Eder, Donna (with Catherine C. Evans & Stephen Parker). (1995). *School talk: Gender and adolescent culture.* New Brunswick, NJ: Rutgers University Press.

Eichstedt, Jennifer L. (1998). Reproducing racial and class inequality: Multiculturalism in the arts. In Jodi O'Brien & Judith A. Howard (Eds.), *Everyday inequalities: Critical inquiries* (pp. 237–252). Malden, MA: Blackwell.

Eisenhart, Margaret (2001). Educational ethnography past, present, and future: Ideas to think with. *Educational Researcher, 30*(8), 16–27.

Elbaz-Luwisch, Freema (1997). Narrative research: Political issues and implications. *Teaching and Teacher Education, 13*(1), 75–83.

Eliasoph, Nina (1998). *Avoiding politics: How Americans produce apathy in everyday life.* Cambridge: Cambridge University Press.

Ellsworth, Elizabeth (1989). Why doesn't this feel empowering? Working through the repressive myths of critical pedagogy. *Harvard Educational Review, 59,* 297–324.

Elster, Jon (1998). Introduction. In Jon Elster (Ed.), *Deliberative democracy* (pp. 1–18). Cambridge: Cambridge University Press.

Epstein, Joyce L. (1990). School and family connections: Theory, research, and implications for integrating sociologies of education and family. *Marriage and Family Review, 15,* 99–126.

Epstein, Joyce L., & Scott-Jones, Dianne (1992). School-family-community connections for accelerating student progress in the elementary and middle grades. In Henry Levin (Ed.), *Accelerated education for at-risk students.* Philadelphia: Falmer.

Ewert, Gerry D. (1991). Habermas and education: A comprehensive overview of the influence of Habermas in educational literature. *Review of Educational Research, 61*(3), 345–378.

Fairclough, Norman (1992). *Critical language awareness.* London: Longman.

Fairtest (1999–2000a, Winter). Court rules for high-stakes Texas test. *Examiner, 14*(1), 1, 11.

Fairtest (1999–2000b, Winter). Florida teachers refuse bonuses for high test scores, *Examiner, 14*(1), 5.

Farazmand, Ali (1999). The elite question: Toward a normative elite theory of organization. *Administration and Society, 31*(3), 321–360.

Feagin, Joe R. (October 15, 1999). Soul-searching in sociology: Is the discipline in crisis? *The Chronicle of Higher Education,* pp. B4–B6.

Fields, A. Belden, & Feinberg, Walter (2001). *Education and democratic theory: Finding a place for community participation in public school reform.* Albany: State University of New York Press.

Felski, Rita (2002, January 25). Why academics don't study the lower middle class. *The Chronicle of Higher Education,* p. B24.

Fine, Michelle (1991). *Framing dropouts: Notes on the politics of an urban public high school.* Albany: State University of New York Press.

Fine, Michelle (1992). *Disruptive voices.* Ann Arbor: University of Michigan Press.

Fine, Michelle, & Roberts, Rosemarie A. (1999). Editors' introduction on Erika Apfelbaum: Public Intellectual. *Feminism & Psychology, 9*(3), 261–265.

Finkelstein, Barbara (1992). Education historians as mythmakers. In Gerald Grant (Ed.), *Review of Research in Education, 18,* 255–297 (Washington: American Educational Research Association).

Foster, Michèle (1997). *Black teachers on teaching.* New York: New Press.

Foucault, Michel (1977). *Discipline and punish: the birth of the prison.* Harmondsworth: Penguin.

Foucault, Michel (1980). Truth and Power. In Colin Gordon (Ed.), *Power/Knowledge: selected interviews and other writings 1972–1977* (pp. 109–133). New York: Pantheon.

Fraser, Nancy (1989). *Unruly practices: Power, discourse and gender in contemporary theory.* Minneapolis: University of Minnesota Press.

Freire, Paolo (1973). *Education for critical consciousness.* New York: Seabury.

Freire, Paolo (1985). *The politics of education: Culture, power, and liberation.* South Hadley, MA: Bergin & Garvey.

Freire, Paulo (1989). *Pedagogy of the oppressed.* New York: Continuum.

Fullan, Michael (1993). *Change forces: Probing the depths of educational reform.* London: Falmer.

Gamoran, Adam, & Berends, Mark (1987). The effects of stratification in secondary schools: Synthesis of survey and ethnographic research. *Review of Educational Research, 57,* 415–435.

Gans, Herbert J. (1996). The so-called underclass and the future of antipoverty policy. In M. Brinton Lykes, Ali Banuazizi, Ramsay Liam, & Michael Morris (Eds.), *Myths about the powerless: Contesting social inequalities* (pp. 87–101). Philadelphia: Temple University Press.

Gardner, Howard (1991). *The unschooled mind: How children think and how schools should teach.* New York: Basic Books.

Garmarnikow, Eva, & Green, Tony (2000, April 25). *Social capital, social class, citizenship and educational policy under new labor.* Paper presented at the American Educational Research Association Annual Meeting, New Orleans.

Gaskins, Suzanne, Miller, Peggy J., & Corsaro, William A. (1992). Theoretical and methodological perspectives in the interpretive study of children. In William A. Corsaro & Peggy J. Miller (Eds.), *Interpretive approaches to children's socialization* (pp. 5–23). San Francisco: Jossey-Bass.

Gee, James (2002, April 5). *What makes discourse analysis critical?* Paper presented at the Annual Meeting of the American Educational Research Association, New Orleans.

Geertz, Clifford (1973). Ideology as a cultural system. In Clifford Geertz (Ed.), *The interpretation of cultures* (pp. 197–207). New York: Basic Books.

Gelberg, Denise (1997). *The "business" of reforming American schools.* Albany: State University of New York Press.

Gerschick, Thomas J. (1998). Sisyphus in a wheelchair: Men with physical disabilities confront gender domination. In Jodi O'Brien & Judith A. Howard (Eds.), *Everyday inequalities: Critical inquiries* (pp. 189–211). Malden, MA: Blackwell.

Gewirtz, Sharon, Ball, Stephen, & Bowe, Richard (1995). *Markets, choice, and equity in education.* Philadelphia: Open University Press.

Gibson-Graham, Julia K. (1996). *The end of capitalism (as we knew it): A feminist critique of political economy.* Malden, MA: Blackwell.

Giddens, Anthony (1987). *Social theory and modern sociology.* Stanford, CA: Stanford University Press.

Gilligan, Carol (1982). *In a different voice: Psychological theory and women's development.* Cambridge, MA: Harvard University Press.

Giroux, Henry A. (1992). *Border crossings: Cultural workers and the politics of education.* New York: Routledge.

Glass, Thomas, Bjork, Lars, & Bruner, C. Cryss (2000). *Study of the American school superintendency: A look at the superintendent in the new millennium.* Arlington, VA: American Association of School Administration.

Glasser, Thomas Lewis, & Bowers, Peggy J. (1999). Justifying change and control: An application of discourse ethics to the role of mass media. In David Demers & K. Viswanath (Eds.), *Mass media, social control, and social change: A macrosocial perspective* (pp. 399–418). Ames: Iowa State University Press.

Glendon, Mary Ann (1991). *Rights talk: The impoverishment of political discourse.* New York: Free Press.

Goffman, Erving (1959). *The presentation of self in everyday life.* New York: Doubleday.

Goffman, Erving G. (1963). *Stigma: Notes on the management of spoiled identity.* Englewood Cliffs, NJ: Prentice Hall.

Goodlad, John I. (1992). On taking school reform seriously. *Phi Delta Kappan, 74*(3), 232–238.

Goodson, Ivor F. (1994). *Studying curriculum: Cases and methods.* New York: Teachers College Press.

Gordon, Michael, & Keiser, Shelby (Eds.). (1998). *Accommodations in higher education under the Americans with Disabilities Act.* New York: Guilford.

Gould, Steven J. (1981). *The mismeasure of man.* New York: Norton.

Gould, Steven J. (1995). Curveball. In Steve Fraser (Ed.), *The Bell curve wars: Race, intelligence, and the future of America* (pp. 11–22). New York: Basic Books.

Gouldner, Alvin W. (1979). *The future of intellectuals and the rise of the new class.* New York: Seabury Press.

Gramsci, Antonio (1971/1929–1935). *Selections from the prison notebooks* (Q. Hoare & G. N. Smith, Eds.). New York: International Publishers (original work published in 1929–1935).

Graue, M. Elizabeth, Kroeger, Janice, & Prager, Dana (2001). A Bakhtinian analysis of particular home-school relations. *American Educational Research Journal, 38,* 467–498.

Greene, Maxine (1993). The passions of pluralism: Multiculturalism and the expanding community. *Educational Researcher, 22*(1), 13–18.

Grimes, J. (1997). Swimming against the tide: Liberal parents and cultural plurality. In Ben Cosin & Margaret Hales (Eds.), *Families, education and social differences* (pp. 190–196). London & New York: Routledge.

Gross, Neal (1976). *Who runs our schools?* New York: John Wiley and Sons.

Gupta, Dipankar (2000). *Culture, spaces and the nation-state.* New Dehli: Sage.

Gutmann, Amy (1996, October 11). Middle democracy. *The Chronicle of Higher Education,* p. B9.

Habermas, Juergen (1971/1978). *Knowledge and human interests* (2nd ed., J. Shapiro, Trans.). London: Heinemann (original work published in 1971).

Hall, Kathy, & Harding, Austin (2002). Level descriptions and teacher assessment in England: Towards a community of assessment practice. *Educational Research, 44*(1), 1–15.

Hall, Stuart (1983). The great moving right show. In Stuart Hall & Martin Jacques (Eds.), *The Politics of Thatcherism* (pp. 19–39). London: Lawrence and Wishart in association with Marxism Today.

Hamilton, David (1998). The idols of the market place. In Roger Slee, Gaby Weiner, & Sally Tomlinson (Eds.), *School effectiveness for whom? Challenges to the school effectiveness and school improvement movements* (pp. 13–20). London: Falmer.

Haraway, Donna (1988). Situated knowledges: The science question in feminism and the privilege of partial perspective. *Feminist Studies, 14,* 575–599.

Harding, Sandra (1998). *Multiculturalism, post-colonialism, and science: Epistemological issues.* Paper presented at the Annual American Educational Research Association Conference, San Diego.

Hargreaves, Andy (1994). Critical introduction. In Ivor Goodson (Ed.), *Studying curriculum: Cases and methods* (pp. 1–11). Buckingham: Open University Press.

Harry, Beth (1992). *Cultural diversity, families, and the special education system: Communication and empowerment.* New York: Teachers College Press.

Harry, Beth (1994). *The disproportionate representation of minority students in special education: Theories and recommendations.* Alexandria, VA: National Association of State Directors of Special Education.

Hartsock, Nancy (1987). The feminist standpoint: Developing the ground for a specifically feminist historical materialism. In Sandra Harding (Ed.), *Feminism and Methodology* (pp. 157–180). Bloomington: Indiana University Press.

Harvey, David (1996). *Justice, nature and the geography of difference.* Cambridge, MA: Blackwell.

Harvey, David (2000). *Spaces of hope.* Berkeley: University of California Press.

Harvey, David (2001, November). *Geographical knowledges/political power.* Lecture at Institute for Advanced Study, Indiana University–Bloomington.

Hatcher, Richard (1998a). Class differentiation in education: Rational choices? *British Journal of Sociology of Education, 19*(1), 1–24.

Hatcher, Richard (1998b). Social justice and the politics of school effectiveness and improvement. *Race, Ethnicity, and Education, 1*(2), 267–289.

Hatton, Elizabeth (1997). Teacher educators and the production of bricoleurs: An ethnographic study. *Qualitative Studies in Education, 10*(2), 237–257.

Hauser, Mary E. (1997). How do we really work? A response to "locked in uneasy sisterhood": Reflections on feminist methodology and research relationships. *Anthropology and Education Quarterly, 28*(1), 123–126.

Hennessy, Rosemary (1993). *Materialist feminism and the politics of discourse.* New York: Routledge.

Henry, Annette (1995). Growing up black, female, and working class: A teacher's narrative. *Anthropology and Education Quarterly, 26*(3), 279–305.

Herr, Kathryn (2000, April 26). *Creating change from within: One school's dance with district mandates and school-wide inquiry.* Paper presented at the American Educational Research Association Annual Meeting, New Orleans.

Herrnstein, Richard, & Murray, Charles (1994). *The Bell Curve.* New York: Free Press.

Hinchey, Patricia H. (1999). Emotion: Educational psychology's pound of flesh. In Joe L. Kincheloe, Shirley Steinberg, & Patricia H. Hinchey (Eds.), *The post formal reader: Cognition and education* (pp. 128–145). New York & London: Falmer Press.

Hirst, Paul, & Thompson, Grahame (1996). *Globalization in question.* Cambridge: Polity Press.

Hofferth, Sandra L., Boisjoly, Johanne, & Duncan, Greg J. (1998). Parents' extrafamilial resources and children's school attainment. *Sociology of Education, 71,* 246–268.

Holland, Dorothy, Lachicotte, William, J. R., Skinner, Debra, & Cain, Carole (1998). *Identity and agency in cultural worlds.* Cambridge, MA: Harvard University Press.

Hollway, Wendy (1989). Subjectivity and method in psychology: Gender, meaning, and science. London, Newbury Park: Sage Publications.

hooks, bell (1989). *Talking back thinking feminist thinking black.* Boston: South End Press.

hooks, bell (1990). *Yearning: Race, gender, and cultural politics.* Boston: South End.

hooks, bell (1994). *Teaching to transgress: Education as the practice of freedom.* New York & London: Routledge.

hooks, bell (2000). *Where we stand: Class matters.* New York & London: Routledge.

Horton, Myles. (1998). *The long haul: An autobiography.* New York: Teachers College Press.

Horvat, Erin M., Lareau, Annette, & Weininger, Elliot B. (2002, April). *From social ties to social capital: Class differences in relations between schools and parent networks.* Paper presented at the Annual Meeting of the American Educational Research Association, New Orleans.

Howe, Kenneth R. (1994). Standards, assessment, and equality of educational opportunity. *Educational Researcher, 23,* 27–33.

Howe, Kenneth R. (1997). *Understanding equal educational opportunity: Social justice, democracy, and schooling.* New York: Teachers College Press.

Hunt, Lynn (2/8/2000). *Tracing the origins of human rights.* Patten Lecture, Indiana University, Bloomington.

Huntington, Samuel P. (1996) *The clash of civilizations and the remaking of the world order.* Cambridge, MA: Harvard University Press.

Hutson, Harry Marshall (1978). *Who controls the curriculum in the local community? A case study of community power and curriculum decision-making,* Unpublished doctoral dissertation, School of Education, Indiana University, Bloomington.

Iran-Nejad, Asghar (1990). Active and dynamic self-regulation of learning processes. *Review of Educational Research, 60*(4), 573–602.

Iran-Nejad, Asghar, McKeachie, Wilbert James, & Berliner, David C. (1990). The multisource nature of learning: An introduction. *Review of Educational Research, 60*(4), 509–515.

Jencks, Christopher (1972). *Inequality: A reassessment of the effect of family and schooling in America.* New York: Harper & Row.

Jencks, Christopher, & Phillips, Meredith (Eds.). (1998). *The black-white test score gap.* Baltimore, MD: Brookes.

Jensen, Arthur R. (1969). How much can we boost IQ and scholastic achievement? *Harvard Educational Review, 39,* 1–123.

Jensen, Robert (1997). Privilege, power, and politics in research: A response to "Crossing sexual orientations." *Qualitative Studies in Education, 10*(1), 25–30.

Jones, Jacqueline (1992). *The dispossessed: America's underclass from the Civil War to the present.* New York: Basic Books.

Jones, Phillip W. (2000). Globalization and internationalism: Democratic prospects for world education. In Nelly P. Stromquist & Karen Monkman (Eds.), *Globalization and education: Integration and contestation across cultures* (pp. 27–42). Lanham, MD: Rowman & Littlefield.

Kailin, Julie (2000, April 27). *The hidden dimensions of liberal racism: An anti-racist response.* Paper presented at the American Educational Research Association Annual Meeting, New Orleans.

Kalra, Paul (1995). *The American Class System: Divide and Rule.* Pleasant Hill, CA: Antenna.

Kantor, Harvey, & Lowe, Robert (1995). Class, race, and the emergence of federal education policy: From the New Deal to the Great Society. *Educational Researcher, 24*(3), 4–11.

Katzenstein, Mary Fainsod (1998). Stepsisters: Feminist movement activism in different institutional spaces. In *The social movement society: Contentious politics for a new century* (pp. 195–216). Lanham, MD; Rowman & Littlefield.

Keddie, Nell (1973). *The myth of cultural deprivation.* London: Penguin.

Keller, Diana (1994). The text of educational ideologies: Toward the characterization of a genre. *Educational Theory, 44*(1), 27–42.

Kenway, Jane (1998). Pulp fictions? Education, markets, and the information superhighway. In Dennis Carlson & Michael W. Apple (Eds.), *Power/knowledge/pedagogy: The meaning of democratic education in unsettling times* (pp. 61–91). Boulder, CO: Westview.

Kincheloe, Joe L. (1993). *Toward a critical politics of teacher thinking: Mapping the postmodern.* Westport, CT: Bergin & Garvey.

Kincheloe, Joe L. (1999a). *Multiple intelligences:* Cultivating post-formal intra/intrepersonal intelligence: Cooperative learning critically considered. In Joe L. Kincheloe, Shirley Steinberg, & Patricia H. Hinchey (Eds.), *The post formal reader: Cognition and education* (pp. 313–328). New York & London: Falmer Press.

Kincheloe, Joe L. (1999b). Trouble ahead, trouble behind: Grounding the post-formal critique of educational psychology. In Joe L. Kincheloe, Shirley Steinberg, & Patricia H. Hinchey (Eds.), *The post formal reader: Cognition and education* (pp. 4–54). New York & London: Falmer Press.

King, Bruce (1995). Locking ourselves in: National standards for the teaching profession. *Teaching and Teacher Education, 10*(1), 95–108.

Kittay, Eva F. (1999). *Love's Labor: Essays on women, equality, and dependency.* New York & London: Routledge.

Koggel, Christine M. (1998). *Perspectives on equality: Constructing a relational theory.* Lanham, MD: Rowman & Littlefield.

Kohn, Alfie (1997). How not to teach values: A critical look at character education. *Phi Delta Kappan, 78*(6), 429–439.

Kohn, Alfie (1998). Only for my kid: How privileged parents undermine school reform. *Phi Delta Kappan, 79,* 569–577.

Kohn, Melvin (1969). *Class and conformity: A study in values.* Homewood, IL: Dorsey.

Kohn, Melvin L. (1994). Social class and parental values. In G. L. Carter (Ed.), *Empirical approaches to sociology: Classic and contemporary readings* (pp. 175–189). New York: Macmillan.

Kohn, Melvin, & Schooler, Carmen (1983). The reciprocal effects of the substantive complexity of work and intellectual flexibility: A longitudinal assessment. *American Journal of Sociology, 84,* 224–252.

Kohn, Melvin L., & Slomczynski, Kazimierz M. (1990). *Social structure and self-direction.* Cambridge, MA: Basil Blackwell.

Kozol, Jonathan (1967). *Death at an early age.* New York: Bantom.

Kozol, Jonathan (1991). *Savage inequalities: Children in America's schools.* New York: HarperPerennial.

Kozol, Jonathan (2001, April 25). *Book review: Ordinary resurrections.* CSPAN, Primetime.

Krueger, Alan B. (2000). *Education matters: Selected essays.* Northhampton, MA: Edward Elgar.

Kunstler, James Howard (2000, May 20). *Can America survive suburbia?* Talk at Bloomington Convention Center. Sponsored by Bloomington Restorations. Bloomington, IN.

Kutchins, Herb, & Kirk, Stuart A. (1997). *Making us crazy: DSM: The psychiatric bible and the creation of mental disorders.* New York: The Free Press.

Lacan, Jacques (1982). Desire and the interpretation of desire in *Hamlet.* In Shoshana Felman (Ed.), *Literature and psychoanalysis: The question of reading, otherwise* (pp. 11–52). Baltimore: Johns Hopkins University Press.

Ladson-Billings, Gloria, & Tate, William (1995). Towards a critical race theory of education. *Teachers College Record, 97,* 47–68.

Ladwig, James G., & Gore, Jennifer M. (1994). Extending power and specifying method within the discourse of activist research. In Andrew Gitlin (Ed.), *Power and method: Political activism and educational research* (pp. 227–238). New York: Routledge.

Lamont, Michele (1992). *Money, morals, and manners: The culture of the French and American upper-middle class.* Chicago: University of Chicago Press.

Lareau, Annette (1989). *Home advantage: Social class and parental intervention in elementary education.* London: Falmer.

Lareau, Annette, & Horvat, Erin M. (1999). Moments of social inclusion and exclusion: Race, class, and cultural capital in family-school relationships. *Sociology of Education, 72,* 37–53.

Lareau, Annette, & Shumar, William (1996). The problems of individualism in family-school policies. [Special issue]. *Sociology of Education,* pp. 24–39.

Larrain, Jorge A. (1992). *The concept of ideology.* Hampshire, England: Gregg Revivals (Routledge).

Lasch, Christopher (1984). *The minimal self.* New York: W. W. Norton.

Lasch, Christopher (1993). What's wrong with the right. In H. Svi Shapiro & David E. Purpel (Eds.), *Critical social issues in American education* (pp. 43–51). New York: Longman.

Lasch, Christopher (1995). *The revolt of the elites and the betrayal of democracy.* New York: W. W. Norton.

Latour, Bruno (1993). *We have never been modern* (Catherine Porter, Trans.). Cambridge, MA: Harvard University Press.

Lauder, Hugh, Hughes, David, Watson, Sue, Waslander, Sietske, Thrupp, Martin, Strathdee, Rob, Simiyu, Ibrihim, Dupuis, Ann, McGlinn, Jim, & Hamlin, Jennie E. (1999). *Trading in futures: Why markets in education don't work.* Buckingham, UK: Open University Press.

Lawrence-Lightfoot, Sarah (1994). *I've known rivers: Lives of loss and liberation.* New York: Penguin.

Lee, Jaekyung (2002). Racial and ethnic achievement gap trends: Reversing the progress toward equity. *Educational Researcher, 31*(1), 3–12.

Lee, Valerie (1993). Educational choice: The stratifying effects of selecting schools and courses. *Educational Policy, 7,* 125–148.

Lee, Valerie (1995). San Antonio school choice plans: Rewarding or creaming? *Social Science Quarterly, 76,* 513–521.

Lee, Valerie, Croninger, Robert, & Smith, Julia (1996). Equity and choice in Detroit. In Bruce Fuller, Richard F. Elmore, & Gary Orfield (Eds.), *Who chooses? Who loses? Culture, institutions, and unequal effects of school choice.* New York: Teachers College Press.

Leistyna, Pepi (1999). *Presence of mind: Education and the politics of deception.* Boulder, CO: Westview Press.

Lexmond, Angela J. (2002). *Challenging secondary education majors' perceptions of middle level students, schools, and teaching.* Unpublished dissertation, Indiana University–Bloomington.

Lien, Hsi Nancy (2001). *Teaching at the crossroads of school reform: A case study of an urban middle school.* Unpublished dissertation, Indiana University–Bloomington.

Lipman, Pauline (1997). Restructuring in context: A case study of teacher participation and the dynamics of ideology, race, and power. *American Educational Research Journal, 34*(1), 3–37.

Lipman, Pauline (1998). *Race, class, and power in school restructuring.* Albany: State University of New York Press.

Lipman, Pauline (2002, April 4). *Chicago school policy and the politics of race: Toward a new discourse of equity and justice.* Paper presented at the Annual Meeting of the American Educational Research Association, New Orleans.

LiPuma, Edward (1993). Culture and the concept of culture in theory of practice. In Craig Calhoun, Edward LiPuma, & Moishe Postone (Eds.), *Bourdieu: Critical perspectives* (pp. 14–34). Cambridge, UK: Polity Press.

Lorde, Audre (1984). *Sister outsider: Essays and speeches.* Trumansburg, NY: Crossing Press.

Lovelace, Tom (2002, April 5). *Who gets what knowledge?* Paper presented at the Annual Meeting of the American Educational Research Association, New Orleans.

Ludwig, Jens, & Bassi, Laurie J. (1999). The puzzling case of school resources and student achievement. *Educational Evaluation and Policy Analysis, 21*(4), 385–403.

Lukacs, Georg (2000). *A defense of history and class consciousness: Tailism and the dialectic.* London: Verso.

Lukas, John (1998). *A thread of years.* New Haven, CT: Yale University Press.

Lukes, Steven (1974). *Power: A radical view.* London: Macmillan.

Lykes, M. Brinton, Banuazizi, Ali, Liem, Ramsay, & Morris, Michael (1996). Introduction. In M. Brinton Lykes, Ali Banuazizi, Ramsay Liam, & Michael Morris (Eds.), *Myths about the powerless: Contesting social inequalities* (pp. 3–13). Philadelphia: Temple University Press.

MacLeod, Jay (1987). *Ain't no making it: Leveled aspirations in low-income neighborhoods.* Boulder, CO: Westview Press.

Marshall, Barbara L. (1994). *Engendering modernity: feminism, social theory and social change.* Boston: Northeastern University Press.

Martin, Hans-Peter, & Schumann, Harald (1997). *The global trap: Globalization and the assault on prosperity and democracy.* New York: Zed Books Ltd.

Martin, James (1998). *Gramsci's political analysis: A critical introduction.* New York: St. Martin.

Martin, Jane R. (Ed.). (1994). *Changing the educational landscape: Philosophy, women, and curriculum.* New York: Routledge.

Marwell, Gerald, & Oliver, Pamela (1993). *The critical mass in collective action: A microsocial theory.* Cambridge: Cambridge University Press.

Mathews, J. (1998). *Class struggle: What's wrong (and right) with America's best public high schools.* New York: Random House.

Mayer, Susan E. (1997). *What money can't buy: Family income and children's life chances.* Cambridge, MA: Harvard University.

McAdams, Dan P. (1997). The case for unity in the (post)modern self: A modest proposal. In Richard D. Ashmore & Lee Jussim (Ed.), *Self identity: Fundamental issues* (pp. 46–78). New York & Oxford: Oxford University Press.

McCarthy, Cameron (1993). Beyond the poverty of theory in race relations: Nonsynchrony and social difference in education. In Lois Weis & Michelle Fine (Eds.), *Beyond silenced voices: Class, race, and gender in United States schools* (pp. 325–346). Albany: State University of New York Press.

McChesney, Robert W. (1997). *Corporate media and the threat to democracy.* New York: Seven Stories Press.

McChesney, Robert W. (1999). *Rich media, poor democracy.* Champaign: University of Illinois.

McDermott, Ray P., & Varenne, Herve (1996). Culture, development, disability. In Richard Jessor, Anne Colby, & Richard A. Shweder (Eds.), *Ethnography and human development: Context and meaning in social inquiry* (pp. 101–126). Chicago & London: University of Chicago.

McGill-Franzen, Anne, & Allington, Richard L. (1993). Flunk 'em or get them classified. *Educational Research, 22*(1), 19–22.

McLaren, Peter (1986). *Schooling as a ritual performance: Towards a political economy of educational symbols and gestures.* London: Routledge & Kegan Paul.

McLeod, Douglas M., & Hertog, James K. (1999). Social control, social change and the mass media's role in the regulation of protest groups. In David Demers & K. Viswanath (Eds.), *Mass media, social control, and social change: A macrosocial perspective* (pp. 305–330). Ames: Iowa State University Press.

McNeil, Linda (1995). Local reform initiatives a national curriculum: Where are the children? In Linda McNeil (Ed.), *The hidden consequences of a national curriculum* (pp. 13–46). Washington, DC: American Educational Research Association.

McNeil, Linda (2000a). The educational costs of standardization. *Rethinking Schools, 14,* 8–13.

McNeil, Linda (2000b). *Contradictions of school reform: Educational costs of standardized testing.* New York: Routledge.

Medovoi, Leerom (2002). Globalization as narrative and its three critiques. *The Review of Education, Pedagogy, and Cultural Studies, 24,* 63–75.

Mehan, Hugh (1992). Understanding inequality in schools: The contribution of interpretive studies. *Sociology of Education, 65,* 1–21.

Mehan, Hugh (1995). Resisting the politics of despair. *Anthropology & Education Quarterly, 26*(3), 239–250.

Mehan, Hugh, Hubbard, Lea, & Villanueva, Irene (1994). Forming academic identities: Accommodation without assimilation among involuntary minorities. *Anthropology & Education Quarterly, 25*(2), 91–117.

Meier, Deborah (1994, Winter). A talk to teachers. *Dissent,* pp. 80–87.

Meier, Deborah (2000, June 12). Interview: Do tests hurt poor kids? *Newsweek,* p. 79.

Merriam, Sharran (1998). *Qualitative research and case study applications in education.* San Francisco: Jossey-Bass.

Merton, Don (1994). The cultural context of aggression: The transition to junior high school. *Anthropology & Education Quarterly, 25*(1), 29–43.

Metcalf, Stephen (2002, January 28). Reading between the lines: The new education law is a victory for Bush and for his corporate allies. *The Nation, 274*(21), 18–22.

Meyer, David S., & Tarrow, Sidney (1998). *The social movement society: Contentious politics for a new century.* Lanham, MD: Rowman & Littlefield.

Meyer, Marshall W., & Zucker, Lynne G. (1989). *Permanently failing organizations.* Newbury Park, CA: Sage.

Mickelson, Roslyn A. (1993). Minorities and education in plural societies. *Anthropology & Education Quarterly, 24*(3), 269–276.

Miller, Alice (1986). *For your own good: Hidden cruelty in child-rearing and the roots of violence.* New York: The Noonday Press.

Miller, Seymour Michael (1996). Equality, morality, and the health of democracy. In M. Brinton Lykes, Aly Banuazizi, Ramsay Liam, & Michael Morris (Eds.), *Myths about the powerless: Contesting social inequalities* (pp. 17–33). Philadelphia: Temple University Press.

Mills, C. Wright (1943). The professional ideology of social pathologists. *American Journal of Sociology, XLIX*(2), 165–180.

Mills, C. Wright (1956). The power elite. New York: Oxford University Press.

Mills, C. Wright (1963). *Power, politics, and people: The collected essays of C. Wright Mills* (I. L. Horowitz, Ed.). New York: Ballantine.

Mintrom, Michael (2000). *Policy entrepreneurs and school choice.* Washington, DC: Georgetown University Press.

Mirel, Jeffrey (1994). School reform unplugged: The Bensenville new American school project, 1991–1993. *American Educational Research Journal, 31,* 481–518.

Morley, Louise, & Rassool, Naz (1999). *School effectiveness: Fracturing the discourse.* London & New York: Falmer.

Morrison, Toni (1993). *Playing in the dark: Whiteness and the literary imagination.* New York: Vintage.

Morrow, Raymond A., & Torres, Carlos A. (1994). Education and the reproduction of class, gender, and race: Responding to the postmodern challenge. *Educational Theory, 44*(1), 43–61.

Mortimore, Peter, & Mortimore, Jo (1999). The political and the professional in education: An unnecessary conflict? In Janet S. Gaffney & Billie J. Askew (Eds.), *Stirring the waters: The influence of Marie Clay* (pp. 221–238). Portsmouth, NH: Heinemann.

Myrdal, Gunnar (1962). *An American dilemma: The Negro problem and modern democracy.* New York: Pantheon Books.

Nader, Laura (1996). Anthropological inquiry into boundaries, power, and knowledges. In Laura Nader (Ed.), *Naked science: Anthropological inquiry into boundaries, power, and knowledge* (pp. 1–25). New York: Routledge.

Nagel, Thomas (1986). *The view from nowhere.* New York: Oxford University Press.

Natriello, Gary (1996). Diverting attention from conditions in American schools. *Educational Researcher, 25*(8), 7–9.

Neill, Monty (1997). *Testing our children: A report card on state assessment systems.* Cambridge, MA: Fairtest.

Neill, Monty (2000, April 28). *The nature and consequences of high-stakes testing in a time of global reaction.* Paper presented at the American Educational Research Association Annual Meeting, New Orleans.

Nespor, Jan (1987). The role of beliefs in the practice of teaching. *Journal or Curriculum Studies, 19,* 317–328.

Newman, Katherine (1998). *Falling from grace: The experience of downward mobility in the American middle class.* New York: Vintage.

Nicholls, John R. (1989). *The competitive ethos and democratic education.* Cambridge, MA: Harvard University Press.

Nielsen, H. Dean (1997). Preface. In H. Dean Nielsen & William K. Cummings (Eds.), *Quality education for all: Community-oriented approaches* (pp. ix–x). New York & London: Garland.

Noddings, Nell (1992). *The challenge to care in schools.* New York: Teachers College Press.

Noddings, Nell (1994). Foreword. In C. M. Brody & J. Wallace (Eds.), *Ethical and social issues in professional education* (pp. ix–x). Albany: State University of New York Press.

Noddings, Nell (1995, January). A morally defensible mission for schools of the 21st century. *Phi Delta Kappan,* pp. 365–368.

Noddings, Nell (2000, April 27). *Address to Division B Annual Meeting.* American Educational Research Association Annual Meeting, New Orleans.

Oakes, Jeannie (1985). *Keeping track: How schools structure inequality.* New Haven, CT: Yale University Press.

Oakes, Jeannie, & Franke, M. (1999, April). *Detracking, mathematics, and the possibility of equitable reform.* Paper presented at the annual meeting of the American Educational Research Association, Montreal.

Oakes, Jeannie, Gamoran, Adam, & Page, Reba N. (1992). Curriculum differentiation: Opportunities, outcomes, and meanings. In Philip W. Jackson (Ed.), *Handbook of Research on Curriculum* (pp. 570–608). Washington, DC: American Educational Research Association.

Oakes, Jeannie, & Guiton, Gretchen (1995). Matchmaking: The dynamics of high school tracking decisions. *American Educational Research Journal, 32,* 3–33.

Oakes, Jeannie, & Quartz, Karen Hunter (1995). *Creating new educational communities.* Chicago: University of Chicago Press.

Oakes, Jeannie, Quartz, Karen Hunter, Ryan, S., & Lipton, Martin (2000). *Becoming good American schools: The struggle for civic virtue in school reform.* San Francisco: Jossey-Bass.

O'Brien, Jodi (1998). Introduction. In Jodi O'Brien & Judith A. Howard (Eds.), *Everyday inequalities: Critical inquiries* (pp. 1–39). Malden, MA: Blackwell.

Oettingen, Gabriele (1996). Positive fantasy and motivation. In Peter M. Gollwitzer & John A. Bargh (Eds.), *The psychology of action: Linking cognition and motivation to behavior* (pp. 236–259). New York: The Guilford Press.

Ogbu, John U. (1995). Understanding cultural diversity and learning. In James A. Banks & Cherry A. Banks (Eds.), *Handbook of research on multicultural education* (pp. 582–593). New York: Macmillan.

Ohanian, Susan (1999). *One size fits all: The folly of educational standards.* Portsmouth, NH: Henineman.

Oliver, Melvin L., & Shapiro, Thomas M. (1995). *Black wealth/white wealth.* New York: Routledge.

Olson, C. Paul (1983). Inequality remade: The theory of correspondence and the context of French immersion in northern Ontario. *Journal of Education, 165,* 75–98.

Olson, Gary A., & Worsham, Lynn (Eds.). (1999). *Race, rhetoric, and the postcolonial.* Albany: State University of New York Press.

Orfield, Gary (1992). Money, equity, and college access. *Harvard Educational Review, 62,* 337–372.

Orfield, Gary (2000, April 27). *What have we learned from school reconstitution?* Paper presented at the American Educational Research Association Annual Meeting, New Orleans.

Orfield, Gary, Eaton, Susan E., & the Harvard Project on Desegregation (1996). *Dismantling desegregation: The quiet removal of Brown versus Board of Education.* New York: New Press.

Ortner, Sherry B. (1996). *Making gender: The politics and erotics of culture.* Boston: Beacon.

Osbourne, A. B. (1996). Practice into theory into practice: Culturally relevant pedagogy for students we have marginalized and normalized. *Anthropology & Education Quarterly, 27*(3), 285–314.

Oswald, Donald P., Coutinho, Martha J., Best, A. M., & Singh, Nirbhay N. (1999). Ethnic representation in special education: The influence of school-related economic and demographic variables. *The Journal of Special Education, 32*(4), 194–206.

Packer, Gary (1992, Winter). Class interest, liberal style: A social conflict in Massachusetts. *Dissent,* pp. 51–56.

Pajares, Michael F. (1992). Teachers' beliefs and educational research: Cleaning up a messy construct. *Review of Educational Research, 62*(3), 307–332.

Patton, James M. (1998). The disproportionate representation of African Americans in special education: Looking behind the curtain for understanding and solutions. *The Journal of Special Education, 32*(1), 25–31.

Peshkin, Alan (2001). *Permissible advantage? The moral consequences of elite schooling.* Manwah, NJ: Lawrence Erlbaum.

Peters, Michael, Marshall, James, & Fitzsimons, Patrick (1999). Poststructuralism and curriculum theory: Neo-liberalism, the information economy, and the crisis of cultural authority. *Journal of Curriculum Theorizing, 15*(2), 111–130.

Piven, Frances Fox, & Cloward, Richard (1979). *Poor people's movements: Why they succeed, how they fail.* New York: Vintage.

Piven, Frances Fox, & Cloward, Richard A. (1996). Welfare reform and the new class war. In M. Brinton Lykes, Ali Banuazizi, A. Ramsay Liam, & Michael Morris (Eds.), *Myths about the powerless: Contesting social inequalities* (pp. 72–86). Philadelphia: Temple University Press.

Plank, David N., & Boyd, W. L. (1994). Antipolitics, education, and institutional choice: The flight from democracy. *American Educational Research Journal, 31*(2), 263–281.

Polakow, Valerie (1992). *Lives on the edge: Single mothers and their children in the other America.* Chicago: University of Chicago Press.

Polanyi, Karl (1957). *The great transformation.* Boston: Beacon.

Popkewitz, Thomas S. (1991). *A political sociology of educational reform: Power/knowledge in teaching, teacher education, and research.* New York: Teachers College Press.

Powell, Arthur G. (1996). *Lessons from privilege: The American prep school tradition.* Cambridge, MA: Harvard University Press.

Proweller, Amy (1998). *Constructing female identity: Meaning making in an upper middle class youth culture.* Albany: State University of New York Press.

Pruyn, Marc (1999). *Discourse wars in Gotham-West: A Latino immigrant urban tale of resistance and agency.* Boulder, Co: Westview Press.

Rawls, John (1971). *A theory of justice.* Cambridge, MA: Harvard University Press.

Ray, Carol A., & Mickelson, Roslyn A. (1990). Corporate leaders, resistant youth, and school reform in Sunbelt City: The political economy of education. *Social Problems, 37,* 178–190.

Reay, Diane (1998). Setting the agenda: The growing impact of market forces on pupil grouping in British secondary schooling. *Journal of Curriculum Studies, 30*(5), 545–558.

Rethinking Schools (2000). A vision of school reform. *Rethinking Schools, 14*(4), 27.

Reynolds, Arthur J., & Wolfe, Barbara (1999). Special education and school achievement: An exploratory analysis with a central-city sample. *Educational Evaluation and Policy Analysis, 21*(3), 249–269.

Ricoeur, Paul (1986). *Lectures on ideology and utopia.* New York: Columbia University Press.

Ringer, Fritz (2000). *Toward a social history of knowledge: Collected essays.* New York: Berghahn Books.

Rizvi, Fazal, & Lingard, Bob (2000). Globalization and education: Complexities and contingencies. *Educational Theory, 50*(4), 419–426.

Rochon, Thomas R. (1998). *Culture moves: Ideas, activism, and changing values.* Princeton, NJ: Princeton University Press.

Rorty, Richard (1998). *Achieving our country: Leftist thought in twentieth-century America.* Cambridge, MA: Harvard University Press.

Rosaldo, Michelle (1984). Toward an anthropology of self and feeling. In Richard A. Shweder & Robert A. LeVine (Eds.), *Culture theory: Essays in mind, self, and emotion.* Cambridge, MA: Cambridge University Press.

Roth, Jeffrey (1992). Of what help is he? A review of Foucault and education. *American Educational Research Journal, 29,* 683–694.

Rothstein, Richard (1999). *The way we were? The myths and realities of America's student achievement.* A Century Foundation Report.

Rubin, Lillian B. (1976). *Worlds of pain: Life in the working class family.* New York: Basic Books.

Ryan, Jake, & Sackrey, Charles (1996). *Strangers in paradise: academics from the working class.* Lanham, MD: University Press of America.

Ryan, Richard M., Sheldon, Kennon M., Kasser, Tim, & Deci, Edward L. (1996). All goals are not created equal: An organismic perspective on the nature of goals and their regulation. In Peter M. Gollwitzer & John A. Bargh (Eds.), *The psychology of action: Linking cognition and motivation to behavior* (pp. 7–26). New York: The Guilford Press.

Ryan, William (1969). *Distress in the city: Essays on the design and administration of mental health services.* Cleveland: Press of Case Western Reserve University.

Ryan, William (1971). *Blaming the victim.* New York: Random House.

Ryan, William (1981). *Equality.* New York: Pantheon.

Saavedra, Elizabeth (2000, April 27). *Teacher study groups as contexts for transformative learning and practice.* Paper presented at the American Educational Research Association Annual Meeting, New Orleans.

Said, Edward (1994). *Representations of the intellectual: The 1993 Reith lectures.* London: Vintage.

Sarason, Seymour B. (1990). *The predictable failure of school reform,* San Francisco: Jossey-Bass.

Scatamburlo, Valerie L. (1998). *Soldiers of misfortune: The New Right's culture war and the politics of political correctness.* New York: Peter Lang.

Schneider, Mark, Teske, Paul, & Marschall, Melissa (2000). *Choosing schools: Consumer choice and the quality of American schools.* Princeton, NJ: Princeton University Press.

Schnog, Nancy (1997). On inventing the psychological. In Joel Pfister & Nancy Schnog (Eds.), *Inventing the psychological: Toward a cultural history of emotional life in America* (pp. 3–16). New Haven, CT: Yale University Press.

Schudson, Michael (1998). *The good citizen: A history of American civic life.* Cambridge, MA: Harvard University Press.

Seiler, Gale, & Tobin, Kenneth (2000, April 26). *Students' perceptions of repression, social justice, and failure to learn science in an inner city high school.* Paper presented at the annual meeting of the American Educational Research Association, New Orleans.

Seldon, Arthur (1990). *Capitalism.* London: Basil Blackwell.

Sennett, Richard, & Cobb, Jonathan (1972). *The hidden injuries of class.* New York: Vintage.

Sergiovanni, Thomas J. (1991). *The principalship, a reflective practice perspective* (2nd ed.). Boston: Allyn and Bacon.

Sexton, Patricia C. (1961). *Education and income: Inequalities of opportunity in our public schools.* New York: Viking.

Shanahan, James, & Jones, Victoria (1999). Cultivation and social control. In David Demers & K. Viswanath (Eds.), *Mass media, social control, and social change: A macrosocial perspective* (pp. 31–50). Ames: Iowa State University Press.

Shapiro, H. Svi (1993). Curriculum alternatives in a survivalist culture: Basic skills and the minimal self. In H. Svi Shapiro & David E. Purpel (Eds.), *Critical social issues in American education* (pp. 288–304). New York: Longman.

Shapiro, H. Svi, & Purpel, David E. (1993). Introduction. In H. Svi Shapiro & David E. Purpel (Eds.), *Critical social issues in American Education* (pp. xiii–xxi). New York: Longman.

Shor, Ira (1999). Preface. In Ira Shor & Caroline Pari (Eds.), *Education is politics: Critical teaching across differences, K–12* (pp. vii–ix). Portsmouth, NH: Boynton/Cook (Heinemann).

Shor, Ira, & Pari, Caroline (1999). *Education is politics: Critical teaching across differences, K–12.* Portsmouth, NH: Boynton/Cook (Heinemann).

Shweder, Richard (1991, March 17). Dangerous thoughts. *NY Times Book Review,* pp. 1, 30, 31, 35.

Sieber, R. Timothy (1982). The politics of middle-class success in an inner-city public school. *Journal of Education, 164,* 30–47.

Silverman, David (2000). *Doing qualitative research: A practical handbook.* London: Sage.

Sleeter, Christine E. (2000, April 28). *Keeping the lid on: Multicultural curriculum and the organization of consciousness.* American Educational Research Association Annual Meeting, New Orleans.

Sleeter, Christine E. (1995). *Multicultural education, critical pedagogy, and the politics of difference.* Albany: State University of New York Press.

Sleeter, Christine, Gutierrez, W., New, C. A., & Takata, S. R. (1992). Race and education: In what ways does race affect the educational process? In Joe L. Kincheloe & Shirley R. Steinberg (Eds.), *Thirteen questions: Reframing education's conversation* (pp. 173–182). New York: Lang.

Smyth, John, & Shacklock, Geoffrey (1998). *Re-making teaching: Ideology, policy and practice.* London & New York: Routledge.

Sober, Elliott, & Wilson, David S. (1998). *Unto others: The evolution and psychology of unselfish behavior.* Cambridge, MA: Harvard University Press.

Spivak, Gayatri C. (1988). Can the subaltern speak? In Cary Nelson & Lawrence Grossberg (Eds.), *Marxism and the interpretation of culture* (pp. 271–313). Urbana: University of Illinois Press.

Spivak, Gayatri C. (1994). Bonding in difference. In Alfred Arteaga (Ed.), *An other tongue: Nation and ethnicity in the linguistic borderlands.* Durham, NC: Duke University Press.

Stallybrass, Peter, & White, Allon (1986). *The politics and poetics of transgression.* Ithaca, NY: Cornell University Press.

Starratt, Robert J. (1994). *Building an ethical school: A practical response to the moral crisis in schools.* London: Falmer.

Stromquist, Nelly P., & Monkman, Karen (2000). Defining globalization and assessing its implications on knowledge and education. In Nelly P. Stromquist & Karen Monkman

(Eds.), *Globalization and education: Integration and contestation across cultures* (pp. 3–25). Lanham, MD: Rowman & Littlefield.

Swartz, Ellen (1993). Multicultural education: Disrupting patterns of supremacy in school curricula, practices, and pedagogy. *Journal of Negro Education, 62*(4), 493–506.

Tarrow, Sidney (1998). *Power in movement; Social movements and contentious politics* (2nd ed.). Cambridge: Cambridge University Press.

Taylor, Steven, Rizvi, Fazal, Lingard, Bob, & Henry, M. (1997). *Educational policy and the politics of change.* London & New York: Routledge.

Thomas, William B., & Moran, Kevin J. (1992). Reconsidering the power of the superintendent in the progressive period. *American Educational Research Journal, 29*(1), 22–50.

Thompson, John B. (1984). *Studies in the theory of ideology.* Berkeley: University of California Press.

Thompson, John B. (1990). *Ideology and modern culture: Critical social theory in the era of mass communication.* Stanford, CA: Stanford University Press.

Thrupp, Martin (1998). The art of the possible: Organizing and managing high and low socio economic schools. *Journal of Education Policy, 13*(2), 197–219.

Tilly, Charles (1999). Durable inequality. In Phyllis Moen, Donna Dempster-McClain, & Henry A. Walker (Eds.), *A nation divided: Diversity, inequality, and community in American society* (pp. 15–33). Ithaca, NY: Cornell University Press.

Tinney, James S. (1983). Interconnections. *Interracial Books for Children Bulletin, 14,* 4–6.

Tomlinson, Sally (1982). *A sociology of special education.* London: Routledge & Kegan Paul.

Tomlinson, Sally (1999, June 15). *Race and special education.* Paper presented at the International Research Colloquium on Inclusive Education, University of Rochester, New York.

Tooley, James (1999). Asking different questions: Towards justifying markets in education. In Nafsika Alexiadou & Colin Brock (Eds.), *Education as a commodity* (pp. 9–19). Suffolk, England: John Catt Educational.

Troyna, Barry, & Vincent, Carol (1996). "The ideology of expertism": The framing of special education and racial equality policies in the local state. In Carol Christensen & Fazal Rizvi (Eds.), *Disability and the dilemmas of education and justice* (pp. 131–144). Philadelphia: Open University Press.

Tyack, David, & Cuban, Larry (1995). *Tinkering toward Utopia: A century of public school reform.* Cambridge & London: Harvard University Press.

Tyack, David, & Hansot, Elisabeth (1982). *Managers of virtue: Public school leadership in America, 1820–1980.* New York: Basic Books.

Tyack, David, & Tobin, William (1994). The "grammar" of schooling: Why has it been so hard to change? *American Educational Research Journal, 31,* 453–479.

Unger, Roberto M. (1987a). *Social theory: Its situation and its task.* Cambridge: Cambridge University Press.

Unger, Roberto M. (1987b) *False necessity: Anti-necessitarian social theory in the service of radical democracy.* Cambridge: Cambridge University Press.

U.S. Census Bureau (1990). 1990 Census of Population and Housing. Washington, DC: U.S. Government Printing Office.

U.S. Department of Education (1983). *A nation at risk.* Washington, DC: Department of Education.

U.S. Department of Education (1991). *America 2000.* Washington, DC: Department of Education.

Useem, Elizabeth L. (1992). Middle schools and math groups: Parents' involvement in children's placement. *Sociology of Education, 65,* 263–279.

Valdes, Guadalupe (1996). *Con repeto: Bridging the distances between culturally diverse families and schools.* New York: Teachers College Press.

Valencia, Richard R. (Ed.). (1997). *The evolution of deficit thinking: Educational thought and practice.* London & Washington, DC: Falmer.

van Manen, Max (1990). *Researching lived experience: Human science for an action sensitive pedaogy.* Albany: State University of New York Press.

Varenne, Hervé (1986). *Symbolizing America.* Lincoln: University of Nebraska Press.

Varenne, Hervé, & McDermott, Ray (1998). *Successful failure: The school America builds.* Boulder, CO: Westview Press.

Veblen, Thorstein (1998/1899). *The Theory of the Leisure Class.* New York: Macmillan.

Viswanath, K., & Demers, David (1999). Mass media from a macrosocial perspective. In David Demers & K. Viswanath (Eds.), *Mass media, social control, and social change: A macrosocial perspective* (pp. 3–30). Ames: Iowa State University Press.

Walker, Alice (1997). *Anything we love can be saved: A writer's activism.* New York: Random House.

Walkerdine, Valerie (2000, April 26). *Feminist and critical perspectives on education and psychology.* Paper presented at the American Educational Research Association Annual Meeting, New Orleans.

Watt, John (1994). *Ideology, objectivity, and education.* New York: Teachers College Press.

Weil, Danny (1999). The education of meaninglessness and the meaninglessness of education: The crisis of the human psyche at the birth of the second millennium. In Joe L. Kincheloe, Shirley Steinberg, & Patricia H. Hinchey (Eds.), *The post formal reader: Cognition and education* (pp. 91–108). New York & London: Falmer Press.

Weinstein, Rhona S., Madison, Sybil M., & Kuklinski, Margaret R. (1995). Raising expectations in schooling: Obstacles and opportunities for change. *American Educational Research Journal, 32,* 121–159.

Weis, Lois (1990). *Working class without work: High school students in deindustrializing America.* New York: Routledge, Chapman & Hall.

Weis, Lois, & Fine, Michelle (1996). Narrating the 1980s and 1990s: Voices of poor and working-class white and African American men. *Anthropology & Education Quarterly, 27*(4), 493–516.

Weiss, Carol H. (1995). The four "I's" of school reform: How interests, ideology, information, and institution affect teachers and principals. *Harvard Educational Review, 65*(4), 571–592.

Wells, Amy Stuart (2000, April 26). *When local control meets the free market: School choice policy for the new millennium.* Paper presented at the American Educational Research Association Annual Meeting, New Orleans.

Wells, Amy Stuart (2002, April 19). *Common school movement: For whom? For what?* Paper presented at the School of Education, Indiana University.

Wells, Amy Stuart, & Crain, Robert L. (1992). Do parents choose school quality or school status? A sociological theory of free market education. *Sociology of Education, 65*(1), 616–618.

Wells, Amy Stuart, & Serna, Irene (1996). The politics of culture: Understanding local political resistance to detracking in racially mixed schools. *Harvard Educational Review, 66*(1), 93–118.

Wenglinsky, Harold (1998). Finance equalization and within-school equity: The relationship between education spending and the social distribution of achievement. *Educational Evaluation and Policy Analysis, 20*(4), 269–283.

Wexler, Philip (1992). *Becoming somebody: Toward a social psychology of school.* London: Falmer.

Whitty, Geoff (2000, April 25). *Schooling and the reproduction of the English middle classes.* Paper presented at the American Educational Research Association Annual Meeting, New Orleans.

Wildman, Stephanie M. (1996). *Privilege revealed: How invisible preferences undermine America.* New York: New York University Press.

Will, George (2002, January 6). No government program can equal stable families. *Hoosier Times,* p. B7.

Willis, Paul (1977). *Learning to labor: How working class kids get working class jobs.* New York: Columbia University Press.

Wilson, Bruce L., & Corbett, H. Dickson (2001). *Listening to urban kids: School reform and the teachers they want.* Albany: State University of New York Press.

Wilson, James K. (1995). *The myth of political correctness: The conservative attack on higher education.* Durham, NC: Duke University Press.

Wilson, William J. (1987). *The truly disadvantaged: The inner-city, the underclass, and public policy.* Chicago: University of Chicago Press.

Wilson, William J. (1996). *When work disappears: The new world of the urban poor.* New York: Knopf.

Wolcott, Harry F. (1987). On ethnographic intent. In George Spindler & Louise. Spindler (Eds.), *Interpretive ethnography of education: At home and abroad* (pp. 37–57). Hillsdale, NJ: Erlbaum.

Wolfe, Alan (1998). *One nation, after all.* Viking.

Worsham, Lynn, & Olson, Gary A. (1999). Hegemony and the future of democracy: Ernesto Laclau's political philosophy. In Gary A. Olson & Lynn Worsham (Eds.), *Race, rhetoric, and the postcolonial* (pp. 129–162). Albany: State University of New York Press.

Wright, Erik O. (Ed.). (1985). *Classes.* London & New York: Verso.

Wright, Erik O. (1989). A general framework for the analysis of class structure. In Erik O. Wright (Ed.), *The debate on classes* (pp. 3–48). London & New York: Verso.

Wright, Erik O. (1994). *Interrogating inequality: Essays on class analysis, socialism, and Marxism.* London: Verso.

Wright, Susan E. (1993). Blaming the victim, blaming society, or blaming the discipline: Fixing responsibility for poverty and homelessness. *The Sociology Quarterly, 34*(1), 1–16.

Wrigley, Julia (1982). *Class politics and public schools: Chicago 1900–1950.* New Brunswick, NJ: Rutgers University Press.

Yeo, Frederick, & Kanpol, Barry (1999). Introduction: Our own "peculiar institution": Urban education in 20th-century America. In Frederick Yeo & Barry Kanpol (Eds.), *From nihilism to possibility: Democratic transformation: Democratic transformations for the inner city* (pp. 1–13). Cresskill, NJ: Hampton Press.

Yonezawa, Susan, Wells, Amy Stuart, & Serna, Irene (2002). Choosing tracks: "Freedom of choice" in detracking schools. *American Educational Research Journal, 39*(1), 37–67.

Young, Iris M. (1990). *Justice and the politics of difference.* Princeton, NJ: Princeton University Press.

Young, Iris M. (2000). *Inclusion and democracy.* Oxford, UK: Oxford University Press.

Zizek, Slavoj (1989). *The sublime object of ideology.* London: Verso.

Zizek, Slavoj (1994). Introduction: The spectre of ideology. In Slavoj Zizek (Ed.), *Mapping ideology* (pp. 1–33). London & New York: Verso.

Zizek, Slavoj (1998). Psycho analysis in post-marxism: The case of Alain Badiou. In Robert Miklitsch (Special Issues Editor), *Psycho-Marxism: Marxism and psychoanalysis late in the twentieth century* (pp. 235–261). *South Atlantic Quarterly, 97*(2).

Subject Index

Author Index